"The volume offers valuable insights about entrepreneurs operating across national boundaries, bridging origins and destinations, spanning their diasporas. As these entrepreneurs find opportunities in their countries of origin as well as with their co-ethnics located in or connected to the place of destination, a new picture emerges of their opportunities and constraints, and the implications for national development. These entrepreneurs build new governance structures and rework their relationships to the states from which they came. An insightful volume for scholars of economic sociology, entrepreneurship, and transnational migration."

— **Frederick F. Wherry**, Townsend Martin, Class of 1917 Professor of Sociology at Princeton University, and the Founding Director of the Dignity and Debt Network

"Transnational entrepreneurs are a special kind of immigrant. Unlike most immigrants, and even unlike most immigrant entrepreneurs, transnational entrepreneurs link sending and reception countries through international business, including the business of labor recruitment. Doing so, they expand and enhance the international linkages that created the immigration in the first place. Transnational entrepreneurship is an engine of change. Any sophisticated understanding of immigration needs to understand how that engine works. The daily practice of transnational entrepreneurs links business, ethnicity, class, and culture, and research on transnational immigrants needs to be multi-disciplinary to do justice to the practice. This volume significantly and consciously advances that crucial interdisciplinary agenda."

— **Ivan Light**, Professor Emeritus of Sociology, UCLA

"The potent forces of migration, entrepreneurship, and high politics combine in this compelling account on the varied and creative ways in which migrants ply their trade across borders. In this skilfully curated collection, a stellar cast of distinguished scholars offers new insights on the changing nature of 'Transnational Entrepreneurship'. Befitting an analysis on globalization, the contributions cover considerable territory, ranging from the lived experience of migrants engaged in cross-border trade, to the playing out of diaspora politics and governance challenges in several entrepreneurial domains. A much-needed contribution."

— **Monder Ram** OBE, Director, Centre for Research in Ethnic Minority Entrepreneurship, Aston Business School, Aston University

"In a world that has seen a reaction against globalisation, the phenomenon of transnational entrepreneurship reminds us that the mixing of cultures can generate new value rather than conflict. Transnational entrepreneurs generate value across migration corridors which too often are seen as one-way streets of human misery. This book delves into the nature and consequences of transnational entrepreneurship, demonstrates the importance of multiple contexts, and sets out an agenda for research on a subject that is likely to become more, not less, important in the future. It is a valuable addition to fast-growing literature."

— **Jonathan Levie**, Professor of Entrepreneurship & Regional Development, J.E. Cairnes School of Business & Economics, National University of Ireland Galway

"Representing years of research from around the world, Zapata-Barrero and Rezaei combine forces to create this collection of articles that advances our knowledge of the interacting causes and consequences of transnational entrepreneurship and how states manage and react to it. *Diaspora Governance and Transnational Entrepreneurship* is a trail-blazing volume and it is truly comparative and international, spanning origins and destinations across the entire world."

— **Edward Telles**, Distinguished Professor, University of California, Irvine

"This book addresses an important topic on migration and transnational diaspora in the age of great uncertainty. It provides insightful observations from a wide range of theoretical perspectives. Another highlight is that leading scholars examine this global phenomenon covering different geographical regions with important policy implications. I highly recommend this book to students of international migration, entrepreneurship, public policy and transnational studies."

— **Yipeng Liu**, Professor in Management and Organisation Studies, Director, Centre for China Management and Global Business, Henley Business School, University of Reading, UK

"In this collection of path-breaking reflections on transnational entrepreneurship, Ricard Zapata-Barrero, Shahamak Rezaei and their colleagues have provided a brilliant analysis of a truly global social pattern. They convincingly employ insights from the studies on diaspora, cross-border identities, business entrepreneurship and transnational practices. The contributions to this volume draw a differentiated portrait of complex cross-border engagements. There are insights to be gained for public policies of immigrant and emigrant states alike. This book is highly relevant for the reorientation of research in the fields of migration and entrepreneurship."

— **Thomas Faist,** Professor Sociology of Transnationalization, Development and Migration Faculty of Sociology, Bielefeld University

"The editors (Ricard Zapata and Shahamak Rezaei) have demonstrated their capacity to fill the gap of the lack of work on transnational entrepreneurship among migrants areas. It is an innovative idea because the economic involvement of migrants as entrepreneurs through borders and citizenships is rarely highlighted. Many of them have been for a long time salaried workers in industry or agriculture and so associated with working-class images. But, thanks to the diversification of migrations, transnational entrepreneurship is an emerging topic, studied here following a multifaceted approach."

— **Catherine Wihtol de Wenden**, Directrice de recherche CNRS, Senior research fellow, CNRS, Sciences-Po Centre de Recherches internationales; Paris

"This highly original and innovative edited collection brings fresh insights into the important global socio-economic phenomenon of transnational entrepreneurship. Appealing to scholars, researchers and policy-makers across many fields - migration, diasporas, transnationalism, business studies and international relations - the chapters range over diverse, multi-sited global contexts, and stress the heterogeneity of transnational entrepreneurs. As a growing global phenomenon, transnational businesses created by migrants, as immigrants and returnees, have considerable developmental potential but also pose challenges to governance and regulation."

— **Russel King**, Professor of Geography, University of Sussex, Sussex Centre for Migration Research, School of Global Studies

"The editors, Ricard Zapata-Barrero and Shahamak Rezaei, make a strong case for further developing a multidisciplinary research agenda on transnational migrant entrepreneurship. Studies on transnational economic activities have been thin on the ground, but this fascinating volume aims to fill that gap and, in so doing, draw particular attention to wider migratory dynamics and diaspora politics. This book is necessary context for any scholar working in migration and business studies."

— **Jan Rath,** Professor, Department of Sociology, University of Amsterdam

"This volume provides a welcome addition to the literature on ethnic entrepreneurship by analyzing its iterations and impacts across borders. Particularly useful is its focus on the cultural, political, and social dimensions of transnational entrepreneurial projects and on the role of states in encouraging them as an integral part of efforts to reinforce membership without residence and promote economic development. An important contribution to migration and mobility studies."

— **Peggy Levitt** Chair, Department of Sociology, Wellesley College, B.A., Brandeis University; M.S., Columbia University USA

Diaspora Governance and Transnational Entrepreneurship

A burgeoning literature is currently exploring the rise of a new migratory profile: migrants engaged in Transnational Entrepreneurship, referring to immigrants who are engaged in cross-border business involving their country of origin and destination, both perceived as lands of opportunity.

Until now, little has been done in linking business studies and migration studies in this particular field of research on diaspora politics and Transnational Entrepreneurship; besides, the focus has mostly been on identifying the key variables, patterns, and developing hypotheses on the favourable and promoting migrant business involvement in the country of origin. The main findings of the European Horizon-2020 interdisciplinary project that has gathered the results in a variety of empirical evidence. This book aims to explore the new global scenario internationally.

The chapters in this book were originally published as a special issue of the *Journal of Ethnic and Migration Studies*.

Ricard Zapata-Barrero is Professor of Political Science at the University Pompeu Fabra, Barcelona, Spain. Director of GRITIM-UPF (Interdisciplinary Research Group on Immigration). His main lines of research deal with contemporary issues of liberal democracy in contexts of diversity, especially the relationship between democracy, citizenship, and migration.

Shahamak Rezaei is Associate Professor at Roskilde University, Denmark. He is the winner of "Danske Bank" 2014 award in "Social Innovation & Social Entrepreneurship". His research focuses on Transnational-Knowledge-Transfer, Migration, Transnational Entrepreneurship and Diaspora Entrepreneurship. During 2015–2019, he was Research Coordinator for the research project "DiasporaLink", financed by EU-REA– 'Horizon 2020–RISE Program'.

Research in Ethnic and Migration Studies
Series editor: Paul Statham, Director, Sussex Centre for Migration Research (SCMR), University of Sussex, UK

The *Research in Ethnic and Migration Studies* series publishes the results of high-quality, cutting-edge research that addresses key questions relating to ethnic relations, diversity and migration. The series is open to a range of disciplines and brings together research collaborations on specific defined topics on all aspects of migration and its consequences, including migration processes, migrants and their experiences, ethnic relations, discrimination, integration, racism, transnationalism, citizenship, identity and cultural diversity. Contributions are especially welcome when they are the result of comparative research, either across countries, cities or groups. All articles have previously been published in the *Journal of Ethnic and Migration Studies (JEMS)*, which has a rigorous peer review system. Collective volumes in this series are either the product of Special Issues published in the journal or published articles that the Editor has selected from individual submissions.

Titles in the series:

Asian Migration and Education Cultures in the Anglosphere
Edited by Megan Watkins, Christina Ho and Rose Butler

Exploring the Migration Industries
New Perspectives on Facilitating and Constraining Migration
Edited by Sophie Cranston, Joris Schapendonk and Ernst Spaan

Aspiration, Desire and the Drivers of Migration
Edited by Francis Collins and Jørgen Carling

The Microfoundations of Diaspora Politics
Edited by Alexandra Délano Alonso and Harris Mylonas

Diaspora Governance and Transnational Entrepreneurship
The Rise of an Emerging Global Social Pattern in Migration Studies
Edited by Ricard Zapata-Barrero and Shahamak Rezaei

Children of the Crisis
Ethnographic Perspectives on Unaccompanied Refugee Youth in and En Route to Europe
Edited by Annika Lems, Kathrin Oester and Sabine Strasser

For a full list of titles please visit https://www.routledge.com/Research-in-Ethnic-and-Migration-Studies/book-series/REMS

Diaspora Governance and Transnational Entrepreneurship

The Rise of an Emerging Global Social Pattern in Migration Studies

Edited by
Ricard Zapata-Barrero and Shahamak Rezaei

LONDON AND NEW YORK

First published 2022
by Routledge
2 Park Square, Milton Park, Abingdon, Oxon, OX14 4RN

and by Routledge
605 Third Avenue, New York, NY 10158

Routledge is an imprint of the Taylor & Francis Group, an informa business

© 2022 Taylor & Francis

All rights reserved. No part of this book may be reprinted or reproduced or utilised in any form or by any electronic, mechanical, or other means, now known or hereafter invented, including photocopying and recording, or in any information storage or retrieval system, without permission in writing from the publishers.

Trademark notice: Product or corporate names may be trademarks or registered trademarks, and are used only for identification and explanation without intent to infringe.

British Library Cataloguing-in-Publication Data
A catalogue record for this book is available from the British Library

ISBN13: 978-1-032-04953-3 (hbk)
ISBN13: 978-1-032-04959-5 (pbk)
ISBN13: 978-1-003-19534-4 (ebk)

DOI: 10.4324/9781003195344

Typeset in Minion Pro
by codeMantra

Publisher's Note
The publisher accepts responsibility for any inconsistencies that may have arisen during the conversion of this book from journal articles to book chapters, namely the inclusion of journal terminology.

Disclaimer
Every effort has been made to contact copyright holders for their permission to reprint material in this book. The publishers would be grateful to hear from any copyright holder who is not here acknowledged and will undertake to rectify any errors or omissions in future editions of this book.

Contents

	Citation Information	ix
	Notes on Contributors	xi
1	Diaspora Governance and Transnational Entrepreneurship: some introductory reflections on the rise of an emerging social pattern in migration studies *Ricard Zapata-Barrero and Shahamak Rezaei*	1
2	Exploring the intersection of transnational, ethnic, and migration entrepreneurship *Benson Honig*	16
3	They are not all the same: immigrant enterprises, transnationalism, and development *Alejandro Portes and Brandon P. Martinez*	33
4	Transnational entrepreneurs: opportunity or necessity driven? Empirical evidence from two dynamic economies from Latin America and Europe *Johannes von Bloh, Vesna Mandakovic, Mauricio Apablaza, José Ernesto Amorós and Rolf Sternberg*	50
5	Harnessing the potential of Moroccans living abroad through diaspora policies? Assessing the factors of success and failure of a new structure of opportunities for transnational entrepreneurs *Ricard Zapata-Barrero and Z. Hellgren*	69
6	Prometheus, the double-troubled – migrant transnational entrepreneurs and the loyalty trap *Shahamak Rezaei and Marco Goli*	87
7	The mixed embeddedness of transnational migrant entrepreneurs: Moroccans in Amsterdam and Milan *Giacomo Solano*	109

8	Exploring the relationship between immigrant enclave theory and transnational diaspora entrepreneurial opportunity formation *Osa-Godwin Osaghae and Thomas M. Cooney*	128
9	Entrepreneurs' transnational networks channelling exports: diasporas from Central & South America, Sub-Sahara Africa, Middle East & North Africa, Asia, and the European culture region *Ye Liu, Rebecca Namatovu, Emine Esra Karadeniz, Thomas Schøtt and Indianna D. Minto-Coy*	148
	Index	169

Citation Information

The chapters in this book were originally published in the *Journal of Ethnic and Migration Studies*, volume 46, issue 10 (2020). When citing this material, please use the original page numbering for each article, as follows:

Chapter 1
Diaspora governance and transnational entrepreneurship: the rise of an emerging social global pattern in migration studies
Ricard Zapata-Barrero and Shahamak Rezaei
Journal of Ethnic and Migration Studies, volume 46, issue 10 (2020) pp. 1959–1973

Chapter 2
Exploring the intersection of transnational, ethnic, and migration entrepreneurship
Benson Honig
Journal of Ethnic and Migration Studies, volume 46, issue 10 (2020) pp. 1974–1990

Chapter 3
They are not all the same: immigrant enterprises, transnationalism, and development
Alejandro Portes and Brandon P. Martinez
Journal of Ethnic and Migration Studies, volume 46, issue 10 (2020) pp. 1991–2007

Chapter 4
Transnational entrepreneurs: opportunity or necessity driven? Empirical evidence from two dynamic economies from Latin America and Europe
Johannes von Bloh, Vesna Mandakovic, Mauricio Apablaza, José Ernesto Amorós and Rolf Sternberg
Journal of Ethnic and Migration Studies, volume 46, issue 10 (2020) pp. 2008–2026

Chapter 5
Harnessing the potential of Moroccans living abroad through diaspora policies? Assessing the factors of success and failure of a new structure of opportunities for transnational entrepreneurs
R. Zapata-Barrero and Z. Hellgren
Journal of Ethnic and Migration Studies, volume 46, issue 10 (2020) pp. 2027–2044

Chapter 6
Prometheus, the double-troubled – migrant transnational entrepreneurs and the loyalty trap
Shahamak Rezaei and Marco Goli
Journal of Ethnic and Migration Studies, volume 46, issue 10 (2020) pp. 2045–2066

Chapter 7
The mixed embeddedness of transnational migrant entrepreneurs: Moroccans in Amsterdam and Milan
Giacomo Solano
Journal of Ethnic and Migration Studies, volume 46, issue 10 (2020) pp. 2067–2085

Chapter 8
Exploring the relationship between immigrant enclave theory and transnational diaspora entrepreneurial opportunity formation
Osa-Godwin Osaghae and Thomas M. Cooney
Journal of Ethnic and Migration Studies, volume 46, issue 10 (2020) pp. 2086–2105

Chapter 9
Entrepreneurs' transnational networks channelling exports: diasporas from Central & South America, Sub-Sahara Africa, Middle East & North Africa, Asia, and the European culture region
Ye Liu, Rebecca Namatovu, Emine Esra Karadeniz, Thomas Schøtt and Indianna D. Minto-Coy
Journal of Ethnic and Migration Studies, volume 46, issue 10 (2020) pp. 2106–2125

For any permission-related enquiries please visit:
http://www.tandfonline.com/page/help/permissions

Notes on Contributors

José Ernesto Amorós, EGADE Business School, Tecnológico de Monterrey, Santa Fe, Mexico City, Mexico.

Mauricio Apablaza, School of Government, Universidad del Desarrollo, Las Condes, Santiago, Chile.

Thomas M. Cooney, School of Marketing, Technological University Dublin, Ireland.

Marco Goli, Copenhagen College, Frederiksberg, Denmark.

Z. Hellgren, GRITIM-UPF (Interdisciplinary Research Group on Immigration, Pompeu Fabra University), Barcelona, Spain.

Benson Honig, DeGroote School of Business, McMaster University, Hamilton, Canada.

Emine Esra Karadeniz, Department of Economics, Yeditepe University, Istanbul, Turkey.

Ye Liu, Department of Public Administration, Zhejiang Sci-Tech University, Hangzhou, People's Republic of China; Department of Entrepreneurship and Relationship, University of Southern Denmark, Kolding, Denmark; Sino-Danish Center for Education and Research, Beijing, People's Republic of China.

Vesna Mandakovic, School of Business and Economics, Universidad del Desarrollo, Las Condes, Santiago, Chile.

Brandon P. Martinez, Department of Sociology, University of Miami, Coral Gables, USA.

Indianna D. Minto-Coy, Mona School of Business & Management, University of the West Indies, Kingston, Jamaica; Management, Wilfrid Laurier University, Waterloo, Canada.

Rebecca Namatovu, Makerere University Business School, Kampala, Uganda.

Osa-Godwin Osaghae, School of Marketing, Technological University Dublin, Ireland.

Alejandro Portes, Department of Sociology, Princeton University and University of Miami, Princeton, USA.

Shahamak Rezaei, Department of Social Sciences & Business, Roskilde University, Denmark.

Thomas Schøtt, Department of Entrepreneurship and Relationship, University of Southern Denmark, Kolding, Denmark; Sino-Danish Center for Education and Research, Beijing, People's Republic of China.

Giacomo Solano, Migration Policy Group, Brussels, Belgium; Department of Sociology and Social Research, University of Milan-Bicocca, Italy; Amsterdam Institute for Social Science Research, University of Amsterdam, the Netherlands.

Rolf Sternberg, Institute of Economic and Cultural Geography, Leibniz Universität Hannover, Germany.

Johannes von Bloh, Institute of Economic and Cultural Geography, Leibniz Universität Hannover, Germany.

Ricard Zapata-Barrero, GRITIM – University of Pompeu Fabra, Barcelona, Spain.

Diaspora Governance and Transnational Entrepreneurship: some introductory reflections on the rise of an emerging social pattern in migration studies

Ricard Zapata-Barrero and Shahamak Rezaei

Rationale and theoretical framework of the special issue

A burgeoning literature is currently exploring the rise of a new migratory profile: migrants engaged in Transnational Entrepreneurship (TE). Roughly speaking TE has been described as a 'social realm of immigrants operating in complex, cross-national domains, with dual cultural, institutional, and economic features that facilitate and require various entrepreneurial strategies' (Drori, Honig, and Wright 2009, 1). Formulated in the simplest way, Transnational Entrepreneurs (TEs) are immigrants who are engaged in border crossing business activities involving their country of origin and destination (Portes, Guarnizo, and Haller 2002; Saxenian 2002; Elo and Freiling 2015).

TE has been articulated as a set of distinctive and dependent variables by business management scholars (Drori, Honig, and Wright 2009; Honig, Drori, and Carmichael 2010) and sociologists (Portes, Guarnizo, and Haller 2002), who analyze the trend as a specific attribute of the globalisation process, linked to the increase of human mobility, and a specific economic dimension of a transnational practice. Technological advances related to cheaper transportation and inexpensive communication have enabled TEs to have a greater amount of social, political and economic influence on their home countries than in the past, through the establishment of economic and political links between their host and home countries.

Migration scholars have previously discussed migrant entrepreneurship, mainly centred on the country of residence, and recent special issues have been centred on domestic migrant entrepreneurship (see list of references below). Researchers have to date identified micro and macro level factors that either encourage or inhibit TE (agency, cultural capital, social capital, institutions) (Drori, Honig, and Wright 2009), but always in the framework of residence countries, without taking into consideration as a core focus of analysis, the home country as an agent influencing the widespread of the new migratory pattern or as the main beneficiary of the effects that this new pattern may have on economic (TE contribute to economical development), social (TE may contribute to social development) and even cultural (TE may contribute to new cultural values) and political spheres and agendas (TE may contribute to the democratisation of home countries).

In migration studies, this new migratory pattern becomes meaningful as it breaks the view that migrants perceive their home countries with resentment and reveals how they rather perceive home countries as lands of opportunities, though the transnational dimension of the migrant entrepreneur has remained widely unexplored. The growing area of research has made great strides in explaining the rise of the TE profile and its distinctions have been examined by a great amount of case studies that, mainly at the micro level, tries to understand its singular features in order to give TE its own specific place as a field of research separated from international migrant entrepreneurs (who do not necessarily focus their entrepreneurial venture in home countries) and domestic migrant entrepreneurs (who do not have relation with their origin countries). The incorporation of TE as a new dependent variable in migration studies has still to be done. As a field, it is neither theorised nor empirically researched by migration studies scholars. Although there are few concrete case studies, they are mainly focused on the US (Morawska 2004; Portes and Yiu 2013; Bagwell 2015; Brzozowski, Surdej, and Cucculelli 2017). Incorporating TE as a new research field will involve maximising the multidisciplinary and multi-methodological character of migration studies. TE is at the crossroad of several current key framework debates and can contribute to develop the research agenda, advancing both empirical knowledge and theoretical understanding of two contemporary forms of cross-border concepts: Transnationalism and Diaspora. These two frameworks have served through the last decades as prominent research lenses through which we have viewed the aftermath of international migration and the shifting of state borders across populations (Brubaker 2005; Bauböck and Faist 2010). With this special issue, we invite researchers to open up the focus and to look more closely at the intersections between the traditionally studied fields of research, namely Ethnic Entrepreneurship (EE), TE, and Migration and Integration, to fully grasp the complexities of TE in the increasingly and rapidly evolving globalised world.

First of all, the transnational research agenda, which already has a long history, has preliminary considered TE as a new economic practice that goes beyond the traditional remittances, since it mobilises the competencies, skills, social and cultural capitals acquired by migrants during their incorporation processes, but it has still not gone further, towards cultural, political and social dimensions as by-products of the migrant TE projects.

Secondly, some debates focus on the exploration of this new practice from the diaspora lens, and even speak about 'Diaspora Entrepreneurs'. This involves a nuance with normative dimensions. Authors coincide that the notion of diaspora is a socio-political formation, whose members regard themselves as of the same ethno-national group, and maintain regular or occasional contacts with what they regard as their homelands and with individuals and groups of the same background (Brubaker 2005; Sheffer 2006; Bauböck and Faist 2010). The use of Diaspora Entrepreneurship is for us too narrow, as it assumes that the migrant who decides to frame his/hers entrepreneurial project as bridging home and residence countries, is doing this with a feeling of belonging to his/hers national group and with national intentions of contributing to create jobs and contribute to economic development of his/hers country of origin. We will rather discuss the governance policies that are being deployed by home countries specially targeting the TE profile, most of them within an external economic development paradigm. The diaspora lens will thus rather be considered as a focus point on how home politics are responding to this new profile and trend, and whether they meet their purposes. The interface between the emerging transnational migratory dynamics and the home diaspora politics is then at the nuclear core focus of this special issue.

There are few recent studies focusing on diaspora institutions and governance (Newland and Tanaka 2010; Gamlen 2014; Brinkerhoff 2016). By mentioning 'Diaspora Governance' in the main title, we aim to broaden the scope to incorporate macro and meso levels, since there are a number of networks, from the stake holders, mainly from civil societies, to the so-called Business Incubators, which are institutions that help entrepreneurs overcome the financial, human, and social capital impediments they face during the business creation (Riddle, Hrivnak, and Nielsen 2010). The function of these networks involved in the diaspora governance is usually to bridge home country governments and TE (Rusinovic 2008; Chen and Tan 2009; Xiaohua and Tao 2012). This particular focus is extremely important, since it allows us to jump to the general current new trend of migration studies and consider the fusion of home country policies towards nationals living abroad, while examining not only the institutional, social, economical and political effects that the recognition of TEs as new actors may have in terms of change and transformation in home countries, but also how it is the epicentre of new actors' networks dynamics in need of exploration. Supportive policies fostering this new transnational practice may also involve normative issues and implications, in terms of externalisation of home politics (between domestic and international politics, i.e. home country governments becoming agents attracting their own national talents), new frameworks to rethinking citizenship (the external citizenship theorised by Baubock 2009, for instance) and nation-state policies beyond national borders of the home countries.

Originality of the focus of the special issue: contribution potential in theoretical and empirical terms

Viewed globally TE is, as all other sociological and interrelational phenomena, a context-embedded phenomenon. What becomes increasingly evident is that this research field's multidisciplinary character dynamics only can be grasped by applying a multiplicity of research sub-fields: Return migrants, diaspora, development studies, ethnic entrepreneurship, international entrepreneurship, transnationalism, circular mobility, etc (see, among others, Kloosterman and Rath 2001; Riddle 2008; McEvoy, Khalid, and Keoy 2010; Adiguna 2012; Mohamoud and Formson-Lorist 2013; Bulmer and Solomos 2014; Valdez and Romero 2017).

All sub-fields and shapes of TE share a common core, but vary across cases as well. A core feature of TE is that many aspects overlap with other related concepts. Qualitative comparisons based on ethnographic methods remain vital to understand how different actors matter in the design and implementation of diaspora policies at different levels, and in different periods of time, but quantitative comparisons are also necessary to measure and evaluate the drivers of diaspora policies and their effects.

Given the origin of the research in business and entrepreneurial studies, the incorporation of the particular field of research in migration cannot be done without them. The research profile of the two Guests Editors illustrates this intention: one coming from migration studies (R. Zapata-Barrero), the other from business studies (S. Rezaei).

Until now, little has been done in linking business studies and migration studies in this particular field of research on diaspora politics and TE, and when it has been done, the focus has mostly been on identifying the key independent variables, patterns and developing hypotheses on the favourable and non-favourable factors promoting migrant business involvement in the country of residence. Given the current scholarly debate on TE (and Diaspora Entrepreneurship), the first stage should be to give a proper place to this new field of research by utilising the existing great amount of empirical researches, mostly case studies and less multi-sited and comparative studies (see most of the seminal references below). What we can keep from these preliminary contributions is a toolkit with a great amount of analytical distinctions that seem meaningful to discriminate *the proper place of TE as a new independent variable in migration studies.*

There appears to be a gap that needs to be filled in the debates on how home countries develop institutions, policies and governance strategies to attract their own expatriates, and how these strategies and efforts work for nationals living abroad while they develop their own personal TE by following different purpose strategies and standards. Maybe TEs assume that they will remain in the residence countries or will develop a specific transnational practice in permanent circularity between home and residence countries. We know that in both receiving and sending countries, the socio-political context is decisive since it governs the structure of opportunities for migrants to put their talent and motivation to work for economic advancement in their home countries and for the sustained development of the places they left behind (Portes and Yiu 2013, 92). It is interesting to explore this interface between diaspora politics, governance and TE purposes, as it is an area that has been under-researched.

To narrow the scope of the specific focus, we can initially keep (by criticising it also) the analytical dimension that has been inspired by Schumpeter (1974, 132), among others, who defined Necessity Entrepreneurs as those who are simply self-employed and Opportunity Entrepreneurs as those who reform or revolutionise the pattern of production. In our terms Necessity Entrepreneurship is need-based, while opportunity entrepreneurs start a business in order to pursue an opportunity, generally involving social mobility. The contrast between necessity- and opportunity-driven entrepreneurship is important because it has been proved that they have a different impact on home countries' economic growth (Brzozowski, Surdej, and Cucculelli 2017). This assumes that not all forms of TE contribute equally to economic development. Necessity entrepreneurs normally contribute little to economic growth, although they do contribute to poverty reduction. While many entrepreneurs traditionally fall into the necessity category, the pattern is changing as members of the diaspora community become more educated and gain more skills. Saying that a necessity-driven TE has no or rather limited effect in the economic sphere does not mean that it has no effect in the social, cultural and certain aspect of economical sphere as well (Mohamoud and Formson-Lorist 2014). The analytical toolkit needs to be deepened and extended beyond the economic sphere. Unfortunately, research that concerns TEs impact on their home countries in terms of social, political and cultural development is minimal.

Research contributions to the special issue

All articles in this special issue cover areas of TE from different angles. They are selected to showcase the underexplored sides of TE and shed light on the intersections with traditional fields of research in migration studies (Ethnic Entrepreneurship (EE), Migrant Transnational Entrepreneurship (MTE), Immigrant Enclave Theory (IET) etc.), all contributing to the growing toolkit proposed to explore the suggested new global social pattern of entrepreneurs doing business transnationally.

In the first article, Honig (2020) examines the importance of entrepreneurship from the multiple perspectives of Transnational, Ethnic and Migration Studies. He points out that in the next few decades growth and labour forces in OECD countries will come mainly from immigration and that there within Europe are extreme cases where some countries (Czech Republic, Italy, Greece, Slovenia and Slovakia) are only growing through immigration. He thereby makes explicit that knowledge on migration is essential, in relation to entrepreneurship in general and in relation to TE in particular, as advanced countries prepare for the arrival of new immigrants and less advanced countries face significant challenges in maintaining and attracting workforces. He points out that research has focused on metropolitan cities and that very little is known of integration and resettlement of newcomers and their contribution of social capital elsewhere. His goal is to provide insights that can assist research perspectives in an interdisciplinary approach to help pave the way for answers needed in policy making.

He further points out that chain migration, initially established by immigrants seeking to link with friends and family across geographical areas, did not originally have political overtones, but was an unpolitical social science term. Today anti-immigration politicians have given it a negatively laden meaning, dividing newcomers into *us* and *them* with a debate between globalizsation and local protectionism, being echoed throughout the world. Honig predicts that some countries will embrace the changes and celebrate multinational differences, whereas others might react negatively and entrench themselves in a nativist, isolationist philosophy, risking to jeopardizse their own economic potential and drive away talented labour with immigrant 'unfriendly' political discourses that may eventually create barriers to entry for TEs and migrants, which will further the negative impact on economic growth.

Historically migrants have provided advantages of economic flexibility and innovation, but Honig makes clear that this will not happen without significant internal adjustments, both culturally and politically, and may provide existential challenges to political entities. Honig concludes that future migration research and scholarship rests at the intersection of political and economic power, and that solving the multi-dimensional puzzle requires innovative targeted interdisciplinary research, as the traditional one-sided approach simply will not cover the development taking place.

Portes and Martinez (2020) also seek to challenge the traditional view that paints all immigration entrepreneurship in the same homogenous colours. They look into details on the sizes, earnings and entrepreneurial span of different ethnic groups in the US, revealing that self-employed in general, regardless of ethnic background, have consistently higher earnings than wage workers. Their data further reveals differences between ethnic groups, showing, for example, that high tech TE human capital is the strongest determinant of economic outcomes and that almost all ethno-national groups are at an economic disadvantage, even after controlling for human capital variables and self-employment. The only immigrant groups whose annual incomes exceed those of native whites are 'The Triple I' (Indians, Iranians, and Israelis), and they do so by sizable margins, further proving the heterogeneous character of the immigration entrepreneurship.

The development is naturally dependent on a positive, or at least neutral, mode of incorporation in the host country. Legal status and the absence of widespread discrimination are necessary conditions to enable immigrants to deploy high levels of expertise for the construction of large-scale companies. A negative reception, either by the government or from society in general, would make it impossible to engage in establishing new companies. What determines the differences has not been properly theorizsed, but in general major causal effects have been ascribed to the level and type of the human capital.

Portes and Martinez (2019) stress two main points. First, that the groups are highly heterogeneous, and secondly that the way immigrants are received affects results and levels of entrepreneurship. The overall conclusion is that context matters and as the title indicates: they are not all the same, but are, quite contrary, a highly heterogeneous group that deserves more attention as a research field on its own.

Using data from the 2016 and 2017 Adult Population Surveys (APS), the Global Entrepreneurship Monitor and DiasporaLink data from Chile and Germany, von Bloh et al. (2020) compare TE in two different national host country contexts and institutional settings. While the two countries share similarities in political stability, immigration patterns and openness to a global perspective, they differ on social welfare. Where Chileans must rely on family for support, Germans can rely on a governmental social security welfare system designed to help people affected by unemployment. Further, in sharp contrast to Germany, the Chilean Government has actively tried to attract foreign entrepreneurs with various programmes such as a programme to reduce bureaucracy and a new bankruptcy law from 2014 that reduces a company's closure proceedings and enables a new start for entrepreneurs that faced failure. Further, the Chilean government launched Startup Chile in 2010 that, among other initiatives, offers a one-year working visa to entrepreneurs with high human capital in the technology services sector to start or develop their business in Chile.

The data revealed considerable differences between TE in the two countries. Chile seemed to attract or form mainly opportunity-driven TE, while the TE in Germany revealed strong evidence of necessity-driven TE. The authors argue that the differences can be related to the different institutional settings and levels of economic development, and they suggest that the different institutional settings attract or form different types of TE.

The authors recommend more research on a micro-, but also meta-, level to develop tailored policy recommendations that take countries of origins into consideration more explicitly than in the past, as the national institutional context seems to play a significant role, as well as the economic development, on what kind of TE emerges in a given host country context.

The aim of Ricard Zapata-Barrero's and Zenia Hellgren's article (2020) is to assess changes in the Moroccan policy paradigm concerning diaspora engagement policy. They seek to contribute to the debate on transnational migrant entrepreneurship by exploring two sets of arguments: First, the *socio-economic argument* and second, the *national identity argument*.

One of their main findings is that the Moroccan approach to economic development is a return-based approach driven by traditional state instruments of promoting belonging and a sense of Moroccan identity (national and/or religious based). But the Authors' exploratory empirical analysis reflects that most of the entrepreneurs who seek to develop their business projects in their country of origin are guided by pragmatic reasons rather than by strong feelings of national identity, contrary to the general mainstream narrative of Moroccan diaspora engagement policies. They conclude that much of the shortcomings of the engagement policy are related to the fact that the philosophy behind it is too economy-driven, without contemplating the potential role that Moroccans living abroad could play in political reform and the democratizsation of Morocco.

They point out that there are many initiatives to help TEs from Morocco, but also many institutional organs with little coordination, and the competition between them is therefore great, with more focus on being the best initiative rather than the actual outcome. Furthermore, the authors point out a lack of coherency in policies on the area, with government officials both encouraging migrants to stay in host countries to help the economy and to come home and work full time in Morocco. The return-based approach is *mono-dimensional* and the way Moroccan policy initiatives set out to attract their skilled nationals reflect a gap between expectations and outcomes. A question raised in the article is whether TEs can be unpolitical and it becomes clear that further knowledge is needed for the Moroccan policy initiatives to have an effect and avoid falling flat in the gap between expectations and outcomes.

Rezaei and Goli (2020), based on extensive research, DiasporaLink data and 126 in-depth qualitative interviews, introduce a new model to research the intersection between Integration, Ethnic Entrepreneurship (EE) and Migrant Transnational Entrepreneurship (MTE). The intersection has not previously been examined, as research traditionally has focused on one field at a time, but to fully grasp the complexities of the field, they suggest, in line with other contributions to this special issue, a broadened scope and bring into light a need for a new focus and interdisciplinary approach.

Their comprehensive research data introduces the lived experience of MTEs. The results clearly reveal a concern from the interviewees on loyalty and dual citizenship, showing how the MTEs, contrary to traditional views, experience a loyalty issue with home countries framing them as 'traitors that left' and host countries framing them as 'strangers not to be trusted'. This leaves the MTE in a vacuum of being a cultural hybrid that does not entirely belong to either country, constantly bumping into obstacles as someone 'nowhere completely trusted – nowhere completely at home'. Rezaei and Goli's (2019) research thus confirm Portes and Martinez's (2019) claim that how an immigrant is received in both host and home country plays a significant role in immigrant business development and TE.

Taking both macro-, meso- and micro- levels into consideration, Rezaei and Goli (2019) further introduce a way to divide MTEs through a *can/want to* model that groups potential MTEs into categories based on likelihood to engage in TE. Based on these findings, they suggest access to training and suggest initiatives to help MTEs, thus laying the groundwork for a focus on how to help MTE evolve and improve policymaking to help MTE.

Solano (2020) offers us a study based on qualitative in-depth interviews of 35 Moroccan transnational entrepreneurs who reside in Milan and Amsterdam, chosen as cities with similar stability, comparable traits and a considerable number of Moroccan migrants, to understand how transnational practices vary according to structural and institutional situations in different contexts. Through the application of a mixed embeddedness approach, revisited from a transnational perspective, he combines different levels of analysis to fully grasp the TE phenomenon, resting on the main question of what factors influence the transnational entrepreneurial patterns of migrants and what resources transnational migrant entrepreneurs employ to conduct their transnational business.

Solano (2019) found that on the one hand institutional embeddedness influenced respondents and on the other hand that transnational entrepreneurs take advantage of their heterogeneous, and often previously acquired, contacts and skills to conduct their business. He remarked that an overall analysis of the driving factors for TE is still underexplored, that existing literature on TE has focused on an individual level and characteristics, and that the previous focus of mixed embeddedness theory has been on the county of residence.

In general, the Author found that the Moroccan TEs had a multifocal perspective, rather than a bi-focal perspective as suggested by most of the existing literature. He also found that the economic context was particularly powerful in influencing choices of what kind of business the TE would engage in. Thus, Moroccans in Milan seem more engaged in the strong goods related sector in the city, whereas Moroccans in Amsterdam were keener to engage in the business-oriented sector that is strongest in that city. Especially, the Milan sample stressed the importance of the economy of the home country as equally important as it allowed for trade, but also the free movement of products within the EU that allowed for the trade of Moroccan products between/to Moroccans residing in other European countries, as important. Social embeddedness showed to be of crucial importance, and Solange discovered that previous to starting a business TEs had substantial geographically-dispersed, non-homogeneous networks combining people from home-, host- and other countries. This is a new finding, underlining that the networks led to the TEs starting their business, and not the other way around. Solange concludes his study with a suggestion for a much needed longitudinal study to shed further light on the dynamics at play between the entrepreneurial profile and TE.

Osa-Godwin Osaghae and Thomas Cooney (2020) examine TE through cross-border movement of people and apply Immigrant Enclave Theory (IET) and Transnational Diaspora Entrepreneurial (TDE) Opportunity Formation as an alternative approach to business development within immigrant enclaves. They define IET as 'an enclave sharing the same group identity with the presence of collective sanctions mechanisms that generate trust, reduce behavioural uncertainty and enhances the immigrant activities within a geographical location' and define TDE as 'settled ethnic minority groups of migrant origins residing and acting in their country of residence, but maintaining strong sentimental, entrepreneurial and material links with their country of origin'.

Resting on these definitions, their desire to understand entrepreneur opportunity formation led them to ask where opportunities come from. By combining existing literature on the realist approach, constructionist approach, and discovery/creation approach, they found that opportunity formation is the result of an individual enabler interacting with an external enabler (environment, infrastructures, and resources). They propose a model to highlight the relationship between IET and TDE, and by the proposed model that highlights the dual connection of the individual enabler and the external enablers, they contribute to the existing literature stressing that the interaction at the individual level embedded in the external context is what forms opportunity.

They finally suggest that further research should seek to identify the importance of the connection of enclave and transnational diaspora entrepreneurship to create greater understanding of economic and social benefits within a national context, given that despite TDEs inherent ability to support economies in both host and home countries, it is an ongoing issue of national divide.

In the last article, Liu et al. (2020) present their findings from a global sample study on 55068 entrepreneurs, including 5212 diasporans, collected between 2012 and 2014, in 75 countries. They wanted to know-how embeddedness of diasporic entrepreneurs in their origins, shape pursuit of transnational networks and trade. By comparing diasporas originating from the five regions of the World: Central & South America, Sub-Sahara Africa, Middle East & North Africa, Asia, and the region of countries dominated by European culture, they found that: Exporting is greater for diasporic entrepreneurs than for domestically located entrepreneurs; Diasporic entrepreneurs network transnationally more than domestically located entrepreneurs, especially those originating from Sub-Sahara Africa; Transnational networking promotes exporting and effects on exporting of being diasporan are partly channelled through transnational networking, but differently across diasporas.

The Authors contribute to theorizsing by demonstrating that the effect of being in a diaspora upon exporting is mediated by transnational networks differently across various diasporas. As other contributors, they find differences within the group of transnational entrepreneurs and their original pioneering study shows that context has an influence on the outcome. In line with most of the above contributions, Liu et al. (2019) recommend and suggest that further research is needed.

Justifying the subtitle: the rise of a new social global pattern in migration studies

The interlink between the framework and focus of this special issue grounds the ambitiously proposed subtitle: *the rise of a new social global pattern in migration studies*. The idea comes from reading the seminal work of A. Portes, where he noticed the rise of transnational communities (Portes 1996), and further by Portes, Guarnizo, and Haller (2002, 2013) who address the rise of transnational entrepreneurial communities in the following terms:

> ... it is the rise of a new class of immigrants, economic entrepreneurs or political activists who conduct cross-border activities on a regular basis, that lies at the core of the phenomenon that this field seeks to highlight and investigate.

Within transnational studies, there is a need to analyze the variety of practices of transnational migrants. The emerging transnational practice can be explored in terms of the formation of a new global social pattern for many different reasons, all of which make this particular pattern unique. The most substantial and obvious one is a common interest of people engaging in the same venture from different contexts and nationalities. It has been shown, for instance, that some governments or business incubators organise collective multinational meetings to address common concerns among their own national TEs and are contributing to the formation of a sense of corporation across otherwise established social stratifications. This is why the dimension of a global social pattern makes sense, following the article by Scott Hartley who also address the *rise of a global entrepreneurship class* (Hartley 2012). The idea of a socio-economic class construction at the global level assumes not only that there is a process of institutional recognition of this new pattern by home countries, but emphasises also its continuity through time as a proper distinctive transnational community with differentiated interests, motivations and with a potential expansive wave beyond the economic sphere, with TEs becoming transformative agents in their home countries. Further TEs follow distinctive values, interests and motivations (we assume that cultural and national based approaches and ties are important, for example, but we do not know the intensity of this cultural national driver, or whether it is a real factor of TE or TEs simply are transnational by pragmatism rather than national affinities).

The uniqueness of TEs as an emerging global social pattern has also been signalled by Saxenian (1999), who gives an interesting example of TEs in her study on Asian immigrant engineers and scientists in Silicon Valley. She describes how these entrepreneurs exploit their social capital by building far-reaching professional business ties that connect them with Asia. They are 'uniquely positioned because their language skills and technical and cultural know-how allow them to function effectively in the business culture of their home countries as well as in Silicon Valley' (Saxenian 2005).

An additional dimension of the singularity of this pattern, seeing it globally and collectively, is how TEs view their home countries as lands of opportunities, most likely in terms of social mobility for necessity-driven TE, and in terms of increasing power and influence for opportunity-driven TE. The uniqueness of this pattern taken collectively as a new global social pattern shows us a need for transnational capital as well. That is a combination of economic capital (money to invest, and/or travel regularly to, or do business in, the country of origin), cultural capital (bilingualism, knowledge of oversea markets, international management experience) and social capital (such as contacts, relatives or family in the country of origin whom one can trust and/or can do business with). In other words, the emerging global social pattern analyzed allows us to focus on the singularity of its potential to structure TEs environment and influence the development of their home countries.

General findings and further research

General findings from the collection of contributions invite us to widen the focus of this particular line of research and to look at intersections of fields. Home countries need more attention in research contexts. It is also crucial to see TEs in the heterogeneous fields they operate in as equally heterogeneous individuals. The overall contributions reflect precisely that there are very diverse forms of transnational entrepreneurship, much more diverse than what has been assumed in earlier research.

Adding this complexity and nuance strengthen even more this new global social pattern. The overall core message that speaks loud and clear through all sample studies selected for this special issue is that context matter, as well as pragmatism, loyalty, belongingness and how new migrants are perceived in both home countries (traitors that left) and host countries (strangers that might be a threat), whether immigrants are welcomed or not, and whether home countries provide support or initiatives to attract TEs.

Finally, this special issue aims to cast light on the development in the rapidly changing world we live in, with migration patterns changing in previously unseen directions. As Honig points out, Europe previously provided US, Canada, Australia and New Zealand with immigrants. Now Western Europe is attracting the Middle East and Eastern

Europeans, not historically resources, and Europe additionally needs to address a shrinking and increasing ageing/elderly population.

This collection helped pave the way for further research, where a suggested longitudinal study seems to be at the forefront of all contributors attention, to shed further light on influences on decision making to engage in, and the success of, TE. Furthermore, additional research is essential to give political advice on how to best make use of, integrate, motivate and benefit from the increasing trend of TE.

The interface between diaspora governance and transnational entrepreneurship: some preliminary key-distinctions and key-questions

This special issue aims to contribute with a step forward in the emerging debate on TE and Diaspora politics by focusing on how home countries' diaspora governance affect the decision to engage in a transnational entrepreneurial venture with home countries. The question of what the attracting or discouraging factors might be is less explored, and we have very limited information on how governments focus on entrepreneurship, either towards necessity or opportunity-driven ventures, and whether they seek to promote mobility from necessity to opportunity or not. Since opportunity-driven entrepreneurship inherently has a transformative potential, all political regimes might not be open to allow it without control.

From the point of view of home countries, there is a need to analyse in-depth home government programmes and how home countries incorporate the transnational practice into their diaspora policy agenda. Why some TEs involve themselves in their home countries while others prefer to follow an international entrepreneurship venture or stay in host countries, still remains unanswered. From a comparative perspective, we may further ask whether the policy narrative behind diaspora governance varies among home countries or not, and further, the differences between home country narratives and TE narratives is also in need of evidence-based theorisation to know if TEs are aware, or not, of being agents of change in their home countries. We suspect that those that enter into contact with home policies are likely to be more aware of their potential to influence beyond their individual business benefits, but there is still not a theorisation on how TEs build their project beyond the individual business scope. TEs have ties with their home countries, but how much these ties influence their decisions, or whether their decision on involvement is simply pragmatic in character, needs to be investigated as many developing countries have had only limited success in attracting their diaspora entrepreneurs.

From the point of view of the TE other different key-questions arise. Some typologies of profiles have been proposed in the literature (we have already noticed the necessity-driven and opportunity-driven distinction), but most of them are based on motivations and social status. We propose to keep an eye on these typologies, but also to incorporate other ones based on mobility, space and territory. One of the first to highlight explicitly the mobility framework is the work of Saxenian (1999). The frequency of travels from home to residence countries make some TEs become an example of a new migratory pattern, which she calls 'brain circulation' as opposed to 'brain drain' (Saxenian 2005). This brain circulation has been the specific focus of a special issue coordinated by Rezaei, Light, and Telles

(2016), but it has not been compared to other TE profiles; those who remain in residence countries and those who decide to return.

The fact that TEs must navigate within very different social and cultural institutional settings and administrative frameworks and business cultures is important. We can expect then that there are several main profiles that deserve analysis. The nature of movement as well as motivation and background are important; while some TEs permanently repatriate to their home country, many more 'migrate circularly'. We know by preliminary studies that this circular TE is a profile that comes in later stages of entrepreneurial projects, but it is becoming an increasingly interesting profile to analyse in the framework of migration studies and in comparison with other TE profiles.

Articulating some key strides all contributions explore in this special issue

TE is seen as a resource and an opportunity for both the country of origin (which develops a new focus, adding to the traditional one of remittances management) and the migrant (who develops a new activity perceiving his or her country of origin as a resource rather than as a constraint). This is being discussed in terms of explanatory variables to understand the new dynamic and the distinctive features of its profile (sharing different cultures and social and cultural capital), but also in terms of the effects on countries of origin (social, economic, political, cultural effects). There is also a new research trend of brain gain policies for countries of origin who attract skilled migrants, but there is less research on how this brain gain operates as a policy for the home countries and for targeting their own diaspora.

Finally, current research shows that factors relating to generation (the future potentials of young migrant generations), education and sense of identity shape how transnational enterprises are created, as this is an essential part of fully comprehending the benefits of TE. We are furthermore interested in discussing how to justify political intervention in these new dynamics, and how to frame this intervention beyond legal and administrative services and assistance by understanding what main programmes, policies and structures that are being developed; the main policy focus; the network of actors involved; and the intercultural aspects of these initiatives linking economically, politically and culturally both the country of origin and the country of immigration.

- *Normative expansive wave of diaspora governance and TE:* The task of normatively evaluating new transnational practices and diaspora policies is to contribute to the development of this field of research. This focus allows us to explore the important transformations that can take place, not only theoretically, in debates on citizenship and externalisation of policies of home countries. Because they project domestic policies beyond territorial borders, formal state policies towards Diasporas fall into a grey area in need of further explorations. More fundamentally, such initiatives disrupt the assumed symmetry of the self-governing national population and its territorial jurisdiction, and give rise to unconventional modes of post-Westphalian citizenship and sovereignty not envisioned in modern geopolitics. These processes both reinforce and undermine the foundations of the nation-state. Indeed, transnational organisations and multiple identifications compel home states to position themselves and develop what is called 'diaspora politics' as a means of maintaining the loyalty of the citizens on both their territory of settlement and 'abroad' (Délano and

Gamlen 2014). For the countries of origin, the process involves then extending their power beyond their territories, which leads to the de-territorialisation of nationhood, which becomes a resource for identity and for mobilisation for individuals and/or groups of immigrant descent.

- ***Deepening and going beyond current theoretical frameworks paradigms:*** The master theoretical framework is based on the hypothesis that TE and economic developments are positively linked. This ground the argument that TEs are not merely immigrant entrepreneurs working in a transnational space, but are instead, distinctive agents of change (Riddle and Brinkerhoff 2011). Following the current economical view of how TE have an active role and added value, we suggest to go beyond the business enterprise focus. Recent research suggests that TE can contribute to development by creating businesses and jobs, stimulating innovation, creating social capital across borders, and channelling political and financial capital toward their countries of origin, beyond the traditional remittances focus and TEs are thus likely to also be agents of social, cultural and political change in home countries. How TEs capacities and capital can be mobilised and utilised beyond the economic development activities, and how TEs can contribute to processes of democratisation and political opening, is still unanswered in current literature and we have no knowledge on to what extent TEs have a greater sense of corporate social responsibility in the homeland. Crucially, we may explore through case studies how TE lead not only to economic change by creating new goods and services, new firms, and innovative solutions to local needs in developing economies, but at the same time, how they might play a vital role in the development of democracy that can expand opportunity, unleash individual initiatives, and cultivate independent citizens who are invested in society and democratic governance.

History shows that a great gain can be made from TE and migration, and foreign trade has existed as long as we have recorded history; Marco Polo and the early explorers were TEs. A remarkable contrast to the still increasing anti-immigration politics to be found across Europe and elsewhere, stressing the need for further research to help policy makers navigate and tailor policies to help national growth from TE.

As seen in the previous, more research is indeed needed. Until recently, no comparable empirical data was available to analyse TE on a global scale, and as our global communication and travel capabilities continue to expand, we can only expect that the importance and impact of immigration will grow as well. How we deal with it is therefore crucial and we need a frame for understanding and fully crasping the rapidly evolving world, to navigate it best.

Disclosure statement

No potential conflict of interest was reported by the authors.

Funding

This work was supported by Research Executive Agency [645471].

ORCID

Ricard Zapata-Barrero http://orcid.org/0000-0002-3478-1330

References

Adiguna, R. 2012. "Exploring Transnational Entrepreneurship: On the Interface between International Entrepreneurship and Ethnic Entrepreneurship." http://orbilu.uni.lu/handle/10993/20767.

Bagwell, S. 2015. "Transnational Entrepreneurship Amongst Vietnamese Businesses in London." *Journal of Ethnic and Migration Studies* 41 (2): 329–349.

Baubock, R. 2009. "The Rights and Duties of External Citizenship." *Citizenship Studies* 13 (5): 475–499.

Bauböck, R., and T. Faist. 2010. *Diaspora and Transnationalism: Concepts, Theories and Methods.* Amsterdam: Amsterdam Univ. Press.

Brinkerhoff, M. J. 2016. *Institutional Reform and Diaspora Entrepreneurs: The In-Between Advantage.* New York: Oxford University Press.

Brubaker, R. 2005. "The 'Diaspora' Diaspora." *Ethnic and Racial Studies* 28 (1): 1–19.

Brzozowski, J., A. Surdej, and M. Cucculelli. 2017. "The Determinants of Transnational Entrepreneurship and Transnational Ties' Dynamics among Immigrant Entrepreneurs in ICT Sector in Italy." *International Migration* 55 (3): 105–125.

Bulmer, M., and J. Solomos. 2014. *Diasporas, Cultures and Identities.* London: Routledge.

Chen, W., and J. Tan. 2009. "Understanding Transnational Entrepreneurship Through a Network Lens: Theoretical and Methodological Considerations." *Entrepreneurship Theory and Practice* 33 (5): 1079–1091.

Délano, A., and A. Gamlen. 2014. "Comparing and Theorizing State-Diaspora Relations." *Political Geography* 41: 43–53.

Drori, I., B. Honig, and M. Wright. 2009. "Transnational Entrepreneurship: An Emergent Field of Study." *Entrepreneurship Theory and Practice* 33 (5): 1001–1022.

Elo, M., and J. Freiling. 2015. "Transnational Entrepreneurship: An Introduction to the Volume." *American Journal of Entrepreneurship* 8 (2): 1–9.

Gamlen, A. 2014. "Diaspora Institutions and Diaspora Governance." *International Migration Review* 48 (1): 180–217.

Hartley, S. 2012. "Rise of the Global Entrepreneurial Class." *Forbes*, March 25.

Honig, B. 2020. "Exploring the Intersection of Transnational, Ethic, and Migration Entrepreneurship." *Journal of Ethnic and Migration Studies* 46 (10): 1974–1990. doi:10.1080/1369183X.2018.1559993.

Honig, B., I. Drori, and B. Carmichael, eds. 2010. *Transnational and Immigrant Entrepreneurship in a Globalized World.* Toronto: University of Toronto Press.

Kloosterman, R., and J. Rath. 2001. "Immigrant Entrepreneurs in Advanced Economies: Mixed Embeddedness Further Explored." *Special Issue, Journal of Ethnic and Migration Studies* 27 (2): 189–201.

Liu, Y., R. Namatovu, E. Esra Karadeniz, T. Schøtt, and I. D. Minto-Coy. 2020. "Entrepreneurs' Transnational Networks Channeling Exports: Diasporas From Central & South America, Sub-Sahara Africa, Middle East & North Africa, Asia, and the European Culture Region." *Journal of Ethnic and Migration Studies* 46 (10): 2106–2125. doi:10.1080/1369183X.2018.1560002.

McEvoy, D., H. Khalid, and K. Keoy. 2010. "Special Issue: Ethnic Minority Entrepreneurship and Management." *International Small Business Journal: Researching Entrepreneurship* 28 (2): 131–135.

Mohamoud, A., and C. Formson-Lorist. 2013. "Harnessing the Bridging Potential of Migrant and Diaspora Entrepreneurs for Transformative and Inclusive Development." Report web: https://www.diaspora-centre.org/wp-content/uploads/2013/10/FINAL_MADE-Policy-Paper_MigrantsEntrepreneurship_Dec2014.pdf.

Mohamoud, A., and C. Formson-Lorist. 2014. "Diaspora and Migrant Entrepreneurs as Social and Economic Investors in Homeland Development." Migration and Development Civil Society Network (MADE).

Morawska, E. 2004. "Immigrant Transnational Entrepreneurs in New York: Three Varieties and Their Correlates." *International Journal of Entrepreneurial Behavior & Research* 10 (5): 325–348.

Newland, K., and H. Tanaka. 2010. "Mobilizing Diaspora Entrepreneurship for Development." Paper for the Diasporas & Development Policy Project, MSI.

Osaghae, O.-G., and T. M. Cooney. 2020. "Exploring the Relationship Between Immigrant Enclave Theory and Transnational Diaspora Entrepreneurial Opportunity Formation." *Journal of Ethnic and Migration Studies* 46 (10): 2086–2105. doi:10.1080/1369183X.2018.1560001.

Portes, A. 1996. "Global Villagers: The Rise of Transnational Communities." *The American Prospect* 7 (25): 74–77.

Portes, A., W. G. Haller, and L. E. Guarnizo. 2002. "Transnational Entrepreneurs: An Alternative Form of Immigrant Economic Adaptation." *American Sociological Review* 67 (2): 278–298.

Portes, A., and B. P. Martinez. 2020. "They Are Not All the Same: Immigrant Enterprises, Transnationalism, and Development." *Journal of Ethnic and Migration Studies* 46 (10): 1991–2007. doi:10.1080/1369183X.2018.1559995.

Portes, A., and J. Yiu. 2013. "Entrepreneurship, Transnationalism, and Development." *Migration Studies* 1 (1): 75–95.

Rezaei, S., and M. Goli. 2020. "Prometheus, the Double-Troubled – Migrant Transnational Entrepreneurs and the Loyalty Trap." *Journal of Ethnic and Migration Studies* 46 (10): 2045–2066. doi:10.1080/1369183X.2018.1559998.

Rezaei, S., I. Light, and E. E. Telles. 2016. "Brain Circulation and Transnational Entrepreneurship: Guest Editorial - Special Issue." *International Journal of Business and Globalisation (IJBG)* 16 (3): 1–7.

Riddle, L. 2008. "Diasporas: Exploring Their Development Potential." *Journal of Microfinance* 10 (2): 28–35.

Riddle, L., and J. Brinkerhoff. 2011. "Diaspora Entrepreneurs as Institutional Change Agents: The Case of Thamel.com." *International Business Review* 20: 670–680.

Riddle, L., G. A. Hrivnak, and T. M. Nielsen. 2010. "Transnational Diaspora Entrepreneurship in Emerging Markets: Bridging Institutional Divides." *Journal of International Management* 16 (4): 398–411.

Rusinovic, K. 2008. "Transnational Embeddedness: Transnational Activities and Networks among First- and Second-Generation Immigrant Entrepreneurs in the Netherlands." *Journal of Ethnic and Migration Studies* 34 (3): 431–451.

Saxenian, A. L. 1999. *Silicon Valley's New Immigrant Entrepreneurs*. San Francisco, CA: Public Policy Institute of California, ISBN: 1-58213-009-4

Saxenian, A. L. 2002. "Silicon Valley's New Immigrant High-Growth Entrepreneurs." *Economic Development Quarterly* 16 (1): 20–31. doi:10.1177/0891242402016001003.

Saxenian, A. L. 2005. "From Brain Drain to Brain Circulation: Transnational Communities and Regional Upgrading in India and China." *Studies in Comparative International Development* 40 (2): 35–61.

Schumpeter, J. A. 1974. *Capitalism, Socialism and Democracy*. 4th ed. London: Unwin.

Sheffer, G. 2006. *Diaspora Politics*. Cambridge: Cambridge University Press.

Solano, G. 2020. "The Mixed Embeddedness of Transnational Migrant Entrepreneurs: Moroccans in Amsterdam and Milan." *Journal of Ethnic and Migration Studies* 46 (10): 2067–2085. doi:10.1080/1369183X.2018.1559999.

Valdez, Z., and M. Romero, eds. 2017. *Intersectionality and Ethnic Entrepreneurship (Ethnic and Racial Studies)*. 1st ed. Abingdon: Routledge.

von Bloh, J., V. Mandakovic, M. Apablaza, J. Ernesto Amorós, and R. Sternberg 2020. "Transnational Entrepreneurs: Opportunity or Necessity Driven? Empirical Evidence From Two Dynamic Economies From Latin America and Europe." *Journal of Ethnic and Migration Studies* 46 (10): 2008–2026. doi:10.1080/1369183X.2018.1559996.

Xiaohua, L., and S. Tao. 2012. "Transnational Entrepreneurs: Characteristics, Drivers, and Success Factors." *Journal of International Entrepreneurship* 10: 50–69.

Zapata-Barrero, R., and Z. Hellgren. 2020. "Harnessing the Potential of Moroccans Living Abroad Through Diaspora Policies? Assessing the Factors of Success and Failure of a New Structure of Opportunities for Transnational Entrepreneurs." *Journal of Ethnic and Migration Studies* 46 (10): 2027–2044. doi:10.1080/1369183X.2018.1559997.

Exploring the intersection of transnational, ethnic, and migration entrepreneurship

Benson Honig

ABSTRACT
In this essay, the importance of entrepreneurship is examined from multiple perspectives: Transnational, Ethnic, and Migration studies. Short historical perspectives are provided to illustrate both the universality of the immigrant entrepreneurship experience, and to highlight the need for multi-dimensional interdisciplinary study. A theoretical framework is suggested to facilitate this research, and discussions of future research opportunities are provided.

Introduction

In the next few decades, growth in the OECD's population and labour force will come almost entirely from immigration (Boubtane, Dumont, and Rault 2015; Clements 2015; Maestas, Mullen, and Powell 2016). Within the European Union, for example, research has shown that positive net migration rates within the EU have significant and positive effects on per capita GDP (Bernskiöld and Perman 2015). This demographic trend can only be countered through higher labour force participation rates, higher retirement ages, and proactive economic immigration policies. However, within Europe there are extremes, where by some countries are only growing due to immigration (Czech Republic, Italy, Greece, Slovenia and Slovakia) while others continue to be in population decline (e.g. Hungary) (Muenz 2007). Notably, research has shown that diversity of immigration populations has a positive economic impact (Bove and Elia 2017). This becomes relevant when considering that out migration will be predicted for emergent economies and in-migration for advanced economies (Clements 2015).

While extensions of the retirement age and encouraging more labour force participation can be helpful, immigration represents the fastest path to solving the aging demographic trends. Advanced economies will need to prepare for these new arrivals, and second- and third-tier cities in particular, face significant pressure to attract permanent and temporary immigrant populations to boost their productivity, transfer economic activity, and counter population aging trends.

World-wide, approximately 3% of the world's population lives in a country other than where they were born (Kerr et al. 2016). In many locations such as high-tech centres, immigrants represent a much larger percentage of the population: for example, in California, 27% of the population are immigrants (Simonson 2016). Yet, many cities are not prepared for a significant influx of multiple immigrant groups, or what Vertovec (2007) terms 'super-diversity.' Super-diversity creates both challenges, such as the integration of minorities into smaller, often homogenous communities, and opportunities, such as the potential benefits of the business endeavours by, and labour contributions of, immigrants to the ongoing development of the OECD's cities and communities.

Existing immigration and ethnicity scholarship generally focuses on metropolitan cities, representing an important research gap. Limited scholarship addresses the processes involved in the integration and resettlement of newcomers, especially the contribution of social capital (SC) in second- and third-tier cities or how these processes differ from those in metropolitan cities. Combining theoretical frameworks from Transnational Entrepreneurship, Ethnic Entrepreneurship and Migration Studies, this essay examines approaches to these issues directed at the following three questions:

- How can policymakers maximise and manage the economic benefits and costs of super-diversity for advanced economies, including second- and third-tier communities?
- How can communities attract and use immigrants, including encouraging entrepreneurship? How can they promote welcoming communities that enhance social capital and develop labour markets while reflecting important values of equity and justice?
- How can advanced economies create sustainable community labour markets for immigrants? What employment and firm creations techniques and processes can be developed that facilitate partnerships across an array of stakeholders, including community, university, and government entities, as well as different communities (e.g. rural–urban, different language, religious, and ethnic attributes)?

The objective of this essay is not to expressly answer the above questions, as each will require considerable research specific to the individual communities where they apply. Rather, the goal is to provide insight through research perspectives that will assist scholars in answering these questions. Doing so requires an interdisciplinary approach related to immigration, entrepreneurship, and labour market integration focussing on the perspectives of the three primary research paradigms: Migration studies regarding entrepreneurship, ethnic and ethnic enclave research, and transnational entrepreneurship. In the last section, an interdisciplinary framework is provided, suggesting how researchers might advance policy development in this arena, followed by suggestions for future research.

Entrepreneurship and its definition

Immigrants have long been associated with entrepreneurial endeavours, and many countries hope to attract and retain an entrepreneurial class that provides emergent industries, innovation, and new employment possibilities (Saxenian 1996, 2005, 2007; Bhachu 2017). Entrepreneurship has entered the public space in almost every forum imaginable – but certainly in the political, economic, business, not-for-profit and environmental domains. It is often presented as a panacea, although critiques have argued that in some circumstances, entrepreneurship may serve primarily to reduce the stresses of social inequality (Honig 2017). Thus, entrepreneurship has become a likely candidate for recognition and focus when examining contemporary problems, particularly those with newsworthy elements. For example, the crisis of refugees in Europe, precipitated both by warfare in Syria Iraq, Afghanistan, and by environmental challenges in North Africa and the Sahel are frequently addressed through entrepreneurial lenses. Public policy actors ask how to facilitate entrepreneurship for newer migrants, how entrepreneurship can improve lives in refugee camps, and even how entrepreneurship can encourage potential migrants to stay put and avoid migrating in the first place (Dos Reis, Koser, and Levin 2017; Sak et al. 2017). Within this span of scholarship we frequently observe different and contradictory definitions of what entrepreneurship is, what is should be accomplishing, and what the overall social and economic goals for migration and entrepreneurship are.

The first step in attempting to bridge across these very different domains of scholarship lies with defining the common word, 'entrepreneurship'. Reams of scholarship have been exhausted in this debate, with scholars arguing entrepreneurs are (1) leaders (2) innovators (3) disrupters (4) managers (5) risk takers (6) inventors (7) idea generators (8) creators of new organisations. While each of these aforementioned definitions have adherents for the purposes of this essay, I will adapt the latter: Entrepreneurs are individuals that create new organisations (see Drucker 1985). I use this definition not because the other are no relevant, but because I believe it captures the essential component of organisational diversity on which our activities incrementally advance and become established. Variation, selection and retention represent a useful model to explain new organisational emergence, grounded in well established evolutionary theory as first documented by Charles Darwin (Van de Ven and Poole 1995; Aldrich 1999). While other factors no doubt contribute to the process of organisational emergence, a focus on the phenomenological characteristics provides a useful domain for interdisciplinary studies (Sorenson and Stuart 2008) particularly valuable for understanding the implications of migration.

Entrepreneurship: the impact and importance of migration

Entrepreneurs are typically over-represented by immigrants (Light 1984; Waldinger 1986; Gold 1988; Razin 2017). Migrants have historically provided trans-national opportunities for ensuring reliability and securing trust and confidence. Thus, Jewish migrant entrepreneurs in the middle ages were able to rely on considerable international information, and also provided a level of contractual certainty other migrants could not offer – if there were problems, local Jewish communities might be held responsible until a resolution was forthcoming (Greif 1989). Beyond these obvious advantages, a number of additional possible causes have been attributed to the correlation between entrepreneurship and migration. First, many migrants are self-selected risk takers. They leave the predictability of their how countries in favour of better opportunities and conditions. Entrepreneurship has risk-taking properties, and so there may be a natural fit between migrants and self-employment. Second, many migrants find themselves in locations where previous status and human capital are not adequately recognised. For example, doctors and lawyers may be prohibited from practicing due to licensing constraints. Foreign degrees and experience may not be recognised in the new destination country. Previous expectations may drive migrants to seek other returns to their human capital that may be outside their professional boundaries offered by entrepreneurial activities. Third, migrants bring with them another perspective or view of the world. They may have preferences for certain types of food or dress, or other cultural norms that are inadequately addressed in their new destination countries, providing for entrepreneurial opportunities. Alternatively, they may be aware of different practices that they believe might be advantageous to apply in their new setting. Finally, they may have particular observations regarding their new environment that lead to recognising opportunities. Having a comparative external frame of reference can be an important inspiration for new ideas, firms and organisations.

The growing relationship between migration and entrepreneurship can also be attributed to the changing nature of international migration and diasporas and to the complex nature of international business activities (Yeung 2002; Zahra and George 2002). While businesses were once frequently national and even localised, they are increasingly subject to global competition, offshore subcontracting and outsourcing, and enhanced expectations of product delivery, service, and pricing. A quick visit to any tourist market in Africa will highlight this new reality. Present will be goods from across the African continent, as well as from China. Few if any of the vendors are aware of the origin of all but the most local goods, as they are typically sold by roving salesmen. Likewise, an informal tour of most European cities provides a window into migratory labour, some legal, others illegal (Rezaei, Goli, and Dana 2013). Africans selling collections of handbags, watches, sunglasses, and jerseys are quite common in subways and tourist locations. The goods are frequently displayed on large cloths looped by rope, such that the vendor can collect all their goods and 'run' from authorities at a moment's notice. Inquiries in some locations reveal that certain communities have learned how to dominate the geographic location. For example, primarily Senegalese can be observed along the Barcelona boardwalk. They monitor and disallow the sales of drugs, alcohol, and tobacco, thus providing a tacit agreement between the authorities and their informal sector sales.

The very demands of the new competitive business environment create and inspire migration. This can be seen from petty traders (Freeman 1997; Marques, Santos, and Araújo 2001) all the way to transnational and born global firms (Knight and Cavusgil 2004) that may demand migratory labour in order to maintain adequate human capital for their research and development, as exhibited by the growth of targeted visas for technical and scientific labour (D'Costa 2008; Ayers and Syfert 2001; Kerr et al. 2016). In sum, the world of entrepreneurship is increasingly on the move, whether it be due to drivers, such as climate change, that reduce the opportunities for individuals to engage in traditional farming or animal husbandry in the Sahal, war, such as that observed in the Middle East, or opportunity such as that provided in the gulf countries and in other high-technology regions world-wide.

Ethnic entrepreneurship, ethnic enclaves, and the entrepreneurship of the 'other'

A rich history has developed around the concept of ethnic entrepreneurship, frequently identifying new practices and recognising the specific needs and opportunities of immigrant communities (Light 1984; Light and Karageorgis 1994; Portes 1995; Zhou 2004; Volery 2007). Initially, certain ethnic groups were targeted and 'imported' to take advantage of cheap labour or to engage in activities locals were unwilling to do (Safa 1981; Cloud and Galenson 1987; Holland 2007). Cities recognised these ethnic enclaves with colloquial names – 'China-town'; 'Little Italy'; 'Japan-town'; 'the barrio as well as more directly derogatory identifiers. Many of these practices, consisting of parallel segmented labour markets for immigrants, continue even until today (Zlolniski 1994).

Institutionally regulated programmes, such as the post-war invitation by Germany to Turkish guest workers, have worked out very differently than initially expected. As Swiss novelist Max Frisch reportedly said regarding the state of European temporary workers: 'We wanted workers … but we got people instead.' (Borjas 2016). Despite not being granted citizenship in Germany, for example, many Turkish immigrants stayed on through multiple generations – eventually creating an ideological challenge for determining precisely what constitutes German nationality. Only recently has Germany systematically opened up the opportunity for citizenship to their immigrant population, often with mixed results (Ehrkamp 2005; Ersanilli and Koopmans 2010). Meanwhile, the proliferation of kebab shops, middle eastern sweets, and other ethnic goods have taken on a nearly universal place in contemporary German life (Ehrkamp 2005). As immigrants play an increasing cultural role, citizenship for some immigrants may include the appropriation of public spaces and even include the gradual reconfiguration of what citizenship in the host country constitutes (Ehrkamp and Leitner 2003). However, research shows that there continue to be significant ideological barriers embodied by the six million Turkish immigrants in Germany, approximately 6% of the population. For example, a recent study found that while Turkish immigrants were generally positive about their German integration, a slight majority felt they were second class citizens and not recognised as part of German society (Pollack et al. 2016). More concerning was that the study revealed that half of the Turkish population indicated there is only one true religion, and that it was more important to follow the commandments of their religion than the laws of the country they were living in. Fully 20% of the population believed that the threat to Islam by Western civilisation justifies Muslims to defend themselves with violence. Further, 27% had somewhat or very negative attitudes towards atheists, and 21% against Jews. These attitudes suggest important contrasts regarding this population's openness to liberal democracy, often persisting three generations after immigration.

Not surprisingly, considerable research, consternation, and public critique continues to centre around where, how, and with what characteristics immigrants establish themselves. Chain migration, initially explaining the process by which immigrants established themselves by linking with friends and family across different geographical locations, was originally a theoretical and sociological explanation lacking political overtones (Castles 2002). Today, the term has taken on explicit negative overtones by anti-immigrant politicians (Kearse 2018). Many are reacting to the impact of neighbourhoods with high immigration from selective areas. In some cases it is voluntary, the outcome of geographical and economic opportunities. In other cases, it is more sociological, an outcome of preferences toward segregation and religious and ethnic bias on the part of the destination population.

In France, for example, immigrants from the Maghreb live in ghettos that surround Paris (Simon 1998), despite the fact that referring to ethnic identities is largely frowned up on in France (Hargreaves 1995). This pattern – whereby immigrants either self-select or are directed to live apart and distinct from the general population, mirrors American ghettos reflecting traditions based on post-slavery and urban immigrant absorption whose certain locations were considered 'appropriate' for recent immigrants. Geographical segregation remains evident in Europe, inclusive of welcoming Scandinavia (Sernhede

2007; Wacquant 2008; Lalander and Sernhede 2011; Stehle 2012) something that the sociologist Pierre Bourdieu concluded was a modern misery (Bourdieu 1999). While some may argue that these are self-selected preferences, few ghettoised locations offer the same standards of education, community services, economic mobility, and civil society as that offered to the general non-immigrant population. Thus, whether by choice, restriction, or probability, ethnic neighbourhoods often institutionalise the very attributes of poverty and lack of inclusion that many governments wish to avoid. The unfortunate results include growing xenophobic and nationalistic movements world-wide (Finzsch and Schirmer 2002).

In contrast to many examples in Europe and North America, high technology centres such as Silicon Valley celebrate their diversity, inclusion, and very lack of ethnic ghettoisation (Saxenian 1996, 2007). Of course, many of these locations reflect an economic homogeneity, whereby only specialised workers can afford the high rents. This creates a type of geographical gated community, as more diverse and less affluent community members depart. Innovative new concepts have sprung up as a reaction, for example, middle class professional (non-technical) San Franciscans are resorting to living in adult dorm rooms with shared communal spaces (Bowles 2018).

While contemporary political responses such as Brexit in the UK and the anti-immigrant movement in the USA led by President Trump seem to tug in one direction, the demands of innovation and flexible high quality labour are pulling the opposite way. High tech firms want to attract the best and brightest immigrants from anywhere in the globe. Unemployed and underemployed former factory workers prefer to see a wall preventing immigration with the belief that it will enhance their employability and job prospects. This debate – between globalisation and local protectionism, is being echoed throughout the world resulting in different entrepreneurial environments (Portes and Martinez 2020). It is likely to increase as global inequality grows (Piketty 2014).

Transnational entrepreneurship and the global diaspora

Increasing mobility, lower costs of transportation, and a new recognition of globalisation precipitated by information flows through the internet have facilitated transnational entrepreneurship, who act as change agents in many locations (Saxenian 1996; Riddle, Hrivnak, and Nielsen 2010; Zapata-Barrero and Rezaei 2020). Transnational entrepreneurs (TEs) utilise multiple cross-border networks to promote their entrepreneurial activities and for developing business opportunities (Drori, Honig, and Wright 2009). Traditionally, TEs have were recognised as petty traders, such as the 'higglers' who travelled throughout the Caribbean trading items purchased and carried in their luggage (Olwig and Sorensen 2003) or the cross-border traders in Africa (Fadahunsi and Rosa 2002). In these cases, TEs emerged following both local obstacles and the pull of trading opportunities often fulfilled by inadequate or inefficient customs regimes. Local contextual knowledge of markets and transaction costs represent the sustained competitive advantage provided by these TEs.

Many of these TEs are low capital activities, sometime resorting to barter, and frequently the solo-self employed. Some enter the informal sector doing illegal work, and a growing feminisation of these opportunities have led to increasing strain in family unit, as women are often asked to take jobs abroad as domestics. Thus, while a neoliberal agenda rewards women in the workplace, the consequences may leave women who enter transnational work and their families whom they leave behind, more venerable (Ribeiro, Rezaei, and Dana 2012).

A newer class of TEs have emerged that reflect more complicated business relationships and more advanced notions and expectations. Saxinian refers to the 'new argonauts' as a distinct class of highly trained specialists who ply their technical expertise on global markets, earning premiums for their specialties (Saxenian 2007). They carry with them the seeds of new enterprise, and have been systematically welcome as 'return migrants and entrepreneurs' by, for example, China (Saxenian 2005). They have also become increasingly evident as small business persons in both developed and emergent markets (Wong and Ng 2002; Saxenian 2005; French 2014; Bhachu 2017; Zapata-Barrero and Rezaei 2020). TE's have led in innovation in many high technology fields. Well cited is the finding that over 25% of the high-technology start-ups in silicon valley have immigrant co-founders. The top ten sending countries include India (33%), China (85) UK (6%), Canada (4%), Germany and Israel (3%), Russia, Korea, Australia and the Netherlands (2%) (Wadhwa, Saxenian, and Siciliano 2012). Concerns have been raised that their return migration to their countries of origin reflect a new reverse brain drain (also referred to as brain circulation, depending on the perspective) (Wadhwa 2009). While specific numbers of TE's by country are very difficult to assess, some research in the USA suggests that 23.5% of the engineering and technology companies established between 1995–2005 has at least one immigrant key founder (Wang and Liu 2015). Thus, TEs have come to be seen as a national resource to be cultivated and protected by some, and as a potential national tragedy, by others.

From a theoretical perspective, the notion of *habitus* and the Theory of Practice (TOP) introduced by Bourdieu provides an important framework for understanding the activities of TEs. *Habitus* is

> a product of history that produces individual and collective practices … It ensures the active presence of experiences, which, deposited in each organism in the form of schemes of perception, thought and action, tend to guarantee the 'correctness' of practices and their constancy over time, more reliably than all formal rules and explicit norms (Bourdieu 1990, 54).

Habitus not only refers to actions on the part of TEs, but also to their way of thinking – what might be referred to as common sense. It includes the norms, patterns, and behavioural dispositions that shape prevailing practices within a given field. *TEs' habitus* is simultaneously 'durable' and open to influences from new experiences and new positions in relation to social structures associated with the multiplicity of environments that characterises transnational operation. Because TEs engage in business in multiple geographical, sociocultural, political, and economic locales, each field has its own logic, specific forms of capital, and stakes, but each field is also part of the social configurations in which fields are themselves embedded. TOP incorporates the view that these boundaries provide locales that differentiate rewards, socializations, network characteristics, and other unique characteristics of the trans-national organisations they develop. They provide both obstacles and opportunities for TEs who navigate multiple environments and exploit opportunities. As observed by Lamont and Molnar (2002, 168) boundaries are conceptual distinctions made by social actors to categorise objects, people, practices and even time and space. They are tools by which individuals and groups struggle over and come to agree upon definitions of reality. Furthermore, boundaries represent 'objectified forms of social differences manifested in unequal access to unequal distribution of resources (material or nonmaterial) and social opportunities.' Thus, the very obstacles that TEs encounter in their efforts to become entrepreneurial represent theoretical distinctions that define their activities.

TE's employ their dual or multiple contexts of habitus in their business practices by leveraging critical resources (Mountz and Wright 1996). Numerous studies of TEs, including those from the Seychelles Islands in Britain and Bangladesh (Gardner 1995), Mexicans in Poughkeepsie, New York (Mountz and Wright 1996), Moroccan women in Italy (Salih 2003), and Ukrainians and Russians in Israel (Remennick 2003) make use of their dual networks in order to advance business activities. It is through their *habitus* that TEs may strive to exert power over the organisational field for the purpose of channelling the forms of capital that fit their individual and societal aspirations (Honneth, Kocyba, and Schwibs 1986).

Finally, it is worth noting that not all TE's are the same – there is considerable variation in the process and objectives of different TE's. They may only be engaged in exporting, they may have an overseas presence or subsidiary, or they may conduct outsourcing. Each of these tasks requires a very different set of capital – human, social, and financial. Overall, however, firms with TE activities have higher payroll per employee than either immigrant or non-immigrant firms, and a positive association with firm performance (Wang and Liu 2015).

Migration at the intersection – where ethnic, transnational and economics meet

When Marco Polo set out from Venice in 1271 toward China and the far east, he left with a merchant's education and a family reputation as travellers and traders, effectively entrepreneurs of the middle ages. Indeed, Venice owed much of its wealth and reputation to entrepreneurship and international trade (Norwich 2003). Nearly six hundred years later, the US navy employed gunboat diplomacy to open the markets of Japan following 220 years of isolation (Walworth 2008). Clearly, migration embodies considerable power and opportunity, one that is both of ongoing economic and political interest. As our global communication and travel capabilities continue to expand, we can only expect that the importance and impact of immigration will grow as well.

The evidence of migration and foreign trade takes us all the way back to the very first known instances of writing, a set of Sumerian accounting clay tablets indicating who owed what for goods, perhaps travelling across the middle east 5000 years ago (Harari 2014). From shell trading in Polynesia, to glass trader beads in Africa and white porcelain and silk from China, migrants have provided the critical mechanism for which good travelled the earth since the dawn of civilisation. Long before there were passports there were traders, merchants, and economic migrants looking for better opportunities and greener pastures.

While the process of migration remains a matter of historical fact – all humans are said to descend from a genetic pool in East Africa 70,000 years ago (Harari 2014), our social construction creates localities, ethnicities, and cultural preferences that not only adhere to particular localities, but often sustain themselves over vast geographical and time boundaries (Anderson 1991, 2006). Although the nation-state is currently the triumphant model (Meyer et al. 1997), it is by no means given that humankind will forever be anchored by nationalistic borders. When ISIS attempted to re-build a caliphate, nation-states attributes with their accompanying flags, songs, animals, and sports teams were no part of their political organisation (Gulmohamad 2014). ISIS, of course, is an organisation composed of migrants from dozens of countries coalescing around a shared ideology. It serves to underscore the increasing complexity that is an outcome of the increasing diversity and complexity of international migration.

The forces of globalisation, that continue to facilitate migration, are both technological and political. Regarding technology, as air travel costs have been reduced substantially around the world, populations have access to migratory opportunities that never existed previously. Politically, neo-liberal policies have been enacted that encourage free trade and mobility, as well as the diffusion of a global culture that both encourages and enables migration. The Syrian refugee crisis, the largest wave of immigration to be seen since the second World War, was enabled and encouraged through the use of smart phones, youtube videos, whatsapp, and other technological innovations. Growing inequality, now observable at the local internet café in nearly every country world-wide, provides important incentives 'pulling' would-be migrants that might be suffering from global climate change, political instability, warfare, or simply corrupt or inefficient leadership. Thus, the range of migrants – their diversity- is also expanding. Added to economic migrants, transnational and migratory entrepreneurs, we now have political refugees, environmental refugees, individuals escaping gender, religious and ethnic discrimination of all sorts, those escaping warfare, racism, ethnocentrism, genocide, instability, slavery, and authoritarianism. This growing cadre of immigrants are both willing and able to go further than in previous years, while many are willing to risk their very lives on the small chance of becoming a successful immigrant.

Globally, immigration trends have changed considerably, as even the immigrant destination countries (USA, Canada, Australia and NZ) are now drawing immigrants from a different and much more diverse set of origin countries (Czaika and Haas 2014). Where once Europe supplied these countries with immigrants, now many Western European countries are attracting immigrants from Eastern Europe and the Middle East, not historically traditional sources. However, in order to maintain continued economic growth, Europeans need to address problems posed by an aging and shrinking population. Europe's 'second demographic transition' (SDT) reports later unions, later and fewer births, and more deaths than births, creating a growing need for elderly care and a crucial role for a supplemental and replacement workforce, hence the need for newcomer integration (Heran 2016). Given the demographic realities of an ageing Europe, this is likely to be a helpful antidote. However, the impact of this shift will be observed in cultural changes that both adjust to new populations, and are precipitated by them.

The resulting outcomes of increasing immigrant diversity suggest a future that might move national political orientations in two very distinctive directions. Some countries may embrace these emergent multicultural dimensions, celebrate them, and learn to benefit from the many transnational entrepreneurial and economic benefits the growing cadre of immigrants embody. Multitudes of ethnic enclaves and explicit strategies for encouraging chain migration, and facilitating the integration and economic vitality of new immigrants, might be developed with the help of settlement assistance agencies. Alternatively, regimes might react to perceived onslaughts brought on by diverse immigration and entrench themselves in a nativist, isolationist philosophy. Doing so may jeopardise their own economic potential, perhaps even serve to drive away talented labour by failing to preserve institutional norms that reward meritocracy and mobility (Medawar and Pyke 2001).

It would seem as though future migration research and scholarship rests at the intersection of political and economic power (Zapata-Barrero and Rezaei 2020). Because the economic advantages of immigration typically take time to play out, and may be difficult to discern, there are many opportunities for nationalists and ideologues to take front and centre state, and effectively control the political agenda. Pressure from various political groups often precedes national action, and these forces are likely to gain additional currency. Brexit and the nationalism of Donald Trump represent important signals, but even welcoming Germany maintains a cadre of critics. For example, a recent bestseller in Germany had the title 'Germany abolishes itself' referring to the asserted negative impact of diverse immigrants on German culture (Sarrazin 2010). Unfortunately, these movements may eventually constrain innovation and entrepreneurship in the countries that espouse ethnocentric policies. Thus, immigrant 'unfriendly' political discourse and regimes my eventually create barriers to entry for TE's and migrants, eventually yielding a negative impact on economic growth.

Irrespective of the tides of cultural fads and fashion, we can predict with near certainty that just as the empirical complexity of immigration patterns will become increasingly convoluted, so will the study of related systems of managing this diversity as well as the range of potential strategies and outcomes. To the 'winners' the future may provide the advantages of economic flexibility and innovation that migrants have historically delivered. However, this will not happen without significant internal adjustments, including cultural and political, some of which may provide existential challenges to various political entities. As more diverse populations continue to take part in the migration equation, and as that equation becomes increasingly more complicated, so, too, are solutions that maximise opportunity and minimise deleterious outcomes. As with the globalisation of trade, the globalisation of human capital presents significant opportunities for those capable of harnessing the rich potential of diversity with the necessary multi-dimensional solutions.

Integrating multiple perspectives: a suggested research framework

Each of the separate fields of entrepreneurship, migration, ethnic, and TE's, have each been examined using different methods and models. Here I propose a single overarching framework capable of examining all three of these different sub-fields and providing concrete policy recommendations utilising a single model, which is subsequently introduced. This is a novel approach that, to the best of my knowledge, has never been implemented.

Managing the increasing complexity of immigration requires managing not only political and economic issues related to labour market integration, but also social issues including ethnicity, social capital, human capital at multiple levels, micro, meso, and macro. The specific objectives should be capable of providing integration on a localised basis but also adjusted according to demographic and regional characteristic. They are as follows:

- Understanding and measuring the importance of critical demographic variables, including age, religion, community/city of origin in order to understand their impact on programmes and policies that support social integration and labour market integration and self-employment.
- Understanding the role of political and community level institutional factors that both facilitate and impeded social and labour market integration. These include geographical living arrangements, ethnic enclaves, political parties, preferences and local opposition to immigrants, and opportunities to engage in TE activities.
- Understanding, measuring and identifying policies that enhance the role of human capital including work experience (non-formal) training and apprenticeship (informal) and educational levels (formal). This requires assessment of immigrant human capital at the local level.
- Understanding, measuring, and identifying policies that enhance the role of social capital including previous social capital embodied and carried from the country of origin; social capital acquired in transit from newly-constituted immigrant activities; and social capital established and developed in the new host country.
- Understanding, measuring and identifying policies that enhance the institutions and regulations currently in place in terms of how they impact social integration and labour market outcomes.
- Understanding and measuring how sex and gender impacts policies, regulations, interventions, and the social and human capital of refugees.

Mastering this complexity calls for a mixed embeddedness model relying on interdisciplinary study (Kloosterman 2010a, 2010b). The mixed embeddedness model provides an important theoretical window through which to engage in cross disciplinary research – linking issues regarding human and social capital to policy and institutional factors often overlooked in economic or management research. The model has previously been used primarily to examine immigrant entrepreneurship, however, applying this concept simultaneously to transnational entrepreneurship and return migration would represent a new approach. Although, concepts such as human capital, social capital and institutional environments are all concepts that have previously been extensively studied, the mixed embeddedness framework enables an understanding that integrates and combines insights from all three concepts, providing a more holistic and realistic picture of social and labour market integration.

Critical variables will be associated with the fields of economics, sociology, political science, anthropology, geography, and cultural and gender studies. Together, each brings a facet that facilitates the role of social and economic integration. The mixed embeddedness model (Kloosterman 2010a, 2010b) facilitates interdisciplinary study examining both regulatory and local governance-related factors. Utilising this model should be helpful to public policy actors attempting to adjust and fine tune their immigration policies in order to facilitate immigration integration.

Figure 1 provides an adapted mixed embeddedness model that should provide important insights for scholars planning to do research regarding facilitating migrant integration. The goal is to examine integration at the appropriate levels for developing policy. National, regional, and local policies must reflect the conditions presented by each unique environment. Notably, the three questions at the beginning of this essay

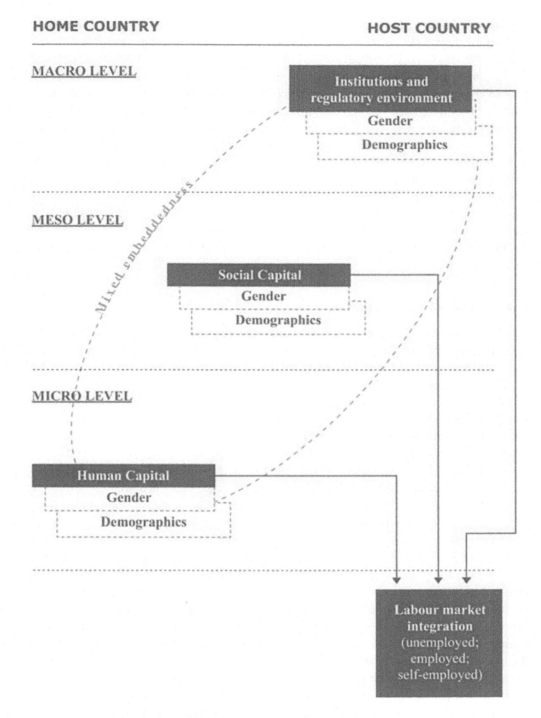

*Developed in collaboration with Kim Klyver.

Figure 1. Theoretical extended mixed embeddedness model for immigrant integration*. *Developed in collaboration with Kim Klyver.

require considerable multifaceted research. Interdisciplinary studies are necessary to understand how policymakers can maximise and manage the economic benefits and costs of super-diversity for advanced economies; how communities can attract and use immigrants and entrepreneurs; how to promote welcoming communities; and how to create sustainable community labour markets for immigrants. Factors involved include promoting social capital and human capital, as well as closely monitoring and enhancing institutional structures that influence access to markets and to economic capital. Focussing on only one element, as scholarship frequently employs, will fail to provide the necessary tools that must be developed on a systemic community-wide basis. The mixed embeddedness model introduced here controls for these factors, as well as gender issues, in identifying pressure points and potential variables to monitor when developing new policies and routines. Successful solutions will require partnerships across an array of stakeholders, including community, university, and government entities, as well as different communities (e.g. rural–urban, different language, religious, and ethnic attributes).

Future research opportunities

Given the aforementioned growth and complexity of global immigration activities, the opportunities for both theoretical and policy driven research are considerable. Solving this multi-dimensional puzzle requires innovative targeted research, appropriate to the particular environment being studies. To begin with, longitudinal studies that examine the actual experiences of immigrants under various institutional arrangements are sorely needed. Much literature focuses primarily on census data, systematic studies of the obstacles and facilitators of immigrant experiences are still rather limited, and rarely extend beyond one or two years. This is problematic because it often takes a decade or more for migrants to adjust to their new environment, obtain credible occupational and social goals, and begin integrating into their acquired new homes. Effective research should periodically and qualitatively study a group of immigrants, comparing them according to either differential institutional exposure, or according to origin or other qualities such as human and social capital variations.

A second critical gap lies in the nexus between political, economic, and social integration. Interdisciplinary studies are necessary to adequately examine what environmental characteristics are most likely to result in effective integration. Granting agencies and public policy designers should target funds specifically for this kind of interdisciplinary study. Further opportunities exist for research that examines particular fields in an attempt to identify positive factors associated with attracting immigrant populations – the effects on elder and health care, the impact on transnational businesses, as well as the growing connection with global cultures that may serve to enrich destination environments. Given that many ageing communities will be forced to depend on immigration for their economic growth and well being, recognising specific contributions through systematic research and socially marketing those findings can result in more welcoming communities.

Finally, important research needs to be done examining the specific institutional factors that facilitate or impede integration at various points of an immigrant absorption, once again, with a longitudinal focus. What is the impact of banking regulations, industrial regulation, and the promotion or constraints for informal and formal sector activities? How can policies be developed that more rapidly assist immigrants in acquiring resources and participating in social, political, and economic life? How do these policies help promote meritocracy and opportunity, and how might they instead constrain mobility and increase inequality?

It seems quite logical to anticipate increasing complexity in the global migration calculus. Climate change, mass communication, and mass transportation all exert forces suggesting policy makers should prepare for ever more nuances in establishing effective working models to integrate migrants into existing populations. Historically, such integration has occurred with little public policy, but much human tragedy. It is our hope that effective research can minimise some of the human suffering that has long accompanied migration patterns.

Disclosure statement

No potential conflict of interest was reported by the author.

References

Aldrich, H. 1999. *Organizations Evolving*. London: Sage.
Anderson, B. 1991. *Imagined Communities*. rev ed. London and New York: Verso.
Anderson, B. 2006. *Imagined Communities: Reflections on the Origin and Spread of Nationalism*. London: Verso Books.
Ayers, K. N., and S. D. Syfert. 2001. "US Visa Options and Strategies for the Information Technology Industry." *North Carolina Journal of International Law and Commercial Regulation* 27: 301.
Bernskiöld, E., and M. Perman. 2015. Free Movement; The Economic Effects of Net Migration within the European Union.
Bhachu, P. 2017. *Immigration and Entrepreneurship: Culture, Capital, and Ethnic Networks*. London: Routledge.
Borjas, G. J. 2016. *We Wanted Workers: Unraveling the Immigration Narrative*. New York: WW Norton & Company.
Boubtane, E., J. C. Dumont, and C. Rault. 2015. Immigration and Economic Growth in the OECD Countries 1986–2006.
Bourdieu, P. 1990. *The Logic of Practice*. Stanford: Stanford University Press.
Bourdieu, P. 1999. *The Weight of the World: Social Suffering in Contemporary Society*. Alhoda: Polity Press.
Bove, V., and L. Elia. 2017. "Migration, Diversity, and Economic Growth." *World Development* 89: 227–239.
Bowles, N. 2018. "Dorm Living for Professionals." *New York Times*, March 5, page. B1.
Castles, S. 2002. "Migration and Community Formation Under Conditions of Globalization." *International Migration Review* 36 (4): 1143–1168.
Clements, M. B. J. 2015. *The Fiscal Consequences of Shrinking Populations*. Washington, DC: International Monetary Fund.
Cloud, P., and D. W. Galenson. 1987. "Chinese Immigration and Contract Labor in the Late Nineteenth Century." *Explorations in Economic History* 24 (1): 22–42.
Czaika, M., and H. Haas. 2014. "The Globalization of Migration: Has the World Become More Migratory?" *International Migration Review* 48 (2): 283–323.
D'Costa, A. P. 2008. "The International Mobility of Technical Talent: Trends and Development Implications." In *International Mobility of Talent and Development Impact*, 44–83. Oxford: Oxford University Press.

Dos Reis, A. A., K. Koser, and M. Levin. 2017. "Private Sector Engagement in the Global Compact on Safe, Orderly, and Regular Migration." In *Migration Research Leaders' Syndicate*, 189. Switzerland: Grand Saconnex.

Drori, I., B. Honig, and M. Wright. 2009. "Transnational Entrepreneurship: An Emergent Field of Study." *Entrepreneurship Theory and Practice* 33 (5): 1001–1022.

Drucker, P. F. 1985. *Innovation and Entrepreneurship: Practice and Principles*. New York, USA: Harper Business.

Ehrkamp, P. 2005. "Placing Identities: Transnational Practices and Local Attachments of Turkish Immigrants in Germany." *Journal of Ethnic and Migration Studies* 31 (2): 345–364.

Ehrkamp, P., and H. Leitner. 2003. "Beyond National Citizenship: Turkish Immigrants and the (RE)Construction of Citizenship in Germany." *Urban Geography* 24 (2): 127–146.

Ersanilli, E., and R. Koopmans. 2010. "Rewarding Integration? Citizenship Regulations and the Socio-Cultural Integration of Immigrants in the Netherlands, France and Germany." *Journal of Ethnic and Migration Studies* 36 (5): 773–791.

Fadahunsi, A., and P. Rosa. 2002. "Entrepreneurship and Illegality: Insights from the Nigerian Cross-Border Trade." *Journal of Business Venturing* 17 (5): 397–429.

Finzsch, N., and D. Schirmer, eds. 2002. *Identity and Intolerance: Nationalism, Racism, and Xenophobia in Germany and the United States*. Cambridge: Cambridge University Press.

Freeman, C. 1997. "Reinventing Higglering Across Transnational Zones." In *Daughters of Caliban: Caribbean Women in the Twentieth Century*, 68–95. Bloomington: Indiana University Press.

French, H. W. 2014. *China's Second Continent: How a Million Migrants are Building a New Empire in Africa*. New York: Vintage.

Gardner, K. 1995. *Global Migrants, Local Lives: Travel and Transformation in Rural Bangladesh*. Oxford: Clarendon.

Gold, S. J. 1988. "Refugees and Small Business: The Case of Soviet Jews and Vietnamese." *Ethnic and Racial Studies* 11 (4): 411–438.

Greif, A. 1989. "Reputation and Coalitions in Medieval Trade: Evidence on the Maghribi Traders." *The Journal of Economic History* 49 (4): 857–882.

Gulmohamad, Z. K. 2014. "The Rise and Fall of the Islamic State of Iraq and Al-Sham (Levant) ISIS." *Global Security Studies* 5 (2): 1–11.

Harari, Y. N. 2014. *Sapiens: A Brief History of Humankind*. New York: Random House.

Hargreaves, A. 1995. *Immigration, 'Race' and Ethnicity in Contemporary France*. Abingdon-on-Thames: Routledge.

Heran, F. 2016. "Looking Forward: Future Migration Trends and Research Needs for Europe." International Conference, Feb. 4-5 2016, Brussels.

Holland, K. M. 2007. "A History of Chinese Immigration in the United States and Canada." *American Review of Canadian Studies* 37 (2): 150–160.

Honig. 2017. "Compensatory Entrepreneurship: Avoiding the Pitfalls of Global Isomorphic Entrepreneurship Research and Activities." *Iberoamerican Journal of Entrepreneurship and Small Business* 6 (3): 452–465.

Honneth, A., H. Kocyba, and B. Schwibs. 1986. "The Struggle for Symbolic Order an Interview with Pierre Bourdieu." *Theory, Culture & Society* 3 (3): 35–51.

Kearse, S. 2018. "Beaten Path." *New York Times Magazine*, March 25. Page MM 15.

Kerr, S. P., W. Kerr, Ç. Özden, and C. Parsons. 2016. "Global Talent Flows." *Journal of Economic Perspectives* 30 (4): 83–106.

Kloosterman, R. C. 2010a. "Matching Opportunities with Resources: A Framework for Analysing (Migrant) Entrepreneurship From a Mixed Embeddedness Perspective." *Entrepreneurship and Regional Development* 22 (1): 25–45.

Kloosterman, R. C. 2010b. "Matching Opportunities with Resources: A Framework for Analysing (Migrant) Self-Employment from a Mixed Embeddedness Perspective." *Self-employment and Regional Development* 22 (1): 25–45.

Knight, G. A., and S. T. Cavusgil. 2004. "Innovation, Organizational Capabilities, and the Born-Global Firm." *Journal of International Business Studies* 35 (2): 124–141.

Lalander, P., and O. Sernhede. 2011. "Social Mobilization or Street Crimes: Two Strategies among Young Urban Outcasts in Contemporary Sweden."
Lamont, M., and V. Molnar. 2002. "The Study of Boundaries in the Social Sciences." *Annual Review of Sociology* 28: 167–195.
Light, I. 1984. "Immigrant and Ethnic Enterprise in North America." *Ethnic and Racial Studies* 7 (2): 195–216.
Light, I., and S. Karageorgis. 1994. "The Ethnic Economy." In *The Handbook of Economic Sociology*, edited by N. J. Smelser and R. Swedberg, 647–671. Princeton, NJ: Princeton University Press.
Maestas, N., K. J. Mullen, and D. Powell. 2016. *The Effect of Population Aging on Economic Growth, the Labor Force and Productivity*. Washington, DC: National Bureau of Economic Research. (No. w22452).
Marques, M. M., R. Santos, and F. Araújo. 2001. "Ariadne's Thread: Cape Verdean Women in Transnational Webs." *Global Networks* 1 (3): 283–306.
Medawar, J. S., and D. Pyke. 2001. *Hitler's Gift: The True Story of the Scientists Expelled by the Nazi Regime*. New York: Arcade Publishing.
Meyer, J. W., J. Boli, G. M. Thomas, and F. O. Ramirez. 1997. "World Society and the Nation-State." *American Journal of Sociology* 103 (1): 144–181.
Mountz, A., and R. A. Wright. 1996. "Daily Life in the Transnational Migrant Community of San Agustín, Oaxaca, and Poughkeepsie, New York." *Diaspora: A Journal of Transnational Studies* 5: 403–428.
Muenz, R. 2007. "Aging and Demographic Change in European Societies: Main Trends and Alternative Policy Options." *World Bank SP Discussion Paper No, 703*.
Norwich, J. J. 2003. *A History of Venice*. Westminster: Penguin.
Olwig, K. F., and N. N. Sorensen. 2003. *Work and Migration: Life and Livelihoods in a Globalizing World*. London: Routledge.
Piketty, T. 2014. Capital in the 21st Century.
Pollack, D., O. Muller, G. Rosta, and A. Dieler. 2016. *Integration and Religion as Seen by People of Turkish Origin in Germany*. Cluster of Excellence. Munster, Germany: Religion and Politics, Munster University.
Portes, A., ed. 1995. *The Economic Sociology of Immigration: Essays on Networks, Ethnicity, and Entrepreneurship*. New York: Russell Sage Foundation.
Portes, A., and B. P. Martinez. 2020. "They Are Not All the Same: Immigrant Enterprises, Transnationalism, and Development." *Journal of Ethnic and Migration Studies* 46 (10): 1991–2007. doi:10.1080/1369183X.2018.1559995.
Razin, E. 2017. "Immigrant Entrepreneurs in Israel, Canada, and California." In *Immigration and Entrepreneurship*, edited by Bhachu, 97–124. London: Routledge.
Remennick, L. 2003. "A Case Study in Transnationalism: Russian Jewish Immigrants in Israel of the 1990s." In *Diasporas and Ethnic Migrants: German, Israel, and and Post-Soviet Successor States in Comparative Perspective*, edited by R. Munz and O. Rainer, 370–384. Hove: Psychology Press.
Rezaei, S., M. Goli, and L. P. Dana. 2013. "Informal Opportunity among SMEs: an Empirical Study of Denmark's Underground Economy." *International Journal of Entrepreneurship and Small Business* 19 (1): 64–76.
Ribeiro, A., S. Rezaei, and L. P. Dana. 2012. "Gender and Family in Transnational Entrepreneurship." *International Journal of Business and Globalisation* 8 (3): 409–420.
Riddle, L., G. Hrivnak, and T. Nielsen. 2010. "Transnational Diaspora Entrepreneurship in Emerging Markets: Bridging Institutional Divides." *Journal of International Management* 16 (4): 398–411.
Safa, H. I. 1981. "Runaway Shops and Female Employment: The Search for Cheap Labor." *Signs: Journal of Women in Culture and Society* 7 (2): 418–433.
Sak, G., T. Kaymaz, O. Kadkoy, and M. Kenanoglu. 2017. *Forced Migrants: Labour Market Integration and Entrepreneurship* (No. 2017-61). Economics Discussion Papers.
Salih, R. 2003. *Gender in Transnationalism: Home, Longing and Belonging among Moroccan Migrant Women*. New York: Routledge.
Sarrazin, T. 2010. Deutschland schafft sich ab: Wie wir unser Land aufs Spiel setzen. dva.

Saxenian, A. 1996. *Regional Advantage*. Boston: Harvard University Press.
Saxenian, A. 2005. "From Brain Drain to Brain Circulation: Transnational Communities and Regional Upgrading in India and China." *Studies in Comparative International Development* 40 (2): 35–61.
Saxenian, A. 2007. *The New Argonauts: Regional Advantage in a Global Economy*. Boston: Harvard University Press.
Sernhede, O. 2007. "Microphone Prophets and Schooling Outside School: The Global Tribe of hip hop and Immmigrant Youth in 'The New Sweden'." In *Reflections on Education in "Multicultural" Societies: Turkish and Swedish Perspectives*, 227–243. Stockholm: Roos Tryckerier.
Simon, P. 1998. "Ghettos, Immigrants, and Integration the French Dilemma." *Netherlands Journal of Housing and the Built Environment* 13 (1): 41–61.
Simonson, S. 2016. "California Has the Most Foreign Born Residents." In SiliconValley Oneworld. http://www.siliconvalleyoneworld.com/2016/04/20/california-has-the-most-foreign-born-residents/.
Sorenson, O., and T. E. Stuart. 2008. "12 Entrepreneurship: A Field of Dreams?" *Academy of Management Annals* 2 (1): 517–543.
Stehle, M. 2012. "White Ghettos: The 'Crisis of Multiculturalism'in Post-Unification Germany." *European Journal of Cultural Studies* 15 (2): 167–181.
Van de Ven, A. H., & Poole, M. S. 1995. "Explaining Development and Change in Organizations." *Academy of Management Review* 20 (3): 510–540.
Vertovec, S. 2007. "Super-diversity and Its Implications." *Ethnic and Racial Studies* 30 (6): 1024–1054.
Volery, T. 2007. "Ethnic Entrepreneurship: A Theoretical Framework." *Handbook of Research on Ethnic Minority Entrepreneurship* 1: 30–41.
Wacquant, L. 2008. "Ghettos and Anti-Ghettos: An Anatomy of the new Urban Poverty." *Thesis Eleven* 94 (1): 113–118.
Wadhwa, V. 2009. "A Reverse Brain Drain." *Issues in Science and Technology* 25 (3): 45–52.
Wadhwa, V., A. Saxenian, and F. D. Siciliano. 2012. *Then and Now: America's New Immigrant Entrepreneurs*, Part VII.
Waldinger, R. 1986. *Through the Eye of the Needle: Immigrants and Enterprise in New York's Garment Trades*. New York: New York University Press.
Walworth, A. 2008. *Black Ships off Japan: the Story of Commodore Perry's Expedition*. New York: Walworth Press.
Wang, Q., and C. Y. Liu. 2015. "Transnational Activities of Immigrant-Owned Firms and Their Performances in the USA." *Small Business Economics* 44 (2): 345–359.
Wong, L. L., and M. Ng. 2002. "The Emergence of Small Transnational Enterprise in Vancouver: The Case of Chinese Entrepreneur Immigrants." *International Journal of Urban and Regional Research* 26 (3): 508–530.
Yeung, H. 2002. "Entrepreneurship in International Business: An Institutional Perspective." *Asia Pacific Journal of Management* 19: 29–61.
Zahra, S., and G. George. 2002. "International Entrepreneurship: The Current Status of the Field and Future Research Agenda." In *Strategic Entrepreneurship: Creating an Integrated Mindset*, edited by M. Hitt, D. Ireland, D. Sexton, and S. Camp, 255–258. Oxford: Blackwell publishers.
Zapata-Barrero, R., and S. Rezaei. 2020. Diaspora Governance and Transnational Entrepreneurship: The Rise of an Emerging Social Global Pattern in Migration Studies. *Journal of Ethnic and Migration Studies* 46 (10): 1959–1973. doi:10.1080/1369183X.2018.1559990.
Zhou, M. 2004. "Revisiting Ethnic Entrepreneurship: Convergencies, Controversies, and Conceptual Advancements." *International Migration Review* 38 (3): 1040–1074.
Zlolniski, C. 1994. "The Informal Economy in an Advanced Industrialized Society: Mexican Immigrant Labor in Silicon Valley." *The Yale Law Journal* 103: 2305–2335.

They are not all the same: immigrant enterprises, transnationalism, and development*

Alejandro Portes and Brandon P. Martinez

ABSTRACT
The literature on immigrant entrepreneurship in the advanced countries tends to paint these initiatives in homogeneous colors. A debate lingers as well on the economic returns to self-employment by immigrant and ethnic groups. We present recent data demonstrating again the significant payoff to autonomous enterprise among all ethnic groups, but also the major differences in such returns among them. This provides the basis for a typology of immigrant enterprises and an analysis of their causes and potential effects for the development of sending nations. Human capital, social capital, and modes of incorporation are the principal determinants of types of immigrant enterprises in host nations. The stance of home country states determines the development potential of high-tech immigrant enterprises. Data and examples supporting these conclusions are presented and their theoretical and practical implications discussed.

Introduction

The character and effects of immigrant entrepreneurship have been long debated in the academic literature. Orthodox economists generally regard ethnic business and ethnic enclaves as 'traps' that confined minorities to a position of occupational and economic subordination by limiting their mobility opportunities (Borjas 1986; Bates 1989). The more recent empirical literature has consistently contradicted this view by documenting the economic progress of immigrant groups that have managed to develop entrepreneurial enclaves in the past and present and by showing that the self- employed have consistently higher earnings than wage workers across a range of different racial and ethnic groups (Rischin 1962; Goldscheider 1986; Portes and Zhou 1996).

Recent evidence from the United States in support of this position will be presented in the next section. For now, it suffices to point out that the empirical literature has further advanced by uncovering two additional trends. First, immigrant entrepreneurs may not be limited to domestic markets in the receiving countries, but may operate transnationally either by sourcing capital, labor, and merchandise or by selling what they produce in

---

*Article written for the Special Issue on 'Diaspora Governance and Transnational Entrepreneurship', edited by R. Zapata-Barrero and S. Rezaei, Journal of Ethnic and Migration Studies 2019.

foreign markets (Landolt, Autler, and Baires 1999; Saxenian 1999; Guarnizo 2003; Lee and Zhou 2015).

Second, immigrant entrepreneurship is not homogeneous. Instead, major differences exist in the size, mode of operation, and market fields where such businesses operate, with significant consequences both for the entrepreneurs themselves and for their ethnic communities. The determinants of these differences have not yet been properly theorized. By and large, the major causal effects are assigned to the level and type of the human capital possessed by different groups and the business experience and progress of firm owners (Light and Rosenstein 1995; Zhou 2004; Portes and Yiu 2013). In this article, we wish to go beyond former conceptualizations by identifying different types and levels of immigrant entrepreneurship; examining under which circumstances they operate transnationally; and discussing forces other than individual human capital that impinge on both dimensions. In agreement with statements in the Introduction to this special issue (Zapata-Barrero and Rezaei 2020) we believe that transnational immigrant enterprise represents a fertile research site. Our focus in this essay is to refine our understanding of this phenomenon and its implications for development.

As it turns out, the social context that immigrants encounter upon arrival in a foreign land can mold the character of their entrepreneurial initiatives and decisively affect their viability and chances for growth. This context is defined by the attitude and practices of the receiving government; the character and stance toward specific foreign minorities of the native population; and the existence and character of the co-ethnic community. This tripartite set of forces is collectively known as the mode of incorporation of particular immigrant groups (Portes and Zhou 1996; Portes and Rumbaut 2014). Their combined effects, both on entrepreneurship and transnationalism is discussed after examining recent data on the extent and economic significance of self-employment.

Self-employment and earnings in the U.S.

This section surveys empirical data on patterns of ethnic entrepreneurship in the U.S. as a prelude and platform for the theoretical typology to be discussed later on. Table 1 presents data on entrepreneurship for selected immigrant and ethnic groups in the United States. The first half of the table includes data on total number of firms while the second half is limited to firms with employees. Several points are noteworthy. First the largest absolute number of firms corresponds to the two ethnic minorities conventionally placed at the bottom of the American occupational and economic hierarchies: African-Americans and Mexican-Americans. However, on a *per capita* basis, both groups exhibit the lowest levels of entrepreneurship.

Most entrepreneurial in terms of firms per 100,000 population are Koreans, closely followed by the Japanese, and then Chinese and Cubans. This pattern corresponds to the known history of these minorities, as described both in the social science and historical literatures (Petersen 1971; Kim 1981; Light and Bonacich 1988; Portes and Stepick 1993). In terms of average receipts per firm, Asian Indians are in a class by themselves, far above any other group. This pattern reflects the high level of human capital brought along by Indian immigrants that enable them to engage in business activities in high-tech sectors of the host economy. With 75% college graduates, Indian immigrants top the American educational ranks, significantly exceeding the mean educational level for

Table 1. Minority firm ownership and indicators of firm performance, 2012.

<table>
<tr><th rowspan="2">Group</th><th colspan="4">All firms</th><th colspan="4">Firms with paid employees</th></tr>
<tr><th>Total numbers of firms</th><th>Firms per 1,000 population</th><th>Sales, receipts, or value of shipments-</th><th>Gross receipts per firm</th><th>Number of firms</th><th>Firms per 1,000 population</th><th>Employees per firm</th><th>Sales, receipts, or value of shipments-</th><th>Gross receipts per firm</th></tr>
<tr><td colspan="10">*Asian:*</td></tr>
<tr><td>Korean</td><td>224,891</td><td>155.05</td><td>107,813,236</td><td>479,402</td><td>81,902</td><td>56.47</td><td>6.4</td><td>99,194,346</td><td>1,211,135</td></tr>
<tr><td>Asian Indian</td><td>377,486</td><td>123.80</td><td>227,148,254</td><td>601,740</td><td>137,720</td><td>45.17</td><td>8.2</td><td>209,778,561</td><td>1,523,225</td></tr>
<tr><td>Japanese</td><td>119,163</td><td>152.73</td><td>44,243,189</td><td>371,283</td><td>23,906</td><td>30.64</td><td>9.2</td><td>39,990,633</td><td>1,672,828</td></tr>
<tr><td>Chinese</td><td>528,702</td><td>144.43</td><td>210,062,246</td><td>397,317</td><td>139,016</td><td>37.98</td><td>8.1</td><td>209,778,561</td><td>1,509,025</td></tr>
<tr><td>Filipino</td><td>193,336</td><td>72.73</td><td>25,845,518</td><td>133,682</td><td>24,548</td><td>9.23</td><td>7.6</td><td>20,460,768</td><td>833,500</td></tr>
<tr><td colspan="10">*Latin American:*</td></tr>
<tr><td>Cuban</td><td>281,982</td><td>144.05</td><td>92,600,303</td><td>328,391</td><td>32,037</td><td>16.37</td><td>8.6</td><td>84,298,660</td><td>2,631,291</td></tr>
<tr><td>Mexican</td><td>1,624,617</td><td>47.73</td><td>204,712,259</td><td>126,006</td><td>14,764</td><td>4.16</td><td>9.0</td><td>156,210,266</td><td>1,101,994</td></tr>
<tr><td>African American</td><td>2,584,403</td><td>65.22</td><td>150,203,163</td><td>58,119</td><td>109,137</td><td>2.75</td><td>8.9</td><td>103,451,510</td><td>947,905</td></tr>
</table>

[a]Sample restricted to males, between ages of 26 and 65 in civilian labor force.
[b]Un-weighted sample. Figures in the table are adjusted using person-level analytical weights.
Sources: US Census Bureau, 2012 Survey of Business Owners; US Census Bureau, 2012 American Community Survey, American Community Survey, 2016.

the *native* population (28%). The percent of working adults classified as professionals is significantly greater among Indians (71.5%) than for the native-born (64.5%) (Portes and Rumbaut 2014: tables 14,17).

Following at a distance are gross receipts per firm for East Asian immigrant groups– Koreans and Chinese. Worth noting is that the bottom category, is again occupied by African Americans whose enterprises are the only ones to fall below the $100,000 threshold in gross annual receipts. These differences already point to significant disparities in the kinds, levels, and profitability of ethnic firms. They are not 'all the same' and the reasons for these differences deserve detailed examination, a task to be pursued in the next sections.

Shifting to the right-hand side of Table 1, we note confirmatory evidence for the trends noted earlier, but also novel ones. Koreans now have the largest number of firms with employees, followed closely by Asian Indians. Of all Asian-origin groups, only Filipinos have less than 10 firms with employees per thousand populations. This result is in line with the known pattern of adaptation of this group in the United States. With 50% college graduates, Filipinos are also significantly above the U.S. average in terms of human capital. However, they have tended to move into salaried employment in a variety of professions, of which nursing, medicine, and academic teaching are paramount. The Filipino median annual household income at the time of the last census was $78,692, comparable to that of Asia Indians and significantly ahead of the comparable native-born population ($50,541) (Portes and Rumbaut 2014: Table 21).

The largest firms in terms of gross receipts correspond to none of these Asian groups, but to Cubans. The number of such firms is not particularly large for this group on a per capita basis, but their size doubles that of most groups in terms of sales. The emergence and development of the Cuban enclave of Miami, documented at length in the research literature, lies behind these contrasting figures (Perez 1992; Nijman 2011; Portes and Rumbaut 2014). The entrepreneurial performance of Cuban immigrants in the United States has become increasingly bifurcated in recent years (Portes and Puhrmann 2015). This latter trend is reflected in the relatively low gross receipts of Cuban firms as a whole, but the very high ones for those with paid employees.

Table 2 presents recent data on self-employment, annual and hourly incomes for the native-born population of the United States and selected immigrant nationalities. The native-born population is divided into its white and black components. Immigrants nationalities include the three largest foreign groups in the country – Mexicans, Indians and Chinese; four Caribbean nationalities – Cubans, Dominicans, Haitians, and Jamaicans; two Middle-Eastern groups – Iranians and Israelis; and four Asian groups – in addition to the Chinese and Indians, Koreans and Vietnamese. The human capital profile and history of immigration and settlement of these foreign groups is generally well-known (Portes and Rumbaut 2014). The data include the most recent available figures from the U. S. Census (American Community Survey 2016).

The first observation of note is that, relative to wage-salaried employees, the self-employed exhibit generally higher earnings, both annually and hourly. This is true for the American working population as a whole, for the two major components of the native-born population, and for most immigrant groups. The difference becomes even clearer when we consider the self-employed who have incorporated their businesses. This category can be considered that of 'true' entrepreneurs since it excludes most

Table 2. Employment type and incomes for native and selected immigrant groups, 2016[a].

Characteristics	Natives						Immigrants						Average
	White	Black	Chinese	Cuban	Dominican	Haitian	Indian	Iranian	Israeli	Jamaican	Korean	Mexican	Vietnamese	
Type of Employment:														
Waged/salaried worker	87.58	93.45	87.94	82.28	90.52	91.34	89.96	74.69	68.17	89.80	80.60	88.00	86.37	88.13
Self-employed–General	12.42	6.55	12.06	17.72	9.48	8.66	10.04	25.31	31.83	10.20	19.40	12.00	13.63	11.87
Self-employed–Incorporated.	5.41	2.27	5.67	7.37	2.87	2.58	5.78	14.70	20.24	3.74	10.10	2.39	5.39	4.93
Annual income Mean:	77,042	46,406	83,005	44,639	40,188	42,176	99,446	104,000	111,885	52,182	86,509	35,117	57,225	70,831
Waged/salaried worker	75,353	46,225	84,263	43,818	40,463	42,440	100,349	100,913	103,477	52,413	87,445	34,987	58,366	69,404
Self-employed – General	88,952	48,987	73,834	48,448	37,563	39,399	91,354	113,111	129,890	50,150	82,579	36,072	49,992	81,418
Incorporated.	120,143	71,361	101,000	68,093	53,050	39,559	117,912	135,354	167,046	74,191	104,910	53,157	61,309	113,757
Hourly income – Mean:	34.29	22.15	38.52	21.09	19.30	20.28	44.31	46.72	46.88	24.48	38.90	16.61	27.57	31.81
Waged/salaried worker	33.24	21.94	38.56	20.25	19.44	20.13	44.89	44.01	45.18	24.63	38.76	16.49	28.04	30.92
Self-employed–General	41.74	25.24	38.26	24.99	17.95	21.84	39.12	54.72	50.54	23.22	39.49	17.53	24.60	38.38
Incorporated.	52.24	32.99	48.44	34.94	27.13	19.16	48.65	57.93	61.67	32.54	50.56	25.11	27.18	49.71
Mean hours worked per week	43.75	41.04	41.43	41.03	40.81	40.37	42.60	43.44	44.55	41.10	43.05	41.92	41.55	43.22
N[b]	378,196	32,746	5,937	2,372	1,201	838	9,626	1,059	208	1,088	2,162	29,161	3,185	467,779

[a]Sample restricted to males, between ages of 26 and 65 in civilian labor force.
[b]Un-weighted sample. Figures in the table are adjusted using person-level analytical weights.
Source: American Community Survey, 2016.

forms of casual or informal activity. Economic differences between incorporated entrepreneurs and their wage-salaried co-ethnics are, without exception, in favor of the first category and, in most cases, by significant amounts. For example, native white entrepreneurs earn over $40,000 more per year than their wage-salaried counterparts; among Israeli immigrants, the difference exceeds $50,000; and, for the country as a whole, it is close to $40,000.

The second important observation are the major differences in the return to entrepreneurship among the different ethno-racial categories, whether for all firms or for the incorporated. For example, incorporated Israeli firms report average annual incomes of $167,046, as contrasted with just $53,157 for Mexicans and a paltry $39,559 for Haitians. Among natives, the difference in business returns is close to $50,000 per year, favoring whites over blacks. The observed differences again point to the lack of homogeneity in the character of immigrant enterprise, a fact that is commonly obscured in past discussions on the topic. A typology of such firms is presented next.

Types of ethnic firms and modes of incorporation

Informal enterprise

Street vendors and casual day laborers are the best examples of ethnic enterprise at the lowest level. These activities are not incorporated, nor are they subject to legal regulations. They are, hence, an integral part of the informal economy. Informal vendors selling contraband watches and imported trinkets from their home countries are a common sight in the streets of New York, Madrid, and Rome. Clusters of men standing by the bus depot and certain parking lots waiting to be picked up for casual daily work are seen by the dozens in Miami, San Diego, Los Angeles, New York and other cities (Sassen 1989; Fernandez-Kelly 1995, 2016; Duneier 1999; Stepick et al. 2001).

A second type of informal enterprise involving poor immigrants is linked to sub-contracted homework paid on a piece-rate basis by middlemen who then market this production to stores and corporate firms in the formal economy. This type of a modern putting-out system often involves women and children who are less eligible for harsh daily work in agriculture and construction, but who can saw and stitch garments and footwear for a fraction of the legal minimum wage (Fernandez-Kelly and Garcia 1989; Ybarra 1989; Zhou 1992). A third variant involves independent female immigrant maids who make a living cleaning house for middle class families, paid in cash and without any social security deductions. By and large, daily laborers, street vendors, home subcontractors, and home maids are unauthorized immigrants, ineligible for legal protection in the host society (Hondagneu-Sotelo 1994; Repak 1995; Menjivar 2000).

Informal immigrant enterprise is consistently linked to a negative mode of incorporation in the receiving society by government authorities, widespread discrimination and prejudice by the native populations, and weak co-ethnic communities. Street vendors are commonly subjected to police raids because of their tenuous legal status and lack of permits; daily laborers are commonly defrauded of their pay by employers who regard them as little more than serfs; middlemen for sub-contracted homework, often co-ethnics, commonly squeeze endless extra hours from women laborers (Beneria 1989; Stepick 1989; Duneier 1999; Fernandez-Kelly 2016).

This is, therefore, a 'resource-less' type of entrepreneurship where the only asset is the co-ethnic community but where the latter is too precarious and too weak to provide any significant support. By the same token, this type of immigrant enterprise is seldom transnational: Poverty and its absence of legal status in the host country make it all but impossible to travel abroad on a regular basis. One-way return trips are possible, but they often mark the end of the foreign sojourn (Repak 1995; Menjivar 2000). Middlemen who subcontract to daily laborers and homeworkers may themselves be involved in transnational ventures, but they belong to a different social class by dint of higher human capital and legal status in the receiving country (Levitt 2001; Guarnizo 2003; Itzigsohn 2009).

Enclaves and petty entrepreneurship

The next type of immigrant enterprise is found in the agglomeration of small businesses serving their co-ethnic communities and providing selected goods and services for the broader market. Such agglomerations are commonly referred in the literature as 'ethnic enclaves' (Light and Gold 2000; Zhou 2004). Characteristic of this form of entrepreneurship is that it compensates for limited economic resources by cohesive ethnic networks that provide an important source of social capital. On that basis, entrepreneurs are able to access start-up capital, as well as markets and cheaper labor.

Rotating credit associations (variously known as *Kye* or *Tanomoshi* in Korean and Japanese) have been key sources of start-up capital for Asian immigrant firms in the United States (Bonacich and Modell 1980; Light and Gold 2000). Their existence depends entirely on social capital as there are no legal restraints on their participants. Similarly, the 'character loans' that were instrumental in the rise of the Cuban ethnic enclave in Miami relied solely on relationships of trust and bounded solidarity among donors and recipients (Portes and Stepick 1993, Ch-6). The recent proliferation of Chinese garment subcontractors in Northern Italian cities and small convenience stores in Madrid and other Spanish cities have largely been built by co-ethnic networks through which capital, information about business opportunities, and access to labor flow (Barbu, Dunfort, and Weidong 2013; Yiu 2013).

Petty immigrant enterprise can be connected, in various ways, with the sending countries. A key finding of the Comparative Immigrant Entrepreneurship Project (CIEP) conducted in the United States in the late nineties is that up to sixty percent of successful businesses among various Latin American immigrant nationalities relied on transnational linkages for credit, labor, or marketable goods (Portes, Haller, and Guarnizo 2002; Guarnizo, Alejandro Portes, and Haller 2003). Similarly in her study of the Salvadorian immigrant communities of New York City and Washington D.C., Landolt uncovered a 'vibrant entrepreneurial community embedded in a web of social relations' (Landolt, Autler, and Baires 1999).

The study identified four types of enterprises built on transnational networks. *Circuit firms* were involved in the transfer of goods and remittances across countries and ranged from an array of small international couriers to large firms like *El Gigante Express*, based in California. *Cultural enterprises* relied on their daily contact with El Salvador, depending on the demand created by immigrants to acquire and consume music, art, and other cultural goods from their home country. *Ethnic enterprises* are retail firms that depend on a steady supply of foodstuffs, beverages, clothing, and other goods from the home country for sale within the immigrant community and in the broader market. Finally, *return migrant microenterprises* are firms created by returnees to El Salvador that rely on their contacts in the United States for capital and business skills. They include restaurants, auto detailing and repairs, laundromats, home deliveries, office supplies, and others (Landolt, Autler, and Baires 1999; Landolt 2001).

Transnationalism and social capital are intimately linked in the case of small ethnic enterprise since social networks within the immigrant community and across international borders provide these firms with their sole competitive advantage. The information, capital, and goods that flow through these networks make all the difference in the survival and growth of these firms (Itzigsohn et al. 1999; Guarnizo 2003; Yiu 2013). The use of such networks presupposes, however, a favorable or at least neutral mode of incorporation by the host society. A hostile reception by government authorities may negate legal status to immigrants and relegate them to a precarious situation. Lack of a secure legal status generally prevents the rise and consolidation of ethnic firms. Any entrepreneurial initiative on the part of immigrants in such condition would be confined to the informal sector.

The same is true when an immigrant group confronts widespread discrimination by the host society. In these cases, enterprises are restricted to serve the co-ethnic community, seldom expanding beyond it. Early Chinatowns in American cities like San Francisco and Los Angeles, created to provide a measure of refuge against widespread external hostility provide an example (Boswell 1986; Zhou 1992). Haitians businesses in Miami have been faced with similar prejudice, being unable to extend beyond the limits of the confines of their own neighborhood (Stepick 1992; Mooney 2009; Portes and Rumbaut 2014, Ch. 4).

While small immigrant enterprises, whether concentrated in enclaves or not, depend on transnational ties for their creation and growth, they seldom make a significant contribution to national development in sending countries. Their limited size and market reach do not allow major capital investments or significant technological transfers abroad. In the aggregate, immigrant enclaves can provide a significant market for some home country exports, as documented by Landolt (2001) for Salvadoreans; Grasmuck and Pessar (1991) and Itizigsohn (2009) for Dominicans; and Zhou (1992, 2004) for the Chinese. But, beyond this function, plus the sending of remittances by successful entrepreneurs, the significance of immigrant enterprises in major developmental projects at home is limited.

High-tech transnational firms

Drawing on the available census data, Table 3 presents results of a multivariable regression of annual incomes on human capital variables, self-employment, and selected ethno-national categories in 2015.[1] These results are presented as a means to introduce and illustrate the third type of immigrant enterprise. Several points are worth nothing. First, human capital is the strongest determinant of economic outcomes. A college degree yields a net gain of $38,900 per year, relative to workers with less than a high school education; the payoff for those with a post-graduate title is $66,000. Second, with all human capital variables controlled, self-employment still has a sizable positive effect on annual incomes. For the self-employed category as a whole, the net gain is over $6,000 per year; but for those who have incorporated their business; it reaches almost $31,000

Table 3. Regressions of annual incomes on self-employment, nationality, and selected predictors in the United States 2015[a].

Predictors	Self-employed vs. Not Coeff.	S.E.	Self-employed Incorporated vs. Not Coeff.	S.E.
Nationality (ref. native whites African American)	−7,590***	194	−7,408***	195
Chinese	−2,399***	498	−2,286***	505
Cuban	−6,607***	836	−6,928***	858
Dominican	−8,637***	1,063	−8,270***	1,083
Haitian	−10,375***	1,298	−10,049***	1,306
Indian	7,757***	455	7,742***	458
Iranian	10,901***	1,286	9,680***	1,329
Israeli	18,550***	3,196	17,308***	3,351
Jamaican	−5,322***	1,081	−4,923***	1,094
Korean	−4,712***	809	−4,589***	837
Mexican	−4,761***	316	−4,242***	325
Vietnamese	−4,061***	702	−3,849***	722
Self-employed	6,322***	176	30,693***	278
Age	554***	4	560***	4
Married, spouse present	11,155***	124	10,771***	127
Number of children	3,768***	55	3,838***	56
Lives in South	−1,311***	113	−1,469***	115
Knows English well	10,806***	384	10,823***	395
Education (ref. less than high school) H.S. graduate	6,445***	207	6,441***	212
Associate degree	15,008***	253	15,170***	258
College graduate	38,662***	222	38,933***	227
Post-graduate degree	66,022***	241	65,888***	247
Adjusted $R2$	0.175		0.191	

***$P < 0.001$.
[a]Annual dollars, unlogged. See Note 1.
Source: Microdata sample, American Community Survey, 2015.

being roughly equivalent to the effect of a college degree. This result is in line with those presented above about the superior economic outcome attached to self-employment and, by extension, entrepreneurship.

Third, relative to native whites, almost all ethno-national groups are at an economic disadvantage, even after controlling for human capital variables and self-employment. That disadvantage includes relatively non-entrepreneurial groups, such as African- Americans and Mexicans, and those whose enterprises seldom surpass the level of informal activity, such as Haitians and Jamaicans. The disadvantage also extends, however, to immigrant groups known for their entrepreneurial prowess such as Chinese, Cubans, and Koreans. The only immigrant groups whose annual incomes exceed those of native whites are Indians, Iranians, and Israelis and they do so by sizable margins: close to $8,000 for Indians; almost $11,000 for Iranians; and a remarkable $18,500 for Israelis.

The sizable income advantage for these three groups, to be labeled thereafter the 'triple I' requires additional explanation and examination of its developmental implications. Previously, we saw the considerable superiority of Indian immigrants in their average level of education. The same characteristic is true of Iranians and Israelis among whom, the number of college graduates exceeds 50% (Portes and Rumbaut 2014: Table 14). In Table 1, we saw that gross receipts of Indian enterprises were among the largest for all groups included, and, in Table 2, that annual incomes of owners of incorporated firms belonging to the 'triple I' were by far the largest, all three exceeding $115,000 per year.

This level of enterprise exceeds that normally associated with immigrant firms, in or out of enclaves, and suggests the presence of better capitalized businesses in fields requiring higher levels of human capital. High-tech firms in such fields as electronics, international trade, advertising, and graphic design are likely candidates for this alternative type of entrepreneurship. Ethnographic accounts of Indian and Israeli entrepreneurs in the United States indicate their involvement in knowledge-based businesses requiring both higher levels of human and physical capital (Lessinger 1992; Saxenian 2006; Light and Gold 2000; Agarwala 2015).

By the same token, knowledge-based immigrant enterprise possesses the potential of not only tapping resources in the home countries to facilitate their emergence, but of being able to transfer technology and capital to these countries. Transnationalism in this instance becomes a two-way street with significant potential for development in home nations. Anna Lee Saxenian who has studied these relations in detail attributes the emergences of poles of high-tech concentration in such cities as Hyderabad and Bangalore in India and Tel Aviv in Israel to the transnational investments made by their respective expatriate professional communities (Saxenian 2002, 2006). Agarwala remarks on the same point:

> Indian Americans in transnational organizations have built new physical and symbolic terrains that allow them to maintain a presence at both ends of the geopolitical spectrum. By focusing on economic development in India, such organized efforts help to bolster a strong presence in India, while at the same time contributing to assimilation in the United States (Agarwala 2015, 105)

The development of this type of enterprise is naturally dependent on a positive or at least neutral mode of incorporation in the host country. Legal status and the absence of widespread discrimination are necessary conditions enabling professional immigrants to deploy their expertise for the creation of high-tech firms. A negative reception, either by the government or the society-at-large, would make it impossible to engage in such undertakings.

If the stance of the receiving state is vital in the emergence of such firms, that of the sending state plays a similar role in their transformation into transnational entities (Portes and Yiu 2013). Successful Indian and Israeli engineers, computer scientists, and other professionals would not have been able to invest at home if a viable institutional framework did not exist for them to do so. Put differently, for immigrant professionals to be able to make a significant contribution to national development in their countries, there must be *something* to return to in the form of economic opportunities and legal protection. Without proactive home state encouragement and support, high-level immigrant entrepreneurship would remain confined to the receiving society without being able to move in a transnational direction (Saxenian 2006; Iskander 2015).

The situation of Iranian businesses in the United States offers a case in point. Despite their economic success, as documented in Table 2, they seldom transfer expertise or capital back home. The fact that they came to the United States as escapees from the ruling theocracy in Iran makes all the difference. Theirs is an instance of 'blocked transnationalism' where a hostile relationship between the sending state and the expatriate community prevents the latter from making anything but occasional charity contributions to their home country (Huynh and Yiu 2015). A second example involves Indian professionals in the

United States whose developmental activities in India vary significantly with the receptivity and initiatives of their respective home states. After a detailed study of Indian transnational organizations and business activities by migrants from the states of Gujarat and Andhra Pradesh, Agarwala concludes:

> In 1995, (Chief Minister) Naidu created the Hyderabad Technology Engineering Consulting City (or Hytec City) where he provided investors with exemptions from statutory power cuts and labor inspections ... Microsoft chose the state's capital, Hyderabad, for its first foreign research and development center ... Andhra Pradesh's investments in education and IT have made Telugu American[2] transnational activities more diverse than those of the Gujaratis (Agarwala 2015, 89)

The Chinese transnational trajectory also bears mention as an illustration of the role of government in the rise of developmental investments and scientific transfers by the overseas community. Chinese immigrant firms do not reach the average profitability exhibited by 'Triple I' ones because their businesses in the United States are bifurcated between petty entrepreneurial activities in ethnic enclaves (i.e. 'Chinatowns') and high-tech enterprises similar to those launched by Indians and Israelis (Zhou and Lee 2015). The Chinese state has paid particular attention to the professional community abroad and engineered all kinds of activities to nurture its loyalty and investments. The state has created specialized offices, known as *Quiao-ban* at the national, provincial, and municipal levels to deal exclusively with its expatriates. These offices host conferences, in the United States and China, in a number of professional and scientific fields involving both China-based and U.S.-based participants. They also sponsor summer camps for the children of expatriate professionals in order to reinforce their knowledge of the language and culture. After their detailed study of the role of the Chinese state in the transnational field, Zhou and Lee conclude:

> Currently, the Chinese government not only considers returned students and scholars a driving force for the country's economic and social development, but it also supports those staying abroad in the belief that they will make contributions to China in various ways ... Since the mid-1990s, the Chinese state has launched a variety of programs to attract the permanent or temporary return of highly skilled immigrants in the fields of science and engineering. The National Ministry of Education has implemented several programs to attract scholars to return and to facilitate their career abroad (Zhou and Lee 2015, 46).

The Chinese government was the first to realize that the contributions to scientific and technological development of the country by its professional expatriates did not depend on their permanent return home. Instead, it deliberately fostered a transnational pattern in which these highly-skilled migrants regularly travel back home and are encouraged to make investments, create their own enterprises, and to participate in technology-transferring conferences, all the while residing abroad. As in the cases of India and Israel, a proactive state by the home country state has been decisive in transforming high-tech immigrant enterprises into a significant vehicle for development (Portes and Fernandez-Kelly 2015).

Immigrant Entrepreneurship and its Determinants

Type	Human Capital	Social Capital	Mode of Incorporation	Home State Reception	Transnational Involvement and Developmental Impact
Informal	Low-skilled	Limited to Cooperation for Survival	Negative	Negative to Neutral	None
Petty-entrepreneurial	Entrepreneurial skills brought from home country	High in ethnic enclaves as a vehicle for capital raising and search for business opportunities	Neutral-to-positive by the state and society at large	Neutral	High for procurement of business inputs; limited otherwise
High-Tech Professional	High skills brought from home country or acquired abroad	Limited, through professional associations and ties with home country institutions	Neutral-to-Positive	Positive and Proactive	High transnational activism and high developmental contributions.

Figure 1. Immigrant entrepreneurship and its determinants.

Returning to theory: human capital, social capital, and modes of incorporation

Figure 1 presents a synthetic portrait of the ways in which the different entrepreneurial paths described above relate to their basic determinants. While all three forms exist, they have very different bearings on the transnational field and on the contributions of immigrant enterprises can make to development. Assuming a positive or at least neutral mode of incorporation to the host society, it is evident that the key factors determining the viability of immigrant enterprises in general and transnational enterprise, in particular, are linked to the expatriates' human capital and social capital. That is the case both at the group level and at the level of individuals.

For illustration of individual determinants of immigrant entrepreneurship, we present results of a study conducted among Latin American immigrants in the United States at the turn of the century. This study, known as the Comparative Immigrant Enterprises Project (CIEP), remains one of the few sources of individual – level data on this topic. The study interviewed representative samples of the three Latin American nationalities in their principal areas of concentration in the U.S. in 2000–01. When weighted, the 1,202 interviews completed are representative of over 187,000 adult immigrants from these nationalities (Guarnizo et al. 2003). The significance of the study was its focus on individual determinants of entrepreneurship in general and transnational enterprise in particular. Table 4 presents evidence from this survey with respondents classified into wage workers, purely domestic entrepreneurs, and transnational entrepreneurs.[3] As the table shows, the latter were better educated, had better occupational qualifications, received higher incomes, and were more likely to have acquired U.S. citizenship, a point to which we will return below. Table 5 presents results of a multinomial logistic

Table 4. Characteristics of Latin American immigrant in the United States by type 2000.

	Wage Worker	Domestic Entrepreneur[a]	Transnational Entrepreneur[b]	Total
Years of Education	9.8	12.2	13.6	11.0
Professional/Executive Background, %	16	31	35	23
Monthly Income[c]	1251	2836	3143	1918
U.S. Citizen, %	26	49	53	36
Years of Residence in U.S.	14.0	18.0	16.4	15.1
Satisfied with Life in U.S., %	29	49	49	57
N	744	181	277	1202

[a]Owners of firms with no transnational linkages.
[b]Owners of firms with regular transitional linkages: markets, sources of supplies, and/or credit.
[c]In 2000 dollars.
Source: Comparative Immigrant Entrepreneurship Project (CIEP), 1998. Center for Migration and Development, Princeton University. Reported in Portes, Haller, and Guarnizo (2002).

regression using wage-workers as the reference category. The table reveals that immigrant businesses of any kind are largely the preserve of married males since both gender (male) and civil status (married) bear strongly on the pursuit of entrepreneurship. This result is no different from those reported consistently in the past research literature (Bonacich and Modell 1980; Zhou 1992; Light and Gold 2000).

Table 5. Determinants of transnational enterprise among Colombian, Dominican, and Salvadoran immigrants.

	Transnational Entrepreneurship (Binomial Logistic Regression)		
Predictors:	Coefficient	S.E.	Δ[a]
Demographic:			
Age	.017	.012	
Sex (Male)	1.035***	.231	.08
Marital Status (Married)	.440*	.215	.03
Number of Children	−.049	.070	
Human Capital:			
Education (Years)	.114***	.026	.01
Professional/Executive Background	1.191***	.331	.10
Assimilation:			
Years of U.S. Residence	.036*	.017	.003
Post-1989 Arrival	−.437	.338	
Downward Mobility[b]	−.402**	.167	−.03
Experiences of Discrimination	.308	.207	
Social Networks:			
Size	.111***	.022	.01
Scope[c]	.226	.121	
Nationality[d]:			
Colombian	−1.519***	.387	−.05
Salvadoran	1.097***	.279	.09
Constant	−6.235	.686	
Chi Square	141.67(14)***		
Pseudo R^2	.256		
N[e]	1,096		

[a]Increase/decrease in the net probability of each outcome per unit change in significant predictors, evaluated at the mean of the weighted sample distribution.
[b]Ratio of occupational status in the country of origin to status of the first U.S. occupation.
[c]Ratio of number of contacts outside city of residence to local contracts.
[d]Dominican immigrants are the reference category.
[e]CIEP weighted sample.
*$P < .05$.
**$P < .01$.
***$P < .001$.
Source: Portes, Haller, and Guarnizo (2002), based on data from CIEP.

Education and professional-executive background increased significantly the probability of self-employment, but these effects are stronger for transnational than for purely domestic enterprises. Based on model coefficients, a married male with a college education has a 37% greater probability of becoming a transnational rather than a domestic entrepreneur; the advantage increases to 45% if wage/salaried workers are the relevant reference category. The notion that transnational activities are a transitional pursuit, to be abandoned as assimilation takes hold – a notion most prominently associated with Waldinger (2015) – is not supported by these results. Longer periods of U.S. residence *increase* the probability of engaging in transnational enterprise and, as seen above, their owners are the most likely to have already acquired U.S. citizenship.

Finally, the effect of social networks lends support to the social capital argument. Business owners have more numerous social ties than wage/salaried workers, and transnational entrepreneurs have stronger social networks than domestic ones. As seen in Table 5, the social network coefficient is very strong. Each additional social contact increases the probability of transnational enterprise by 1.5%. While CIEP results are in need of actualization and replication, they lead to the conclusion that at both, collective and individual levels, determinants of immigrant enterprise are the same. The tripartite set of determinants summarized in Figure 1 decisively affect whether immigrants are able to engage in business at all, the type of enterprise that they are able to create, and the incidence of such activities on prospects for development in the sending countries.

In contrast to a past literature that painted the phenomenon of immigrant and ethnic entrepreneurship in homogenous terms, it is in reality quite heterogeneous, since immigrant groups adopt quite diverse economic adaptation strategies. In particular, professional migration can represent a significant 'brain drain' for exporting countries or a major 'brain gain', depending on the motivations of the immigrant themselves and, in particular, the stance of home country states and their capacity to influence those motivations. As the cases of China, India and Israel show, immigrant transnationalism can play an important, even decisive role in the future of sending nations. While small businesses in ethnic enclaves have been shown to be a means for economic survival and mobility for immigrants themselves, a winning formula for development of the source nations requires the emergence of a strong professional/business community abroad with which sending states can engage in a sustained relationship.

Notes

1. Income regressions in Table 3 use raw annual incomes, rather than the familiar logarithmic transformation. The latter is commonly employed by economists and sociologists to smooth skewed earnings distributions, as well as neutralize the effect of outliers. By the same token however, it tends to obscure the economic effect of entrepreneurship (self-employment) that is commonly associated with the highest income levels (positive outliers). See Portes and Zhou (1996).
2. 'Telugu' is the self-designation of natives from the state of Andhra Pradesh.
3. This section reproduces material originally presented in Portes, 2010: Chapter 9.

Disclosure statement

No potential conflict of interest was reported by the authors.

References

Agarwala, Rina. 2015. "Tapping the Indian Diaspora for Indian Development." In *The State and the Grassroots: Immigrant Transnational Organizations in Four Continents*, edited by A. Portes and P. Fernandez-Kelly, 84–110. Oxford, UK: Berghahn Books.
Barbu, Mirela, Michael Dunfort, and Liu Weidong. 2013. "Employment, Entrepreneurship, and Citizenship in a Globalised Economy: The Chinese in Prato." *Environment and Planning A* 45: 2420–2441.
Bates, Timothy. 1989. "The Changing Nature of Minority Business: A Comparative Analysis of Asian, Nonminority, and Black-Owned Businesses." *The Review of Black Political Economy* 18: 25–42.
Beneria, Lourdes. 1989. "Subcontracting and Employment Dynamics in Mexico City." In *The Informal Economy: Studies in Advanced and Less Developed Countries*, edited by A. Portes, M. Castells, and L. A. Benton, 173–188. Baltimore, MD: The Johns Hopkins University Press.
Bonacich, Edna, and John Modell. 1980. *The Economic Basis of Ethnic Solidarity: Small Business in the Japanese-American Community*. Berkeley: University of California Press.
Borjas, George J. 1986. "The Self-Employment Experience of Immigrants." *The Journal of Human Resources* 21: 485–506.
Boswell, Terry E. 1986. "A Split Labor Market Analysis of Discrimination Against Chinese Immigrants, 1850–1882." *American Sociological Review* 51: 352–371.
Duneier, Mitch. 1999. *Sidewalk*. New York: Farrar, Strauss, and Giroux.
Fernandez-Kelly, M. Patricia. 1995. "Social and Cultural Capital in the Urban Ghetto: Implications for the Economic Sociology of Immigration." In *The Economic Sociology of Immigration: Essays in Network, Ethnicity, and Entrepreneurship*, edited by Alejandro Portes, 213–247. New York: Russell Sage Foundation.
Fernandez-Kelly, Patricia. 2016. *The Hero's Fight*. Princeton, NJ: Princeton University Press.
Fernandez-Kelly, Patria, and Anna M. Garcia. 1989. "Informalization at the Core: Hispanic Women, Homework, and the Advanced Capitalist State." In *The Informal Economy: Studies in Advanced and Less Developed Countries*, edited by A. Portes, M. Castells, and L. Benton. Baltimore, MD: Johns Hopkins University Press.
Goldscheider, Calvin. 1986. *Jewish Continuity and Change: Emerging Patterns in America*. Bloomington, IN: Indiana University Press.
Grasmuck, Sherri, and Patricia Pessar. 1991. *Between Two Islands: Dominican International Migration*. Berkeley: University of California Press.
Guarnizo, Luis E. 2003. "The Economics of Transnational Living." *International Migration Review* 37 (Fall): 666–699.
Guarnizo, Luis, E. Alejandro Portes, and William J. Haller. 2003. "Assimilation and Transnationalism: Determinants of Transnational Political Action among Contemporary Migrants." *American Journal of Sociology* 108: 1211–1248.
Hondagneu-Sotelo, Pierrette. 1994. *Gendered Transitions: Mexican Experiences of Immigration*. Berkeley, CA: UC Press.
Huynh, Jennifer, and Jessica Yiu. 2015. "Breaking Blocked Transnationalism: Intergenerational Change in Homeland Ties." In *The State and the Grassroots: Immigrant Transnational Organizations in Four Continents*, edited by A. Portes and P. Fernandez-Kelly, 160–186. New York: Berghahn Books.
Iskander, Natasha. 2015. "Partners in Organizing: Engagement between Migrants and the State in the Production of Mexican Hometown Associations." In *The State and the Grassroots: Immigrant Transnational Organizations in Four Continents*, edited by A. Portes, and P. Fernandez-Kelly, 111–138. Oxford, UK: Berghahn Books.

Itzigsohn, Jose. 2009. *Encountering American Faultlines: Race, Class, and the Dominican Experience*. New York: Russell Sage Foundation.

Itzigsohn, Jose, Carlos Dore, Esther Fernandez, and Obed Vazquez. 1999. "Mapping Dominican Transnationalism: Narrow and Broad Transnational Practices." *Ethnic and Racial Studies* 22: 316–339.

Kim, Ilsoo. 1981. *New Urban Immigrants: the Korean Community in New York*. Princeton, NJ: Princeton University Press.

Landolt, Patricia. 2001. "Salvadoran Economic Transnationalism: Embedded Strategies for Household Maintenance, Immigrant Incorporation, and Entrepreneurial Expansion." *Global Networks* 1: 217–242.

Landolt, Patricia, Lilian Autler and Sonia Baires. 1999. "From 'Hermano Lejano' to 'Hermano Mayor': The Dialectics of Salvadoran Transnationalism." *Ethnic and Racial Studies* 22: 290–315.

Lee, Jennifer, and Min Zhou. 2015. *The Asian American Achievement Paradox*. New York: Russell Sage Foundation.

Lessinger, Johanna. 1992. "Investing or Going Home? A Transnational Strategy among Indian Immigrants in the United States." *Annals of the New York Academy of Sciences* 645: 53–80.

Levitt, Peggy. 2001. *The Transnational Villagers*. Berkeley: University of California Press.

Light, Ivan, and Edna Bonacich. 1988. *Immigrant Entrepreneurs: Koreans in Los Angeles, 1965–1982*. Berkeley: University of California Press.

Light, Ivan, and Steven J. Gold. 2000. *Ethnic Economies*. San Diego, CA: Academic Press.

Light, Ivan, and Carolyn Rosenstein. 1995. "Expanding the Interaction Theory of Entrepreneurship." In *The Economic Sociology of Immigration*, edited by A. Portes, 166–212. New York: Russell Sage.

Menjivar, Cecilia. 2000. *Fragmented Ties: Salvadoran Immigrant Networks in America*. Berkeley, CA: University of California Press.

Mooney, Margarita. 2009. *Faith Makes Us Live: Surviving and Thriving in the Haitian Diaspora*. Berkeley, CA: University of California Press.

Nijman, Jan. 2011. *Miami: Mistress of the Caribbean*. Philadelphia, PA: University of Pennsylvania Press.

Perez, Lisandro. 1992. "Cuban Miami." In *Miami, Now!*, edited by G. J. Grenier and A. Stepick, 83–108. Gainesville, FL: University of Florida Press.

Petersen, William. 1971. *Japanese Americans: Oppression and Success*. New York: Random House.

Portes, Alejandro, and Patricia Fernandez-Kelly. 2015. *The State and the Grassroots: Immigrant Transnational Organizations in Four Continents*. Oxford, UK: Berghahn Books.

Portes, Alejandro, William Haller, and Luis E. Guarnizo. 2002. "Transnational Entrepreneurs: An Alternative Form of Immigrant Economic Adaptation." *American Sociological Review* 67: 278–298.

Portes, Alejandro, and Aaron Puhrmann. 2015. "A Bifurcated Enclave: The Economic Evolution of the Cuban and Cuban American Population of Metropolitan Miami." *Cuban Studies* 43: 40–63.

Portes, Alejandro, and Ruben G. Rumbaut. 2014. *Immigrant America: A Portrait*. 4 ed. Berkeley, CA: University of California Press.

Portes, Alejandro, and Alex Stepick. 1993. *City on the Edge: The Transformation of Miami*. Berkeley: University of California Press.

Portes, Alejandro, and Jessica Yiu. 2013. "Entrepreneurship, Transnationalism, and Development." *Migration Studies* 1: 1–21.

Portes, Alejandro, and Min Zhou. 1996. "Self-employment and the Earnings of Immigrants." *American Sociological Review* 61: 219–230.

Repak, Terry A. 1995. *Waiting on Washington: Central America Workers in the Nation's Capital*. Philadelphia, PA: Temple University Press.

Rischin, Moses. 1962. *The Promised City: New York Jews 1870–1914*. Cambridge, MA: Harvard University Press.

Sassen, Saskia. 1989. "New York City's Informal Economy." In *The Informal Economy: Studies in Advanced and Less Developed Countries*, edited by A. Portes, M. Castells, and L. A. Benton, 60–77. Baltimore, MD: The Johns Hopkins University Press.

Saxenian, Anna Lee. 1999. *Silicon Valley's New Immigrant Entrepreneurs*. San Francisco: Public Policy Institute of California.

Saxenian, Anna Lee. 2002. *Local and Global Networks of Immigrant Professionals in Silicon Valley*. San Francisco: Public Policy Institute of California.

Saxenian, Anna Lee. 2006. *The New Argonauts: Regional Advantage in a Global Economy*. Cambridge, MA: Harvard University Press.

Stepick, Alex. 1989. "Miami's Two Informal Sectors." In *The Informal Economy:Studies in Advanced and Less Developed Countries*, edited by A. Portes, M. Castells, and L. A. Benton, 111–134. Baltimore, MD: The Johns Hopkins University Press.

Stepick, Alex. 1992. "The Refugees. Nobody Wants: Haitians in Miami." In *Miami Now!*, edited by G. J. Grenier, and A. Stepick, 57–82. Gaineseville: University of Florida Press.

Stepick, Alex, Carol D. Stepick, Emmanuel Eugene, Deborah Teed, and Yves Labissiere. 2001. "Shifting Identities and Generational Conflict: Growing up Haitian in Miami." In *Ethnicities: Children of Immigrants in America*, edited by R. G. Rumbaut, and A. Portes, 229–267. Berkeley, CA: University of California Press.

U.S. Bureau of the Census. 2016. *American Community Survey*. Washington, DC: US Department of Commerce.

Waldinger, Roger. 2015. *The Cross-Border Connection: Immigrants, Emigrants, and Their Homelands*. Cambridge, MA: Harvard University Press.

Ybarra, Josep-Antoni. 1989. "Informalization in the Valencian Economy: A Model for Underdevelopment." In *The Informal Economy: Studies in Advanced and Less Developed Countries*, edited by A. Portes, M. Castells, and L. A. Benton, 216–227. Baltimore, MD: The Johns Hopkins University Press.

Yiu, Jessica. 2013. "Calibrated Ambitions: Low Educational Ambition as a Form of Strategic Adaptation among Chinese Youth in Spain." *International Migration Review* 47: 573–611.

Zapata-Barrero, R., and S. Rezaei. 2020. "Diaspora Governance and Transnational Entrepreneurship: The Rise of an Emerging Social Global Pattern in Migration Studies." *Journal of Ethnic and Migration Studies* 46 (10): 1959–1973. doi:10.1080/1369183X.2018.1559990.

Zhou, Min. 1992. *New York's Chinatown: The Socioeconomic Potential of an Urban Enclave*. Philadelphia: Temple University Press.

Zhou, Min. 2004. "Revisiting Ethnic Entrepreneurship: Convergences, Controversies, and Conceptual Advancements." *International Migration Review* 38: 1040–1074.

Zhou, Min, and Renne Lee. 2015. "Traversing Ancestral and New Homelands: Chinese Immigrant Transnational Organizations in the United States." In *The State and the Grassroots: Immigrant Transnational Organizations in Four Continents*, edited by A. Portes and P. Fernandez-Kelly, 27–59. Oxford: Berghahn Books.

Transnational entrepreneurs: opportunity or necessity driven? Empirical evidence from two dynamic economies from Latin America and Europe

Johannes von Bloh, Vesna Mandakovic, Mauricio Apablaza, José Ernesto Amorós and Rolf Sternberg

ABSTRACT
Transnational Entrepreneurship (TE) is an increasingly important phenomenon, symptomatic for a globalised world with a large extent of migrants and interchanges between their countries of origin and residence. Our article deploys a unique data set which compares TE for two different national contexts and institutional settings: Chile and Germany. Using data from 2016 and 2017 Adult Populations Surveys (APS) of the Global Entrepreneurship Monitor (GEM), we relate the probability of being an opportunity-driven entrepreneur with the condition of being a transnational entrepreneur. Our findings suggest that varying institutional settings attract or form different types of TE. While Chile seems to attract mainly opportunity-driven TE, TE in Germany reveals strong evidence of necessity-driven TE. In addition, we explore different traits on the probability of being involved in TE based on the presumption that transnational entrepreneurs show signs of higher opportunity recognition and network embeddedness and can thereby be a major driver of entrepreneurial ecosystems as well as act as linkages between different national systems.

1. Introduction

Transnational Entrepreneurship (TE) is an increasingly important phenomenon, symptomatic for a globalised world with a large extent of migrants and interchanges between their countries of origin and of residence. Since Saxenian's (2006) study on 'New Argonauts', TE receives a lot of attention from researchers and policy makers which more than justifies a special issue and its different valuable contributions towards theoretical and empirical progress on TE research (see Zapata-Barrero and Rezaei 2020). TE is associated with huge economic development potentials for both countries of origin and host countries, spurred by visions of establishing a Silicon Valley of their own by creating or supporting TE, based on a 'class' of highly mobile and embedded re-migrant transnational (diaspora) entrepreneurs. However, there is still a lack of comparable research with a certain kind of 'analytical rigor' as stated by Portes, Guarnizo, and Landolt (1999, 218; see also Drori, Honig, and Wright 2009). Despite the lack of empirical data, TE will gain in relevance for entrepreneurship support policies in host countries. Those countries are characterised by very different institutional and other framework conditions and most of them provide better economic conditions than the migrants home countries.

Another very relevant topic of entrepreneurship research is entrepreneurial ecosystems (EES; see Alvedalen and Boschma 2017; Sorenson 2017). EES looks at entrepreneurship within a given spatial territory as a system with interdependently linked actors and organisations intertwined with a context of formal and informal institutions influencing entrepreneurial activity. EES, although a very recent, empirically virtually unproven concept, are gaining almost worldwide acceptance among practitioners. While there are good reasons for applying the EES concept mainly on the sub-national level of (city) regions (see Malecki 2018), the basic idea has also relevance for the national level, i.e. when comparing countries to each other (see Acs, Autio, and Szerb 2014).

Surprisingly enough, the role of transnational entrepreneurs within an EES is almost completely ignored although the latter has developed to one of the most intensively debated topics in entrepreneurship research in recent years. This leaves the link between TE and EES unexplored and opens up an important research gap. While some EES scholars stress the relevance of (ethnic) diversity (Stangler and Bell-Masterson 2015) as an important success factor of an EES, the role of TE has not yet been conceptually or empirically studied. The empirical part of our article is focused on two main motives to start a firm: recognising an opportunity to start a firm or a lack of alternative employment options. Opportunity entrepreneurship is related to growth potentials of young firms, not just because their founders more often have competencies, capacities, and will to grow than founders who start the firm mainly because of having no other choice to earn their own living. Consequently, if policymakers intend to revitalise their national or sub-national economies by supporting new firms, they search for opportunity entrepreneurship, and less so for necessity entrepreneurship. It is not a surprise, therefore, that the EES concept is dedicated to 'ambitious' entrepreneurship (Stam and Spigel 2018), i.e. young entrepreneurs who want to grow, who are able to grow and who intend to develop innovative products or services. We argue that transnational entrepreneurs, different from migrant entrepreneurs in general, are more driven by opportunity motivations than by necessity motivations, meaning that transnational entrepreneurs would be relevant actors in an EES. EES, however, do differ between countries, and they exert country-specific influences on transnational entrepreneurs. Thus, it is useful to test our idea in two countries with many similarities, but also some differences regarding their EES. Until recently, no comparable empirical data was available to analyse TE on a global scale. As part of the EU funded research project 'DiasporaLink', researchers associated with the Global Entrepreneurship Monitor (GEM) developed a unique set of questions to capture TE and included them into many GEM national team's adult population and national expert surveys in 2016 and 2017. Two of those countries are presented and compared in this article: Chile and Germany.

Our research intends to contribute to the TE and EES literature in two ways: We expect that, among other traits, (1) transnational entrepreneurs have a higher probability of engaging in opportunity-based entrepreneurial activities with higher growth expectations, and that this probability differs between both countries based on contextual peculiarities, i.e.

ecosystem conditions. We hypothesise that the more enabling entrepreneurial environment in Chile will create more and more successful policy instruments to support TE in Chile than in Germany. Additionally, (2) we intend to explore the relationship between country embedded TE and EES. We suggest that transnational entrepreneurs are the 'right kind of entrepreneurs' with personal ties to different countries and, acting as potential bridging agents, such entrepreneurs could connect ecosystems across the globe, which would allow them to play a crucial role in keeping EES vital and progressing. They can do this by supplying role models and contacts for local entrepreneurs to internationalise and by providing an inflow of new knowledge and routines from other EES. But also through having a unique opportunity recognition which helps the EES in a variety of ways, such as: Maximising its potency by pushing opportunity-driven entrepreneurship, enhancing the social capital of both EES by connecting their actors with each other and by inducing positive development in both EES. We argue that transnational entrepreneurs can fit this role because they can perceive more opportunities for start-ups and have higher embeddedness into entrepreneurship networks (i.e. they have more contacts).

The majority of the literature on TE is dominated by qualitative case studies that are necessary for in-depth understanding (Brzozowski, Cucculelli, and Surdej 2018); we want, however, to contribute to increase the number of quantitative empirical studies.

The remainder of the article is structured as follows: Section 2 addresses the differences and commonalities of the institutional and economic national contexts of Chile and Germany. In Section 3, we look at the theoretical background of the applied concepts. We then pursue the empirical part by relating the probability of being an opportunity-driven entrepreneur with the condition of being a transnational entrepreneur for both countries in Section 4 after which we compare two different national contexts in terms of entrepreneurship (Section 5). Section 6 will cover our findings, critical remarks and insight into further research.

2. Comparing national entrepreneurial contexts: Chile and Germany

Despite the socio-political and economic problems of the last 10 years, many countries in Latin America have been able to create political stability and growth during the last three decades. This has been followed by trade openness and better global integration, leading to a new environment which fosters transnational entrepreneurs in the region and particularly in Chile. In Germany, too, the economic and the political situation are rather stable during the recent decades. The economy performed quite well, with low unemployment rates and modest but steady GDP growth rates (see ec.europa.eu/eurostat), even during the global financial and economic crisis of 2007/2008. Another parallel of both countries is the heavily increased immigration in recent years which poses both challenge and opportunity. Differences between both countries are the deepness of the social welfare system and unemployment benefits. While in Chile people have to rely on family and friends to seek a job, in Germany exists a government agency handling unemployment benefits and the search for employment. Long-term unemployed are also supported by the state to keep a minimum standard of living. While this social security net keeps people away from critical situations where their lives are at stake, it might reduce the incentives to become self-employed along the way.

Following the assessment of the World Economic Forum (WEF), Chile is listed as efficiency driven and Germany as innovation-driven economy. While we argue that both countries are comparable in many ways, there is a gap in economic development, with Germany's economy mostly driven by human capital, knowledge and innovation, and Chile's economy by more efficient and comparative productions as well as resource mining and export. The national context influences how entrepreneurial activities and attitudes are formed. Between both countries, both similarities and significant differences in terms of entrepreneurial attitude, culture and climate are observable. If Chile and Germany are compared with the recently developed Entrepreneurial Spirit index of GEM (GESI), this becomes especially visible (see GERA 2018, 29). Chile ranks 10th in comparison with 54 countries which are listed in the most recent GEM Global Report. Germany ranks 37th. And while media coverage of entrepreneurship and the view on whether entrepreneurship is a good career choice are quite similar for both countries, the overall reputation of entrepreneurs shows noticeable differences. The social status of entrepreneurs in general is lower in Germany. The differences in entrepreneurial spirit and climate, amongst other socio-economic factors, result in diverging levels of entrepreneurial activity. While Chile is characterised by high start-up rates, Germany has one of the lowest total early-stage entrepreneurial activity rates (TEA). If compared to TEA rates of all other GEM countries, oblivious of the level of development, Germany ranks 48th of 54 countries while Chile comes in 5th. For a long time, in Germany TE has neither been an important empirical phenomenon nor has it been the object of government policies. Both has changed in recent years, partially related to the proposed relationship between significantly increased in-migration, assumed increase of start-up rate, and policy responses in terms of specific means to steer migration, (migrant) entrepreneurship and TE. While Germany seems to be the destination of migration more or less involuntarily, the Chilean Government actively tried to attract foreign entrepreneurs with various programmes.

Both entrepreneurial climate and activity hint at significant differences in the configuration of the national EES. In light of this institutional variance between Germany and Chile, we expect to see differing types of transnational entrepreneurs in both countries.

3. Theoretical framework

3.1. Transnational entrepreneurship

Since the conceptualisation of transnationalism related with 'the process by which immigrants forge and sustain multi-stranded social relations that link together their societies of origin and settlement, and through which they create transnational social fields that cross-national borders' (Basch, Glick Schiller, and Szanton-Blanc 1994, 6), there are different attempts to delimitate what a transnational phenomenon is. Portes, Guarnizo, and Landolt (1999) and Portes, Guarnizo, and Haller (2002) argue that the concept is restricted to circumstances in which travels that imply cross-border connections are extensive, regular and resilient. Wong and Ng (2002) relate the concept with the ethnic economy which involves both operational components and the transmigration of the owners. These enterprises are socially embedded in both their home and host countries, potentially providing them with access to networks and resources in both entrepreneurial environments. Some other efforts are in the direction to define typologies for translational entrepreneurs (Landolt, Autler, and Baires 1999; Rusinovic 2008; Elo 2016) that put emphasis on the transnational involvements but also the degree and the extent of transnational inputs and activities in the business.

More recently, transnational entrepreneurship seems to be a phenomenon which is closely connected to globalisation, decreasing barriers for migration and trade or modern fast ways for communication and travel (see Riddle, Hrivnak, and Nielsen 2010).

The brain drain was long thought of as the inevitable negative result when developing countries invested in education to increase human capital which then would migrate to more advanced countries. The view on this changed in the last 10–15 years (see Saxenian 2006). In several cases emigrants returned, equipped with a plethora of experience, (technological) know how, know who, personal and professional networks and formed by the informal institutions of the host country, leading to reverse brain drain or even brain circulation in the form of continued transnational business ties. If transnationals found new businesses based upon this unique mix of skills and their embeddedness in two different national contexts they could become important motoric units for economic development and the exchange of new knowledge for their country of origin. But even if no permanent remigration takes place, transnational entrepreneurs can establish corridors for knowledge flows between both country of origin and stay (see Saxenian 2006). In their case study of the incubator IntEnt in the Netherlands, Riddle, Hrivnak, and Nielsen (2010) found evidence that transnational entrepreneurs show cyclic migratory patterns which led to increased opportunities for starting up a new business, leading to the hypothesis that transnational entrepreneurs have a higher opportunity recognition than non-transnational entrepreneurs.

Brzozowski, Cucculelli, and Surdej (2014) state that home country conditions have not been thoroughly reviewed. They were able to show that institutional peculiarities as well as socio-economic contexts of the country of origin impact transnational connections of migrant entrepreneurs.

For this article we adopted the definition which was used as foundation of creating the TE questions for the GEM surveys: transnational entrepreneurs are operating within cross-border networks shaping and exploiting economic opportunities by maximising their resource base by committing at least one of the following economic activities at both ends of the migration corridor: exporting, forming overseas establishments, outsourcing jobs, mobilising business knowledge. The definition also includes remigration as well as cyclic migration. However, we focus on transnational entrepreneurs who are embedded in two countries. The operationalisation of this will be covered in Section 4.

3.2. Entrepreneurship motivations

According to the GEM framework among others (Reynolds et al. 2005), there are two different main types of entrepreneurial motivations: opportunity- and necessity-based entrepreneurial actions. A differentiation between both types of entrepreneurship is necessary because they are considerably different in their economic impact as well as dependence on factors, both individual and contextual (see Wong, Ho, and Autio 2005; McMullen, Bagby, and Palich 2008). Opportunity-based entrepreneurship (OPP) covers entrepreneurial activities started voluntarily in order to gain more income or independence. In the other hand, necessity-based entrepreneurial activity (NEC) is the creation of a new business out of need, when no other appropriate employment is available to the individual in the formal job market (Reynolds et al. 2005; Bosma et al. 2008).

Because of the potential relevance of entrepreneurship in social and economic development, a lot of research mainly puts special focus on opportunity-based entrepreneurship (Acs 2006; Bowen and De Clercq 2008; Levie and Autio 2011). But in less developed economies, necessity-based entrepreneurship is very important since it is a source of income for individuals excluded from the formal labour market (Amorós et al. 2017).

3.3. Transnational entrepreneurship, motivations and opportunity

From the perspective of transnational entrepreneurship, motivations could be linked with the propensity to be engaged in new business creation. Among different factors that could determine the motives behind these entrepreneurial endeavours, one of the most relevant is the diversity related with (in-)migrants' groups (Sepulveda, Syrett, and Lyon 2011; Brzozowski, Cucculelli, and Surdej 2018). Diversity includes 'a wide variety of political refugees, asylum seekers, and "economic" migrants from a large number of both developed and less-developed countries, [that] is much more diverse' (Kloosterman, Rusinovic, and Yeboah 2016, 914). Diversity is more accentuated in the last two decades. It is not the same being a refugee that starts a new (informal) business out of necessity than an immigrant looking for a genuine business opportunity in a more developed market, maintaining strong relationships with the country of origin. We are not arguing that opportunity-driven entrepreneurs (OPP) have pre-eminence over necessity-driven entrepreneurs (NEC), because the social and economic relationships between these types of entrepreneurship activities are more complex than the simple dichotomy (McMullen, Bagby, and Palich 2008; Amorós et al. 2017), but highlights that motivations could be dynamics and interconnected with the contexts.

Transnationalism could be related with elements that enhance OPP rather than NEC. First, transnational entrepreneurs potentially have access to an extended range of social capital (Simba and Ojong 2018). This social capital is complemented with different types of capital that could include cultural and human capital (multilingualism, international management experience, knowledge of overseas markets) and economic capital (different sources of funding or access to multiple national financial systems). Second, transnational entrepreneurs could be linked to strong networks. Networks help to maintain contacts, relatives or family in the country of origin in whom one can trust and/or do business with, providing access to new markets and increase sales (Rusinovic 2008; Kariv et al. 2009). Finally, transnational entrepreneurs, because of their engagements in different cultural and economics settings, could be more exposed to better opportunity recognition. This is related to experience, skills, know-how, access to technology, and also socio-cultural awareness (Brzozowski, Cucculelli, and Surdej 2018).

The above stated traits of transnational entrepreneurs make them into EES actors with high potential for driving roles based on their opportunity recognition, social capital and openness as well as enabling them to link EES. We argue that transnational entrepreneurs can play an important role as bridging agents not only between countries or regions but between distinct entrepreneurial systems in which they are embedded in home and host country, acting as pipelines by potentially enhancing flows of knowledge, ideas and informal institutions creating more opportunities for start-ups in both countries. We define our understanding of an EES as a geographically located interlinked system of conditions and components which both influence entrepreneurial activities and are also influenced by it. The conditions cover context factors such as culture, formal and informal institutions, availability of financial capital but also the existence of highly active networks consisting of EES actors and support structures amongst others. Components are actors and organisations (Stam and Spigel 2018).

Considering the differences in national EES, entrepreneurial climate and activity between Chile and Germany, we abstain from testable hypotheses and turn towards explorative statements deriving from the research questions whether being a transnational entrepreneur affects the entrepreneurial motive and whether the traits assigned to transnational entrepreneurs through case studies and theory can be shown for Chile and Germany. We estimate that being a transnational entrepreneur has a significant impact on the motivation why someone is an entrepreneur. (1) We expect TE to have an overall positive influence on opportunity-driven entrepreneurship. (2) And an overall negative impact on necessity-driven entrepreneurship. (3) However, we expect to see major differences between the impact of the transnational entrepreneur status between both countries based on their institutional settings and stage of economic development. (4) Lastly, we expect that the probability of someone being a transnational entrepreneur is higher for persons with a high degree of network embeddedness or entrepreneurial awareness and opportunity recognition.

4. Data, methodology and results

4.1. Data and methodology

We use data from the Global Entrepreneurship Monitor (GEM) Adult Population Survey (APS). The GEM annually collects comparable data on the entrepreneurial activity, attitudes and aspirations of individuals in about 60 countries worldwide. GEM classifies the motives of entrepreneurial activities as opportunity and necessity-driven new ventures. GEM members of the national teams from the U.K., Chile and Germany that have been involved into an EU funded project fostering mobility of researchers, *DiasporaLink*, developed and proposed a set of questions for the 2016 GEM APS to measure TE and TDE (transnational diaspora entrepreneurship).

Table 1 shows an overview of the data set description. While both samples border at around 8000 cases (3301 entrepreneurs), the number of entrepreneurs varies significantly with Chile having roughly 2.5-times more.

Following the above stated definition, a transnational entrepreneur is an entrepreneur that either has lived in another country for several years before returning to his or her country of origin and still has business relations with that country or immigrants that still have business related connections with the country of origin. To establish this in the data set, we utilised two variables of the GEM APS TDE set: 'Have you lived in another country for several years and still have business related connections with that country' and 'Do you have business related connections with your country of origin?' We do not include second generation transnational entrepreneurs because we believe they show significant behavioural differences.

Table 1. Descriptive statistic from Chile and Germany.

	Chile			Germany			Total		
	Obs.	Mean	SD	Obs.	Mean	SD	Obs.	Mean	SD
Opportunity-Driven Entrepreneur (OPP)	2344	49.1%	0.594	957	47.6%	0.345	3301	49.9%	0.529
Necessity-Driven Entrepreneur (NEC)	2344	37.7%	0.172	957	26.4%	0.075	3301	35.4%	0.147
Age	2344	40.88	12.07	957	44.68	11.50	3301	41.86	12.04
Female	2344	49.1%	0.404	957	47.0%	0.329	3301	48.7%	0.384
Tertiary Education	2344	49.6%	0.438	957	47.7%	0.349	3301	49.3%	0.415
Knows an Entrepreneur	2344	49.0%	0.600	957	49.9%	0.541	3301	49.3%	0.585
Opportunity Recognition	2344	49.9%	0.536	957	48.5%	0.621	3301	49.7%	0.558
Self-Efficacy	2344	34.6%	0.861	957	34.9%	0.858	3301	34.7%	0.860
Fear of Failure	2344	41.6%	0.222	957	38.0%	0.175	3301	40.7%	0.210
Transnationals	2344	21.7%	0.050	957	27.2%	0.080	3301	23.3%	0.058

We use a probit regression model due to the structure of the dependant variable. It estimates the probability for an individual to engage in opportunity or necessity entrepreneurial activity, using TE as the main explicative variable, including individual level controls that explain the probability of engaging in entrepreneurial activity such as age, gender and education and other controls regarding self-perception of individuals about entrepreneurship. We use interactions in order to capture enhancing or attenuating effects of the traditional entrepreneurial traits.

4.2. Results

To address research statements (1) and (2) influence of being a transnational entrepreneur on being opportunity driven or necessity driven was estimated for a data set consisting of the pooled data from both countries ($N = 3031$). We argue that this shows overall behaviour of TE regarding opportunity-driven entrepreneurship despite the mentioned institutional differences (addressed by a country dummy). At pool level, we observe that the transnationals in Germany are less likely than in Chile to engage in any kind of entrepreneurial activity, necessity ($\beta=-0.58$; $p < .001$) and opportunity driven ($\beta=-0.49$; $p < .001$). When interacting the Germany-Dummy with TE, we find that being German decreases the positive effect TE has on opportunity-driven entrepreneurship and the negative effect of TE on necessity-driven entrepreneurship turns positive, meaning that TE in Germany is more likely to be necessity driven oriented while in Chile it is opportunity driven oriented (Table 2). To shed light on research statement (3) each country was additionally looked upon separately in the next two sub-sections and compared with each other in Section 5.

4.2.1. Chile

Chile provides an interesting case study due to its increasing trend of migration over the last decade (the national census of 2012 accounted that 1.2% of the population in Chile where immigrants, 2.7% in 2015) and the presence of the most dynamic and EESs in this global region. Transition to a free market system and open economy exposed Chilean businesses to a significant amount of turbulence and adjustments to international challenges. Increased international trade taught business owners important lessons to compete in global markets, increasing the quality and global competitiveness of the labour force (Lepeley, Pizarro, and Mandakovic 2015). Chile has free trade agreements

Table 2. Pooled data probit model regression.

	Pooled Data			
	Opp	Nec	Opp	Nec
Transnational	0.23*	−0.10	0.41**	−0.54**
	(0.10)	(0.14)	(0.14)	(0.20)
Tertiary Education	0.35***	−0.36***	0.35***	−0.35***
	(0.05)	(0.06)	(0.05)	(0.06)
Female	−0.12*	0.22***	−0.11*	0.22***
	(0.05)	(0.06)	(0.05)	(0.06)
Age	−0.02	0.03	−0.02	0.03
	(0.01)	(0.02)	(0.01)	(0.02)
Age Squared	−0.00	−0.00	−0.00	−0.00
	(0.00)	(0.00)	(0.00)	(0.00)
Knows an Entrepreneur	0.23***	−0.13*	0.24***	−0.13*
	(0.05)	(0.06)	(0.05)	(0.06)
Opportunity Recognition	0.26***	−0.15*	0.26***	−0.16**
	(0.05)	(0.06)	(0.05)	(0.06)
Self-efficacy	−0.17*	−0.10	−0.17*	−0.09
	(0.07)	(0.08)	(0.07)	(0.08)
Fear of Failure	−0.10	0.03	−0.10	0.02
	(0.06)	(0.07)	(0.06)	(0.07)
Germany	−0.58***	−0.49***	−0.55***	−0.57***
	(0.06)	(0.07)	(0.06)	(0.08)
Germany#Transnational			−0.47*	1.12***
			(0.22)	(0.28)
Constant	1.12***	−1.13***	1.12***	−1.15***
	(0.29)	(0.33)	(0.29)	(0.34)
Pseudo-R-squared	0.138	0.050	0.140	0.056
Observations	3301	3301	3301	3301

Notes: Standard errors in parentheses, *p < .05, **p < .01, ***p < .001. Opp: opportunity-driven entrepreneur; Nec: necessity-driven entrepreneur; Germany#Transnational: interaction between country dummy and transnational entrepreneur.

with more than 30 countries and double taxation avoidance agreements, which is attractive to foreign investors and entrepreneurs.

One of the main factors that influences the construction and consolidation of the Chilean EES is government policies and programmes that have been created in order to promote entrepreneurial activity through incentives for business start-ups (Mandakovic, Cohen, and Amorós 2015). The GEM 2017 expert rating of the national entrepreneurial framework shows that Chile is in the 15th position over 63 countries in government entrepreneurship programmes dimension and first place among Latin American economies. During the last decade, the Chilean government has taken important regulatory initiatives pointing to reduce bureaucracy associated to firm's dynamics. Another initiative was the creation of a new bankruptcy law renamed 're-entrepreneurship law' that reduces the firms' closure proceedings and enables a new start for entrepreneurs that faced failure. As seen in the results, Chilean transnationals show lower levels of fear of failure than non-transnationals and German transnationals.

Those are mainly improvements in formal institutional settings in which entrepreneurial activity takes place, but Chile has also presented advances concerning informal institutions, that arise directly from the influence of government programmes, that aimed to generate a cultural change towards entrepreneurship (Welter and Smallbone 2011). In 2010 the Chilean government launched Startup Chile,[1] a programme that aspired to transform Chile into the innovation and entrepreneurship hub of Latin America, through incentives given to foreign entrepreneurial teams to locate their businesses in Chile and develop global connections (Melo 2012). The programme offers start-ups access to investors, local experts and capital to develop their projects. It still exists and is administered by the Chilean economic development agency (CORFO). The programme keeps its international focus, and offers a one-year working visa to entrepreneurs with high human capital in the technology services sector to start or develop their business in Chile, within a maximum period of 15 working days. The entrepreneurs come mainly from the U.S., Argentina, India and Canada. While quite the significant amount of Chilean TE are from Chile and lived abroad, the most frequent countries of origin of immigrant transnational entrepreneurs are from Argentina, Perú and Brazil, mostly border countries.

Table 3 shows the results of the Chilean estimations; transnationals have a positive and significant probability of becoming an opportunity-driven entrepreneur ($\beta=0.39; p < .01$) and a negative probability of becoming a necessity-driven entrepreneur ($\beta=-0.53; p < .01$). In the case of necessity-based entrepreneurs, the negative effect of TE is driven by the self-efficacy level of the entrepreneur. This can be seen by the interaction effect presented in column 8, being a TE only has a negative effect in the probability of being a necessity-driven entrepreneur if the entrepreneur declares to have a high self-efficacy. Another interesting interaction can be seen in columns 10, where fear of failure has no effect on the likelihood of becoming a necessity-based entrepreneur; however, if the entrepreneur is TE, the effect of fear of failure becomes positive and significant for that subgroup.

4.2.2. Germany

With the recent in-migration Germany faces a challenge both politically and economically. Politically because populistic parties hugely gained votes in recent elections, capitalising on prejudice and fanned fear. Economically because Germany needs to invest in opportunities for immigrants to integrate them into the labour market, either in employment or as entrepreneurs. This is a unique opportunity for the country and since many of the migrants might return once their countries of origin are safe again, this could establish new bridges for economic development and knowledge flows if some of them become transnational entrepreneurs.

Traditionally the German economy relies heavily on exports with car manufacturing being one of the most important industries. Although big global players such as Volkswagen, Daimler or Bayer dominate the outside picture of the German economy, the bulk of its businesses is rather small or medium sized and often family businesses. Wealth distribution is increasingly uneven and taxation and social security contributions are weighing quite heavy on the lower and middle-income households. Whilst generally highly educated, Germany has quite a low count of tertiary educated inhabitants compared to other EU countries. However, the renowned secondary education, the German 'Ausbildung' (apprenticeship) covers the largest part of the German workforce and compensates for the comparatively low (but growing) share of tertiary educated people. The current economic prosperity cycle is leading to historically low unemployment and high wages which takes its toll when it comes to entrepreneurial activity. A secure employment option is quite easy to come by which increases the opportunity costs of becoming self-employed, but it also increases the current share of opportunity-driven entrepreneurs compared to necessity-driven ones.

Since GEM collects data on total early-stage entrepreneurial activity (TEA), Germany was under the lowest scoring countries, even if only compared to other innovation-driven countries. Interestingly, migrants show a higher propensity to engage in TEA than the

Table 3. Chile models estimations.

	Opp	Nec	Opp	Nec	Opp	Nec	Opp	Nec	Opp	Nec	Opp	Nec
Transnational	0.39**	−0.53**	0.11	−0.54	0.32	−0.50	−0.42	0.61	0.48**	−0.82***
	(0.14)	(0.20)	(0.22)	(0.30)	(0.20)	(0.29)	(0.58)	(0.59)	(0.15)	(0.25)
Tertiary Education	0.41***	−0.41***	0.41***	−0.41***	0.41***	−0.41***	0.41***	−0.42***	0.41***	−0.42***
	(0.06)	(0.07)	(0.06)	(0.07)	(0.06)	(0.07)	(0.06)	(0.07)	(0.06)	(0.07)
Female	−0.17**	0.26***	−0.17**	0.26***	−0.17**	0.26***	−0.17**	0.26***	−0.18**	0.27***
	(0.06)	(0.06)	(0.06)	(0.06)	(0.06)	(0.06)	(0.06)	(0.06)	(0.06)	(0.06)
Age	0.01	0.03	0.01	0.03	0.01	0.03	0.01	0.03	0.01	0.03
	(0.02)	(0.02)	(0.02)	(0.02)	(0.02)	(0.02)	(0.02)	(0.02)	(0.02)	(0.02)
Age Squared	−0.00*	−0.00	−0.00*	−0.00	−0.00*	−0.00	−0.00*	−0.00	−0.00*	−0.00
	(0.00)	(0.00)	(0.00)	(0.00)	(0.00)	(0.00)	(0.00)	(0.00)	(0.00)	(0.00)
Knows an Entrepreneur	0.12*	−0.22***	0.10	−0.23***	0.12*	−0.22***	0.12*	−0.23***	0.13*	−0.23***
	(0.06)	(0.07)	(0.06)	(0.07)	(0.06)	(0.07)	(0.06)	(0.07)	(0.06)	(0.07)
Opportunity Recognition	0.32***	−0.16**	0.32***	−0.16**	0.31***	−0.16*	0.32***	−0.16*	0.32***	−0.16*
	(0.06)	(0.06)	(0.06)	(0.06)	(0.06)	(0.07)	(0.06)	(0.06)	(0.06)	(0.06)
Self-efficacy	−0.14	0.03	−0.14	0.03	−0.14	0.03	−0.16	0.06	−0.15	0.04
	(0.08)	(0.09)	(0.08)	(0.09)	(0.08)	(0.09)	(0.08)	(0.09)	(0.08)	(0.09)
Fear of Failure	−0.10	−0.06	−0.11	−0.06	−0.10	−0.06	−0.10	−0.06	−0.08	−0.09
	(0.07)	(0.08)	(0.07)	(0.08)	(0.07)	(0.08)	(0.07)	(0.08)	(0.07)	(0.08)
Knows an Entrepeneur#Transnational			0.44	0.02						
			(0.28)	(0.39)						
Opportunity Recognition#Transnational					0.12	−0.06				
					(0.27)	(0.39)				
Self-Efficacy#Transnational							0.85	−1.26*		
							(0.59)	(0.62)		
Fear of Failure#Transnational									−0.61	1.28**
									(0.37)	(0.46)
Constant	0.67*	−1.41***	0.65*	−1.41***	0.67*	−1.41***	0.67*	−1.42***	0.67*	−1.42***
	(0.33)	(0.37)	(0.33)	(0.37)	(0.33)	(0.37)	(0.33)	(0.37)	(0.33)	(0.37)
Pseudo-R-squared	0.116	0.050	0.117	0.050	0.117	0.050	0.117	0.052	0.117	0.054
Observations	2344	2344	2344	2344	2344	2344	2344	2344	2344	2344

Notes: Standard errors in parentheses, *$p < .05$, **$p < .01$, ***$p < .001$. Opp: opportunity-driven entrepreneur; Nec: necessity-driven entrepreneur.

indigenous population and although migrants and Germans with a migratory background contribute massively towards the success of the German economy, in-migration is not necessarily perceived positively by the 'standard' citizen (German GEM's National Expert Survey, NES data 2016 and 2017). Germany is quite sufficiently equipped with government programmes aimed at fostering entrepreneurship, with financing possibilities and market openness. Shortcomings are found when it comes to politics prioritising entrepreneurship, entrepreneurial culture and most significantly entrepreneurship education in schools.

While a significant number of German transnationals are German born re-migrants, the most frequent countries of origin of immigrant transnational entrepreneurs are Morocco, Poland, Ethiopia, Turkey, the U.S.A., Austria, Switzerland and Russia.

About 47.6% of German Entrepreneurship pursued with the motive of following an opportunity whilst just 26.4% is done out of better alternatives for employment. Roughly 27% of the German entrepreneurs qualify either as migrant or re-migrant transnational entrepreneurs which is quite high. Amongst the early-stage entrepreneurs, males are more frequent and more than a third have a tertiary education background. Low fear of failure, high self-efficacy, above average opportunity recognition and knowing other entrepreneurs are also characteristics of German early-stage entrepreneurs (Table 4).

In Germany, transnational entrepreneurs have a positive and significant effect on the likelihood of becoming a necessity-driven entrepreneur ($\beta=0.43$; $p < .05$), and seemingly no effect in opportunity driven. Interactions show a positive effect of TE over necessity-driven entrepreneurship if the entrepreneur has high levels of self-efficacy. The effect of TE in opportunity-driven entrepreneurship appears to be negative and significant if the entrepreneur has a fear of failure, and the effect turns out to be negative. The research statement proposing a negative impact of TE on necessity-driven entrepreneurship (2) falls short in the case of Germany but is very accurate for Chile. However, as suggested, there seems to be a major difference in TE between both countries. This comparison will be picked up in Section 5.

4.3. Traits of transnational entrepreneurs: country comparison

A comparative analysis of entrepreneurs' traits influences on being transnational in both countries is shown in Table 5. The results suggest a strong positive and significant relationship between tertiary education and the TE condition using the pooled and each country data. Additionally, opportunity recognition and self-efficacy are also positively related to TE using the pooled data. In Chile, TE is associated with age, self-efficacy and fear of failure. In the case of Germany, TE is associated only with opportunity recognition. This evidence supports research statement (3) regarding country-specific differences. However, although the kind of traits associated with transnational entrepreneurs (opportunity recognition, networked: approximated by knowing other entrepreneurs) is found in Germany where TE is strongly related to necessity entrepreneurship. A sign that German institutions clearly do not enable the potential of TE.

5. Discussion: Parallels and differences

Having much higher levels of entrepreneurial activity than Germany, Chile also performs well on the quality side of those activities. With high levels (relative) of opportunity-driven

Table 4. Germany models estimations.

	Opp	Nec	Opp	Nec	Opp	Nec	Opp	Nec	Opp	Nec
Transnational	−0.07 (0.18)	0.43* (0.22)	−0.90 (0.50)	0.98** (0.38)	0.14 (0.41)	0.15 (0.54)	−0.69 (0.58)	1.61** (0.57)	0.25 (0.20)	0.24 (0.28)
Tertiary Education	0.21* (0.10)	0.09 (0.15)	0.21* (0.10)	0.09 (0.15)	0.20* (0.10)	0.10 (0.15)	0.20 (0.10)	0.11 (0.15)	0.18 (0.10)	0.11 (0.15)
Female	0.10 (0.10)	−0.03 (0.15)	0.09 (0.10)	−0.01 (0.15)	0.09 (0.10)	−0.03 (0.15)	0.09 (0.10)	−0.01 (0.15)	0.08 (0.10)	−0.01 (0.15)
Age	−0.09** (0.03)	−0.02 (0.04)	−0.09** (0.03)	−0.02 (0.04)	−0.09** (0.03)	−0.02 (0.04)	−0.09** (0.03)	−0.03 (0.04)	−0.09** (0.03)	−0.02 (0.04)
Age Squared	0.00* (0.00)	0.00 (0.00)	0.00* (0.00)	0.00 (0.00)	0.00* (0.00)	0.00 (0.00)	0.00* (0.00)	0.00 (0.00)	0.00* (0.00)	0.00 (0.00)
Knows an Entrepreneur	0.56*** (0.10)	0.26 (0.15)	0.51*** (0.11)	0.35* (0.16)	0.56*** (0.10)	0.26 (0.15)	0.56*** (0.10)	0.23 (0.15)	0.56*** (0.10)	0.26 (0.15)
Opportunity Recognition	0.14 (0.10)	−0.20 (0.15)	0.14 (0.10)	−0.20 (0.15)	0.15 (0.11)	−0.23 (0.15)	0.15 (0.10)	−0.23 (0.15)	0.16 (0.10)	−0.21 (0.15)
Self-efficacy	−0.28* (0.14)	−0.59*** (0.17)	−0.27 (0.14)	−0.62*** (0.17)	−0.29* (0.14)	−0.58*** (0.17)	−0.33* (0.14)	−0.45* (0.18)	−0.33* (0.14)	−0.56** (0.17)
Fear of Failure	−0.12 (0.13)	0.32* (0.16)	−0.12 (0.13)	0.32 (0.17)	−0.12 (0.13)	0.32 (0.16)	−0.10 (0.13)	0.26 (0.17)	0.03 (0.13)	0.23 (0.18)
Knows an Entrepeneur#Transnational			1.01 (0.54)	−0.78 (0.46)						
Opportunity Recognition#Transnational					−0.26 (0.46)	0.34 (0.59)				
Self-Efficacy#Transnational							0.69 (0.61)	−1.41* (0.62)		
Fear of Failure#Transnational									−1.83** (0.57)	0.62 (0.48)
Constant	1.89** (0.61)	−0.39 (0.81)	1.92** (0.61)	−0.44 (0.81)	1.87** (0.61)	−0.36 (0.81)	1.86** (0.61)	−0.27 (0.81)	1.95** (0.62)	−0.40 (0.81)
Pseudo-R-squared	0.115	0.081	0.119	0.088	0.116	0.082	0.117	0.094	0.128	0.085
Observations	957	957	957	957	957	957	957	957	957	957

Notes: Standard errors in parentheses, *$p < .05$, **$p < .01$, ***$p < .001$. Opp: opportunity-driven entrepreneur; Nec: necessity-driven entrepreneur.

Table 5. TE traits results.

	Transnational		
	Pooled Data	Chile	Germany
Tertiary Education	0.40***	0.46***	0.33*
	(0.08)	(0.10)	(0.14)
Female	−0.14	−0.14	−0.10
	(0.08)	(0.10)	(0.15)
Age	0.03	0.07*	−0.04
	(0.02)	(0.03)	(0.04)
Age Squared	−0.00	−0.00*	0.00
	(0.00)	(0.00)	(0.00)
Knows an Entrepreneur	0.09	−0.03	0.30*
	(0.08)	(0.10)	(0.15)
Opportunity Recognition	0.24**	0.17	0.48**
	(0.08)	(0.10)	(0.16)
Self-efficacy	0.35*	0.49*	0.17
	(0.14)	(0.20)	(0.22)
Fear of Failure	−0.11	−0.33*	0.26
	(0.10)	(0.13)	(0.17)
Germany	0.25**		
	(0.08)		
Constant	−3.00***	−3.82***	−1.38
	(0.50)	(0.65)	(0.87)
Pseudo-R-squared	0.054	0.063	0.064
Observations	3301	2344	957

Notes: Standard errors in parentheses, *$p < .05$, **$p < .01$, ***$p < .001$.

entrepreneurship both countries show similar patterns. Surprisingly Chilean entrepreneurs seem to know fewer other entrepreneurs than German ones, given the fact that Chile has more entrepreneurs per capita, with many of them in a single concentrated geographical area (Santiago). The German sample is more skewed towards male entrepreneurs but the difference is small. The characteristics of German and Chilean entrepreneurs are quite similar and comparable. The only significant difference is the share of transnational entrepreneurs compared to all entrepreneurs. With 27.2% transnational entrepreneurs, Germany has a higher percentage of transnationals than Chile (21.7%). Since Chile has more entrepreneurs in total, Germany has less transnational entrepreneurs per capita.

The models show very different pictures. While the statement that being a transnational entrepreneur increases the likelihood of being an entrepreneur driven by opportunity receives a positive result for Chile, the opposite is the case for Germany. Having a high level of education also pushes the probability of being opportunity driven in Chile while it does not seem to have an effect in Germany. This, however, might be due to the fact that Germany has quite a high level of education on the secondary education level. More than 40% of German TEA is accountable to people having 'just' a secondary education degree. Comparing levels of education between different countries always poses some difficulties regarding the comparability. When it comes to gender influence, Chile shows a significant impact of the female control variable. Women more often seem to have to rely on becoming self-employed because of necessity and are less often entrepreneurs to exploit an opportunity than men in Chile. This implies gender specific imbalances within the entrepreneurial and work culture such as a more restrictive access to capital or job availability. In Germany, gender has no effect on whether an entrepreneur is opportunity or necessity driven. Although women less often found businesses, they seem to do it out of the same motives as men do.

In both countries, public institutions are major players in the support structure for entrepreneurship and new firm foundations. The difference is that the Chilean government is heavily subsidising new firms with financial capital whilst the German programmes mainly supply non-monetary support although migrant entrepreneurship (but not TE support in particular) nowadays belongs to the most important elements of government policies to support 'inclusive entrepreneurship' in Germany (see Sternberg 2017).

Mining and exporting ore, especially copper, was one of the core income generators for Chile and still is very important. Trying to refocus towards a more diverse economic structure the Chilean government focuses intensely on promoting entrepreneurship and supports start-ups through accelerators, co-working spaces and specific programmes. This is definitely not the case in Germany. For many parties, entrepreneurship is not part of their main agenda and entrepreneurship support that does exist focuses on guidance, counselling and networking rather than subsidising with no strings attached. However, in terms of market openness, Germany seems to offer a better context for growing businesses. The influence of traits on being transnational or not differs for both countries as well. Surprisingly the combination of traits contrasts to the country-specific influence that TE has on being opportunity driven. While the kind of TE that is hypothetically good for fostering EES is found in Germany, those entrepreneurs seem to have to become necessity-driven entrepreneurs, without being fully enabled to contribute to the country's EES.

Chile seems to be more successful when it comes to attract opportunity-driven transnational entrepreneurs. This might indicate better policy or incentives for attracting the right kind of transnational migrant entrepreneurs. Chile spends a lot more 'direct' money on entrepreneurship than Germany in terms of financing the start-ups. However, programmes like Start-Up Chile do not only supply money, co-working and networking, they demand some feedback into the EES from the entrepreneurs they as well.

At first glance the opposing effects of TE in Germany and Chile are surprising results. However, if the institutional contexts and entrepreneurial climate are factored into the consideration, it is not unlikely that both countries attract and harbour different manifestations of TE. Both countries' most frequent country of origin for immigrant transnational entrepreneurs is less developed than the host country (Germany: Morocco, Chile: Peru and more recently Haiti). The latter fact would speak in favour of attracting the same type of TE. Since this is not the case, differences in the elements of the national system of entrepreneurship like entrepreneurial culture (i.e. spirit or climate), in institutional context and in policy, could also explain not only different levels of entrepreneurial activity but also the share and type of transnationals.

Only seen in case studies so far, it is now empirically proven that there are different types of TE regarding their motivation for entrepreneurship. As presumed in theory, TE seems indeed to be subject to heterogeneity. Hypothetically at least one factor influencing the behaviour of transnationals could be whether the motive for migration was being pulled into Chile or Germany or rather pushed out of the country of origin. However, when looking at the different kinds of TE and their potential to contribute to EES, the answer does not seem to be so easy as suggested in the 4th research statement and opens up a compelling new field of research.

6. Conclusions

With TE being increasingly relevant as well as harbouring an untapped potential for economic development and thriving EES there was still almost no quantitative empirical analysis available to explore this phenomenon. By employing data recently collected by GEM we could show distinct influence of TE on opportunity- and necessity-driven entrepreneurship. Furthermore, the data hints, that transnationals display traits such as higher opportunity recognition and know more entrepreneurs, are less afraid of failure and have a higher degree of self-efficacy than non-transnationals. We could show considerable differences in TE behaviour between Chile and Germany and argue that those can be related to differing institutional contexts and levels of economic development. This implies differences in TE impact on EES depending on the country-specific framework conditions. While Chile displays TE with such traits higher opportunity recognition, Germany does not. There cannot be drawn a conclusive finding on the relationship between EES and TE, but our article opened up some interesting path for further research in this direction.

Our exploratory empirical article contains some shortcomings: Due to low levels of TEA in Germany and thus low levels of TE within the German sample, instead of the more precise measure for entrepreneurial activity (TEA), owner-managers of established businesses had to be included to receive robust results. Additionally, Chilean data is from one year, German data was compiled from 2016 and 2017. Furthermore, the data did not allow for a more in-depth analysis of the interdependent relationship between EES and TE. Also due to sample size restrictions and TE being a rare event within a rare event a rather wide interpretation of the TE definition had to be applied. With more data available in the future, the results have to be replicated and refined.

Government policies to support entrepreneurship are an important aspect of the institutional environment (see Terjesen, Bosma, and Stam 2016). However, while having recently grown significantly in numbers, such government policy initiatives and programmes rarely explicitly address TE (see Murdock 2012; Pickernell et al. 2013). Therefore, we provide some country-specific implications for governments' entrepreneurship support policies in favour of TE.

In Chile, transnationals are mainly opportunity-driven entrepreneurs, highly skilled and with a high self-assessment of their entrepreneurial skill set. This addresses the needs of a developing economy that searches to exploit its opportunities in order to increase the levels of productivity. Policies and programmes that focus on expanding opportunities and promoting TE, must be implemented in a deeper way. Restrictions in terms of visas for foreign entrepreneurs and more active participation of the private sector, especially in terms of entrepreneurial finance are needed.

For Germany empirical results clearly prevail that transnational entrepreneurs are, in relative terms, more frequent than in Chile, and that their likelihood of becoming a necessity-driven entrepreneur is obvious. While German government's entrepreneurship support policies have developed a noticeable number of programmes to support migrant entrepreneurship in recent years (Sternberg 2017), none of these programmes explicitly address opportunity entrepreneurship or even growth-oriented, ambitious entrepreneurship. Future government policies to support migrant entrepreneurship should address growth potentials of transnational entrepreneurs, since both the number of self-employed as well as the start-up rate rather continuously decreased in recent years. While the total number of self-employed decreased by 5% between 2007 and 2016, those born in Germany even decreased by 8.1%. Thus, immigrants helped to attenuate the decrease of self-employment. Future government policies are suggested to address male immigrants from other innovation-driven economies in particular as in Germany those are more entrepreneurial than non-migrants and female migrants (see Brixy, Sternberg, and Vorderwülbecke 2013). Government support policies may, thus, consider the countries of origin of the migrants more explicitly than in the past. This seems also be significant as migrants in general and from some countries in particular benefit much more from the treatment effect (the income effect solely due to the decision for self-employment) than Germans. Furthermore, migrant entrepreneurs in general and transnational entrepreneurs in particular should also be considered to be an option when it comes to one of the biggest problems of the German 'Mittelstand' in the long run: although there is an increasing number of companies still led by entrepreneurs who will soon retire but do not find someone who is willing to take over the company, the proportion of inter-ethnic take-overs is very low.

Continued data gathering on TE will allow a deeper understanding of how TE influences and is being influenced by entrepreneurial motives but also contexts such as the EES. The institutional (national) contexts as well as level of economic development seem to play a decisive role in which form of TE emerges in a given context. Additionally, the linkages between TE and EES need to be explored further when a profound empirical analysis is possible through newly developed data sets. Especially interdependencies of both phenomena as well as on a meta as on the individual level need to be explored to develop special tailored policy recommendations to fully utilise the potential of TE.

Note

1. http://www.startupchile.org/

Disclosure statement

No potential conflict of interest was reported by the authors.

References

Acs, Z. J. 2006. "How is Entrepreneurship Good for Economic Growth?" *Innovations: Technology, Governance, Globalization* 1 (1): 97–107.

Acs, Z., E. Autio, and L. Szerb. 2014. "National Systems of Entrepreneurship: Measurement Issues and Policy Implications." *Research Policy* 43: 476–494.

Alvedalen, J., and R. Boschma. 2017. "A Critical Review of Entrepreneurial Ecosystems Research: Towards a Future Research Agenda." *European Planning Studies* 25: 887–903.

Amorós, J. E., L. Ciravegna, V. Mandakovic, and P. Stenholm. 2017. "Necessity or Opportunity? The Effects of State Fragility and Economic Development on Entrepreneurial Efforts." *Entrepreneurship Theory and Practice*. doi:10.1177/1042258717736857.

Basch, L., N. Glick Schiller, and C. Szanton-Blanc. 1994. *Nations Unbound: Transnational Projects, Postcolonial Predicaments, and Deterritorialized Nation-States*. London: Routledge.

Bosma, N., K. Jones, E. Autio, and J. Levie. 2008. *Global Entrepreneurship Monitor 2007 Executive Report*. London: Global Entrepreneurship Research Association.

Bowen, H. P., and D. De Clercq. 2008. "Institutional Context and the Allocation of Entrepreneurial Effort." *Journal of International Business Studies* 39 (4): 747–767.

Brixy, U., R. Sternberg, and A. Vorderwülbecke. 2013. *Business Start-ups by Migrants*. IAB-Brief Report 25/2013. Nuremberg: Institute for Employment Research.

Brzozowski, J., M. Cucculelli, and A. Surdej. 2014. "Transnational Ties and Performance of Immigrant Entrepreneurs: The Role of Home-Country Conditions." *Entrepreneurship & Regional Development* 26 (7–8): 546–573. doi:10.1080/08985626.2014.959068.

Brzozowski, J., M. Cucculelli, and A. Surdej. 2018. "Exploring Transnational Entrepreneurship. Immigrant Entrepreneurs and Foreign-Born Returnees in the Italian ICT Sector." *Journal of Small Business & Entrepreneurship*, 1–19. doi:10.1080/08276331.2018.1429803.

Drori, I., B. Honig, and M. Wright. 2009. "Transnational Entrepreneurship: An Emergent Field of Study." *Entrepreneurship Theory and Practice* 33 (5): 1001–1022.

Elo, M. 2016. "Typology of Diaspora Entrepreneurship: Case Studies in Uzbekistan." *Journal of International Entrepreneurship* 14 (1): 121–155.

GERA. 2018. *Global Entrepreneurship Monitor Global Report 2017/2018*. www.gemconsortium.org/report.

Kariv, D., T. Menzies, G. Brenner, and L. J. Filion. 2009. "Transnational Networking and Business Performance: Ethnic Entrepreneurs in Canada." *Entrepreneurship and Regional Development* 21 (3): 239–264. doi:10.1080/08985620802261641.

Kloosterman, R. C., K. Rusinovic, and D. Yeboah. 2016. "Super-diverse Migrants – Similar Trajectories? Ghanaian Entrepreneurship in the Netherlands Seen from a Mixed Embeddedness Perspective." *Journal of Ethnic and Migration Studies* 42 (6): 913–932.

Landolt, P., L. Autler, and S. Baires. 1999. "From Hermano Lejano to Hermano Mayor: The Dialectics of Salvadoran Transnationalism." *Ethnic and Racial Studies* 22 (2): 290–315. doi:10.1080/014198799329495.

Lepeley, M. T., O. Pizarro, and V. Mandakovic. 2015. "Women Entrepreneurs in Chile: Three Decades of Challenges and Lessons in Innovation and Business Sustainability." In *Female Entrepreneurship in Transition Economies*, V. Ramadani, S. Gërguri-Rashiti, and A. Fayolle, 247–264. London: Palgrave Macmillan.

Levie, J., and E. Autio. 2011. "Regulatory Burden, Rule of law, and Entry of Strategic Entrepreneurs: An International Panel Study." *Journal of Management Studies* 48 (6): 1392–1419.

Malecki, E. J. 2018. "Entrepreneurship and Entrepreneurial Ecosystems." *Geography Compass* 12. doi:10.1111/gec3.12359.

Mandakovic, V., B. Cohen, and J. E. Amorós. 2015. "Entrepreneurship Policy and Its Impact on the Cultural Legitimacy for Entrepreneurship in a Developing Country Context." In *Entrepreneurship, Regional Development and Culture*, 109–125. Cham: Springer.

McMullen, J. S., D. R. Bagby, and L. E. Palich. 2008. "Economic Freedom and the Motivation to Engage in Entrepreneurial Action." *Entrepreneurship Theory and Practice* 32 (5): 875–895.

Melo, H. 2012. "Prosperity Through Connectedness (*Innovations Case Narrative*: Start-Up Chile)." *Innovations: Technology, Governance, Globalization* 7 (2): 19–23.

Murdock, K. A. 2012. "Entrepreneurship Policy: Trade-offs and Impact in the EU." *Entrepreneurship & Regional Development* 24 (9–10): 879–893.

Pickernell, D., J. Senyard, P. Jones, G. Packham, and E. Ramsey. 2013. "New and Young Firms: Entrepreneurship Policy and the Role of Government–Evidence from the Federation of Small Businesses Survey." *Journal of Small Business and Enterprise Development* 20 (2): 358–382.

Portes, A., L. E. Guarnizo, and W. J. Haller. 2002. "Transnational Entrepreneurs: An Alternative Form of Immigrant Economic Adaptation." *American Sociological Review* 67 (2): 278–298. doi:10.2307/3088896.

Portes, A., L. E. Guarnizo, and P. Landolt. 1999. "The Study of Transnationalism: Pitfalls and Promise of an Emergent Research Field." *Ethnic and Racial Studies* 22 (2): 217–237. doi:10.1080/014198799329468.

Reynolds, P., N. Bosma, E. Autio, S. Hunt, N. De Bono, I. Servais, P. Lopez-Garcia, and N. Chin. 2005. "Global Entrepreneurship Monitor: Data Collection Design and Implementation 1998–2003." *Small Business Economics* 24 (3): 205–231.

Riddle, L., G. A. Hrivnak, and T. M. Nielsen. 2010. "Transnational Diaspora Entrepreneurship in Emerging Markets: Bridging Institutional Divides." *Journal of International Management* 16: 398–411.

Rusinovic, K. 2008. "Transnational Embeddedness: Transnational Activities and Networks among First and Second-Generation Immigrant Entrepreneurs in the Netherlands." *Journal of Ethnic and Migration Studies* 34 (3): 431–451. doi:10.1080/13691830701880285.

Saxenian, A. 2006. *The New Argonauts. Regional Advantage in a Global Economy*. Cambridge, MA: Harvard University Press.

Sepulveda, L., S. Syrett, and F. Lyon. 2011. "Population Superdiversity and new Migrant Enterprise: The Case of London." *Entrepreneurship & Regional Development* 23 (7–8): 469–497.

Simba, A., and N. Ojong. 2018. "Diaspora Networks: A Social Capital Source for Entrepreneurship in Low-Income and Emerging Economies in Africa." In *African Diaspora Direct Investment. Palgrave Studies of Entrepreneurship in Africa*, edited by D. Hack-Polay and J. Siwale, 113–143. Cham: Palgrave Macmillan.

Sorenson, O. 2017. "Regional Ecologies of Entrepreneurship." *Journal of Economic Geography* 17: 959–974. doi:10.1093/jeg/lbx031.

Stam, E., and B. Spigel. 2018. "Entrepreneurial Ecosystems." In *The Sage Handbook of Small Business and Entrepreneurship and Small Business*, edited by R. Blackburn, D. De Clercq, J. Heinonen, and Z. Wang, 407–422. London: SAGE.

Stangler, D., and J. Bell-Masterson. 2015. *Measuring an Entrepreneurial Ecosystem*. Kansas City, MO: Kauffman Foundation.

Sternberg, R. 2017. *Inclusive Entrepreneurship Policies: Country Assessment Notes: Germany, 2017* (prepared as part of Local Economic and Employment Development (LEED) program). Paris: OECD, Brussels: European Union.

Terjesen, S., N. Bosma, and E. Stam. 2016. "Advancing Public Policy for High-Growth, Female, and Social Entrepreneurs." *Public Administration Review* 76(2): 230–239.

Welter, F., and D. Smallbone. 2011. "Institutional Perspectives on Entrepreneurial Behavior in Challenging Environments." *Journal of Small Business Management* 49 (1): 107–125.

Wong, P. X., Y. P. Ho, and E. Autio. 2005. "Entrepreneurship, Innovation and Economic Growth: Evidence from GEM Data." *Small Business Economics* 24 (3): 335–350. doi:10.1007/s11187-005-2000-1.

Wong, L. L., and M. Ng. 2002. "The Emergence of Small Transnational Enterprise in Vancouver: The Case of Chinese Entrepreneur Immigrants." *International Journal of Urban and Regional Research* 26 (3): 508–530. doi:10.1111/1468-2427.00396.

Zapata-Barrero, R., and S. Rezaei. 2020. "Diaspora Governance and Transnational Entrepreneurship: The Rise of an Emerging Social Global Pattern in Migration Studies." *Journal of Ethnic and Migration Studies* 46 (10): 1959–1973. doi:10.1080/1369183X.2018.1559990.

Harnessing the potential of Moroccans living abroad through diaspora policies? Assessing the factors of success and failure of a new structure of opportunities for transnational entrepreneurs

Ricard Zapata-Barrero and Z. Hellgren

ABSTRACT
In the framework of the emerging field of research on transnational migrant entrepreneurship at the crossroads of business and migration studies, the main purpose of this article is to assess the change of the Moroccan policy paradigm concerning their diaspora engagement policy, which has shifted from a guest-workers policy narrative (remittances based approach) to a transnational policy narrative (skills-mobilisation based approach) during the last decade. Once we have framed this process, we proceed to analyse the factors of success and failure of this new structure of opportunities for Moroccan transnational entrepreneurs. We have interviewed Moroccan migrant entrepreneurs in Morocco and Spain and stakeholders from different Moroccan institutions, and our findings indicate that there is a gap between the aims of the Moroccan engagement policy and the experiences of these Moroccan entrepreneurs. We argue that the Moroccan government has a too narrow view of transnationalism (only focused on return), a false identity premise (assuming that attraction towards Morocco can only be achieved by fostering a sense of 'Moroccanness' that appears to be far from reality), and a false socioeconomic premise that those that take this entrepreneurial route are motivated by opportunity rather than necessity.

Introduction: the Moroccan diaspora engagement policy paradigm

Though remittances play a decisive role in supplying currencies and reducing poverty (VV.AA. 2009), it is increasingly admitted that Moroccans Living Abroad (MLAs) can bring other forms of beneficial transfers to their land of origin, in the shape of technological, managerial and entrepreneurial know-how. Some nationals who return home may have acquired professional experience, social and cultural capital that stimulate the local economy. MLAs also begin to be viewed as drivers of innovation, employment and economic growth. The main purpose of this article is to assess this change of the Moroccan diaspora policy paradigm, which is shifting from a guest-workers policy narrative (remittances-based approach) to a transnational policy narrative (skills-mobilisation-based approach) in line with the growing interest in migrants as actual or potential transnational entrepreneurs described by Zapata-Barrero and Rezaei (2020) in the introduction to this volume.

The approach of this article is first descriptive: to place the diaspora engagement policy paradigm within the Moroccan migration dynamics context and overview its main features reviewing the main literature both from migration and business studies. Once we have framed this process, the rationale will turn to assessing the factors of success and failure of this structure of opportunities building process for Moroccan Transnational Entrepreneurs (MTEs). We have interviewed Moroccan migrant entrepreneurs in Morocco and Spain, and also stakeholders and public policy officers from different key Moroccan institutions.

We seek to contribute to the debate on transnational migrant entrepreneurship by exploring two sets of arguments: First, the *socio-economic argument* concerning the profile this policy is targeting, which does not take into account the differences between opportunity-driven and necessity-driven entrepreneurs that are often referred to in the literature (e.g. Newland and Tanaka 2010); and second, the *national identity arguments* which assume that in promoting a feeling of belonging ('Moroccanness'),[1] MLAs will be motivated to keep ties through professional and/or entrepreneurial ventures.

The main unit of the empirical analysis will follow the mainstream scholarship framework, which identifies incoherencies between policy expectations and outcomes (the so called 'policy gap' in migration studies). In part, this is probably because the policy does not manage to reach the appropriate profiles of people, and it may tend to assume the 'Moroccanness' premise, which could be less important in practice in the process of individual decisions, as our exploratory empirical findings indicate.

These two main arguments will be complemented by some additional arguments based on the empirical findings: that the Moroccan application of transnational policies through this engagement policy is probably too narrow and only focused on return (*return transnationalism*), but does not contemplate other possibilities to practice transnationalism. We will also conclude that much of the shortcomings of this engagement policy are probably related to the fact that the philosophy behind it is too economy-driven, without contemplating the potential role that MLAs could play in political reform and the democratisation of Morocco.

Contextualising the Moroccan case study within the migrant transnational entrepreneurs area of studies: shaping a framework for the analysis

The fact that OECD in 2016–17 released two reports on Moroccan public policies; development and skilled migrants, is an indicator of the international interest in this policy paradigm change. These diaspora policies consist of an array of measures, including ministerial and consular reforms, and investment policies to manage a specific profile of MLAs: skilled nationals. In fact we can identify diaspora policies as a specific transnational pro-active policy developed by home countries, including economical, political (e.g. dual citizenship and the right to vote abroad, which still encounters some resistance from authorities) and even symbolic, culture-related national actions. This case study illustrates the difficulties in consolidating a policy paradigm change that has been progressively implemented since the 1990s, and that now seems to have the shape of a 'governance of a structure of opportunities', engaging Moroccan authorities, but also private and public partnerships, programmes, institutions and government departments.

Taking recent theories of policy paradigm change (Hogan and Howlett 2015) it becomes clear that when emerging policies are contradicted by evidence or are shown to not meet their initial expectations, there are probably less chances that this new paradigm will be consolidated over time, and can only survive if some changes of the initial orientation are produced. The first literature examining the policy paradigm change from a remittances-based approach to a skills-mobilisation-based approach shares the diagnosis that after some decades of implementation, it is much more of a policy rhetoric than an efficient policy (Boukharouaa 2014). This article will not only confirm this conclusion, but it will also propose additional arguments that seem meaningful to explain this policy gap.

Diaspora policy paradigm change in Morocco: main philosophy

The Moroccan Diaspora engagement policies suppose the advancement of capacity building policies aimed at developing a set of state institutions to govern the diaspora, and probably belong to the most extended dimension of engagement diaspora policies. The other two contemplated by Gamlen (2006), namely extending rights to the diaspora and extracting obligations, are probably the least developed. This particular focus is situated in the broad process of change already described by Haas (2007), which explored the shift from controlling the diaspora to including it. This shift occurred due to the high contributions of their remittances, and after recognising that Moroccan authorities were working with a false premise in assuming that integration of their nationals in the host country would reduce national engagement and remittances. In this framework, this article seeks to enter into this second phase, centred on the mobilisation of skilled MLAs in general. We seek to question the Moroccan philosophy, which assumes that the only way for young generations to keep their ties with Morocco and be engaged in productive investments, is by promoting national identity. Within transnational studies, this policy has some interest because it adds to the migration literature the value of considering transnationalism as something that does not necessarily exist naturally, but can be constructed politically from the country of origin. That is, the same transnational policy that was practiced earlier by Morocco with the purpose to prevent their nationals from integrating in the country of residence, now intends to mobilise one important population sector of their diaspora, the best educated and skilled, so that they may contribute to the development of Morocco. These transnational politics appear to be considered a pull factor. The problem, as we will see later through interview analysis, is that the Moroccan government has a very narrow view of transnationalism (only focused upon return).

This policy shift from a guest-workers narrative (remittances-based approach) to a transnational policy narrative (skills-mobilisation-based approach) must be understood as the broad mainstream focus of Moroccan diaspora governance today. This new policy dynamics certainly needs to be placed in a context where Morocco is itself changing from being considered an emigration to an immigration country. Morocco got its first immigration law in 2013 (see first report 2013–2016; Royaume du Maroc 2016a), basically changing its social landscape with black Africans who stayed in the country instead of trying to cross the Mediterranean. These African migrants were controlled as part of

Morocco's commitments with the European (and Spanish) externalisation of their policies. Numerous researches stress that this shift can also be interpreted as an indicator of the political and economic reforms made these last decades, willing to become a much more attractive country to live and invest in. The constitutional reform of 2011, among others, cemented the role of the government on migration issues. It first made the protection of MLAs a priority, before granting them the right to participate in Moroccan political life (OECD 2017, 52–54). Without this general process of change, the diaspora engagement policy would not gain legitimacy in placing economic development as one of its basic strategies for the coming years (OECD 2017) and its efforts to have a place in the global market and the African political landscape. The complex relation to Europe, and having taken the lead of the 'African migration dossier' during its recent incorporation in the African Union are certainly additional factors shaping this context, and making Morocco an interesting dynamic model to analyze within the TME debate.

Three basic pillars sustain the Moroccan diaspora engagement policy philosophy (RdM 2016b): (a) Preservation of the identity of the Moroccans of the World; (b) Protection of rights and interests of MLAs; and (c) Contribution of MLAs to the development of the country.

This diaspora policy focus seeks to profit from the know-how accumulated by MLAs for the benefits of Morocco. It is defined by one of the leading institutions, the CCME (*Conseil de la Communauté Marocaine à lEtranger*), as targeting to manage nationals living abroad with professional, scientific, technical, artistic, cultural or associative expertise who could satisfy a well-identified need of the public or private sector; or meet the human resource needs of sectoral development plans and programmes; or participate in any project at the territorial or national level in need of a strengthening of human resources in Morocco (El Asri 2012). It is within this broad policy scope that the promotion of Moroccan entrepreneurs living abroad is focused. This policy is directly linked to the economic strategy to develop Morocco (OECD 2017) and belongs to its most important strategy regarding their diaspora in Horizon 2025 (Belguendouz 2010, 29). In fact this policy seeking to mobilise MLAs is not new. It allows the home country to capitalise on pre-existing resources, without the need for significant infrastructure investment (Charef 2008). This policy can be interpreted as a Moroccan transnational field of action that seeks to foster a sense of belonging among those living abroad. Transnational spaces have been developed not only where migration flows, entries and exits are managed, but also where the identities, sense of belonging and unique forms of citizen development that are part of more intricate international relations are negotiated (Planet Contreras and Hernando de Larramendi Martinez 2015). It also already existed as a strategy to involve Moroccan associations in the development of Morocco (Østergaard-Nielsen 2009). What is probably new is the institutional attention towards Moroccan individuals living abroad through a series of policy structures and programmes, and within the general scheme of attracting the 'best' nationals.

This mobilisation strategy is explicitly a politics of attraction (*Marhaba*) of high-skilled Moroccan migrants that have acquired a social and cultural capital abroad, and that now are 'seduced' to contribute to the national economical development.[2] The narrative policy logic behind this can be roughly defined as giving rights, services and facilities in order to consolidate duties towards Morocco, expressed through investments and creating jobs through entrepreneurship projects. This policy is mainly focused towards the productive economy rather than the in-productive one, which was one of the main destinations of the old remittances promotion policy model. As the majority of policy officers we interviewed recognised, they have difficulties reaching entrepreneurs living abroad. This approach to economic development is basically driven by traditional state instruments of promoting belonging and a sense of Moroccan identity (national and/or religious based). But as our exploratory empirical analysis reflects, most of the entrepreneurs who seek to develop their business projects in their country of origin are guided by pragmatic reasons rather than by strong feelings of national identity, contrary to the general mainstream narrative of Moroccan diaspora engagement policies. This constitutes one of our main findings, together with some other arguments strengthening what is already a general diagnosis shared by the literature: that Moroccan policy initiatives set out to attract their skilled nationals reflect a gap between expectations and outcomes. Most authors point out that the lack of an integrative view of the different policy initiatives, and the incoherence between different departments, institutions and programmes seeking to create a structure of opportunities for their nationals living abroad, may be some of the main causes (Boukharouaa 2014; OECD 2017, 55).

Distinctive features (and weaknesses) of the diaspora policy paradigm: setting up the governance of transnational Moroccan entrepreneurs

Viewed from comparative migration studies, Morocco is doing the same as most European (such as Germany) and other Western countries (such as Canada): linking migration policies and development. But there are probably few that apply this policy focus to their own national population living abroad. This can certainly be interpreted as a change of policy paradigm from 'brain drain' to 'brain gain': from seeing emigration as a national loss preventing Morocco from developing, to a resource if there is a possibility to politically revert the direction of their own national flows, and make their own nationals living abroad active agents of Moroccan development. Instead of seeking primarily to reduce the brain drain, the focus is on finding the benefits of this 'bleeding'. By inverting the question, it is considered that the rich and diversified expertise accumulated by Moroccans residing abroad can advantageously be involved in the national development process (Belguendouz 2010).

Viewed as a policy dynamics and in broad historical terms, it is some sort of 'boomerang policy'. Morocco is apparently a great case study to know how origin countries take a pro-active attitude towards their own nationals and try to have an impact in their attitudes, behaviours and life expectations (Weimar, Unterreiner, and Fargues 2017), and consider their own diaspora as an opportunity, a resource and an asset. Migrants' relationship with their home countries becomes central when they are expected to develop transnational businesses; these countries gain a new interest in attracting investments from those who formerly emigrated and who may have mixed feelings about the country they once left (Zapata-Barrero and Rezaei 2020). Through a series of programmes and policies, Morocco has been fighting during the last decades to change the view of their own national citizens living abroad who have been forced to leave their country, and who probably have some emotional resentment towards the country, to change their mind and see their own country as a land of opportunities. This is certainly directly related to the historical period of migration dynamics that allowed the linkage between this emerging transnational-based narrative policy to an inter-generational-based narrative. The Moroccan diaspora in Europe is entering the second and third generations, and most young Moroccans have limited knowledge of their origin, mainly filtered by their parents and in holiday periods. In spite of having very few demographic data, the majority of studies exploring the profile of these skilled nationals finds that they are young, well-educated and in European universities, male, and they have kept a link to Morocco through family ties, holidays, etc., and have been in the country of residence for a long time (Gubert and Nordman 2011; Hamdouch and Wahba 2015). Some add that most were engaged in social activities and participated in various organisations in their countries of residence (Hamdouch and Wahba 2015), and have the ambition to contribute through their acquired social and cultural capital (skills and expertise) to the development of their country of origin. Through this pro-active diaspora policy it is evident that Morocco wants to strengthen the ties with young people in its diaspora.

The distinctive features of this diaspora engagement policy have four main pillars, which may actually be its weakness according to our findings:

(a) It is economics-based, framed within the development strategy of the government, with the danger of neglecting political rights distribution and the MLAs as political actors. In some sense this policy paradigm change still does not present a change in terms of the view of MLAs as primarily economic actors.

(b) Following (a) it belongs to a broad strategy of attracting the best and highest skilled migrants abroad (including entrepreneurs and investors of the productive economy), leaving aside those who are still worse off, who may suffer a double exclusion (from the country of origin and the host country). The MLAs who are not qualified still suffer discrimination and exclusion and seems now to be the forgotten population of its own government of origin. This is what has been recently claimed by several reports (FEF 2015; OECD 2017, 52). Moreover, the diaspora policy does not foster entrepreneurship abroad; it has no pro-active approach seeking to influence MLAs and motivate them to take this new vital path. Its focus is rather on care and welfare (legal, information, economical and administrative dimensions) but without a campaign abroad motivating workers not to send their remittances, as the previous policy paradigm, but to engage in entrepreneurial activities with their country of origin.

(c) The transnational dimension of the diaspora policy is basically concentrated on return, assuming that Morocco sees the results of the transnational policy they have promoted for years, now basically affecting new generations supposedly committed to Moroccan identity (*return transnationalism*). The Moroccan diaspora policy ignores other transnational strands indicated by the TDE literature, namely what we will call *circular transnationalism* and *residence transnationalism*.

(d) Finally, in the same vein as Haas (2007), who argued that the remittances-approach policy paradigm was constructed under a false premise in assuming that integration in the host country would reduce national engagement and remittances, there is still a new identity-based assumption in this new policy approach: that most of the politics of attraction (*Marhaba*) are possible if they are politically driven by fostering a sense of Moroccanness (which may include national identity, language and/or religion).[3]

Our findings show that the motivations of Moroccan entrepreneurs living abroad are much more pragmatism-driven than identity-driven.

These four features, but also shortcomings, may help us understand why these policies, in spite of being implemented through different stages since the 1990s, still have difficulties being successful, as some reports show us, including the last OECD reports (2016, 2017).

Mapping the institutional diaspora governance: building a new structure of opportunities to promote a new profile of Moroccans living abroad (Moroccan transnational entrepreneur)

The structure of the Moroccan diaspora governance has three basic institutions. In 2007, the Ministry of Moroccans Residing Abroad (*Ministère des Marocains Résidant à l'Etranger, MMRE*) was (re)-founded to follow up on this engagement strategy towards MLAs giving administrative and legal support; the Council of the Moroccan Community Abroad (*Le C. de la Communauté Marocaine à lEtranger, CCME*), a national consultative and prospective institution placed with King Mohammed VI, and constitutionalised on the occasion of the reform approved by the referendum of 1st July 2011. The CCME mainly assesses public policies towards MLAs, gives advice and develops studies, but also has the aim to become a 'network of networks', as its president Driss El Yazami declared in 2009 (interview in *Les Echos Quotidiens*, Casablanca, 1/12/2009). Finally, there is the *Hassan II Foundation*, founded in 1990 with the purpose of ensuring that MLAs maintain ties with their country of origin through religion, education, cultural and linguistic devices. There are also several departments seeking to provide juridical and administrative support such as the Directorate of Consular and Social Affairs of the Ministry of Foreign Affairs and Cooperation, the Ministry of Labour and Professional Education, the Regional Centre for Investment (Ministry of Interior), the Moroccan Council of Ulemas for Europe and the Mohammed V Foundation for Solidarity.

As the Moroccan government wants to direct transfers to productive investments, it has set up, starting in 2002, regional investment centres that provide assistance for investment and business creation. In order to stimulate investment, Morocco set up several programmes under the already existing *MDM Invest* since 1949 to jointly finance, alongside banks, the creation or development of companies promoted by Moroccans living abroad. For instance in 2009–2012 a strategic national plan providing services to small and medium enterprises, and in 2013–2016 a new strategic development plan focused on reinforcing guarantee and co-financing services with regional development. There are also some private firms such as *Bank Al Amal*, which was created in 1989 with the objective of financially contributing to projects of creation or development of companies in general, and now specifically addresses enterprises launched by MLAs. Another institution that plays a role in shaping this structure of opportunities is the Advisory Council on Human Rights. The Global Innovation Index, Boukharouaa's chapter (coord. 2014) shows us the variety of programmes targeting skilled MLAs. There are several public-private partnerships such as, for instance, the Fincome (*Moroccan Forum of International Competences Abroad*) aiming to involve Moroccan professionals residing abroad in supporting the economic, social, and cultural development of Morocco in terms of training, research, expertise, consultancy, or investment initiatives of their own. Recently there is also the so called *Marhaba Operation* ('Marhaba' means 'attraction'), focused on attracting nationals to contribute to Morocco's development offering services, information, assistance, and learning procedures. New bilateral and multilateral non-governmental networks, such as the *German-Moroccan Skills Network* or the *Moroccan Association of Grandes Ecoles*, are the privileged interlocutors in the context of skills transfer.

Some strategic partnerships with incubators play a role in channelling people and bridging Morocco with its diaspora, such as *Maroc Entrepreneurs*, a non-profit organisation created in 1999 to promote economic development through three main levers: to encourage MLAs to start their own business in Morocco; to discover the universe of the creation of companies and the socio-economic news; and to establish a synergy between companies based in Morocco and Moroccan skills abroad. We can also mention the *Maghribcom platform* created in January 2013, providing a place for MLAs to learn about the initiatives and policies of the Ministry in Charge of MLAs. Both provide Moroccan professionals information regarding business opportunities, ad hoc collaboration, investment, and employment. There are also other examples of programmes, such as 'Mobilization Program Skills', which encourage investors in Moroccan enterprises.

As we can see, there is a large array of government departments engaged in the multifaceted implementation of this skills-mobilisation-based policy approach. Precisely one mainstream criticism by experts, which is recognised by members of the main institutions interviewed, is that there is a need for an integral and comprehensive approach that can interconnect all institutions. At present, the repetition of services provided, the lack of coordination between institutions dependent on the government and others linked directly to the Kingdom (such as CCME), and overlapping policies, create unnecessary internal competition between them affecting the outcomes. In 2012, a major study on the 25 years of Morocco's mobilisation policy (El Asri 2012) highlighted the lack of a coherent policy in this area. The first review of this structure of governance is that the way it is implemented affects the relation between Morocco and MLAs (Belguendouz 2006). The policies carried out and the political tools put in place so far are failing because they lack efficiency. It is clear that, apart from the direct action of the Fincome programme, the different programmes noted above were not much more than announcements (Boukharouaa 2014, 130). But we are not directly interested in assessing how this policy paradigm is implemented but rather to infer what mainstream narrative philosophy exists within this structure of governance.

Regarding policy narratives, there is first some ambivalence in how to understand transnationalism as an asset: either promoting return or to promote that MLAs stay in their residence abroad. This became clear when Abdallatif Maâzouz, Minister of Foreign Trade, in the first meeting called *Autumn University* (20-21 November 2009 in Fès) invited MLAs abroad: 'Stay in Germany, dear emigrants, to play a big role in the marketing of Moroccan products in Germany!' In the same meeting, however, the Minister of Industry and Trade, Ahmed Réda Chami, claimed 'Do not stay on horseback in both countries. Come thus to Morocco to work full-time!' (Belguendouz 2010, 19). There is no mention of the potential circularity of MLAs, having their home in both countries. But what is most important for us is that the only focus that seems to be contemplated in analyzing the structure of governance and the main missions of key-institutions is *return promotion* through a *Marhaba philosophy*. This return-based approach is *monodimensional*, seeing the transnational dimension of MLAs as a resource that can only be enjoyed upon return (*return transnationalism*), without incorporating mobility in the same policy agenda. These policy limitations could also be a factor of failure. A mobility programme could certainly contemplate other potential profiles ignored by this diaspora policy, potentially also contributing to development: *circular transnationalism* or *residencial transnationalism*. One of the first to explicitly highlight this mobility framework in MTE studies is Saxenian's work (1999). The frequency of travels from home to residence countries makes some MTEs become an example of a new migratory pattern, which she calls 'brain circulation' as opposed to 'brain drain' (Saxenian 2006). This brain circulation has been the specific focus of a special issue coordinated by Rezaei, Light, and Telles (2016). The circularity of entrepreneurs who may work and reside in both origin and host countries (*circular transnationalism*) is only one typology of transnational entrepreneurs, which has to be analytically distinguished from those who remain in residence countries and may contribute to the Moroccan economy from abroad (*residence transnationalism*), and those who decide to return (*return transnationalism*). Most of the studies are precisely focused on the strong correlation between return intentions, and planned and executed investment in the country of origin (in general see McCormick and Wahba 2001; Gubert and Nordman 2011, and more recently for Morocco, see Hamdouch, and Wahba 2015). On the other hand, the training of the vast majority of unskilled Moroccan migrants before, during or after migration has not received the same attention to date.

We may conclude that entrepreneurial activity amongst returnees has emerged as a desired profession for authorities, as the last OECD reports show us (OECD 2016, 2017) and the few surveys done on MLA entrepreneurs (Bensouda et al. 2006). These studies also share the concern that although returnees show a high ability to create small or medium businesses and to generate jobs, there are still many hurdles that return migrants face when setting up their businesses. This will also be confirmed in our interview findings. We can infer from the policy narrative that there are two specific main priorities. First, the diaspora's loyalty to the country is aimed to be preserved by the formation of a strong national identity, where especially the second and third generations of Moroccan migrants play an important role. Transnational policy is directly viewed as inter-generational. The Moroccan diaspora policy gradually became aware that it is no longer so much the emigrant workers but their children and grandchildren who determine the current national issues. A policy of the '2.0' diaspora, openly directed towards the new generations is therefore essential. Current policies focus on preserving a Moroccan identity through linguistic, religious and cultural dimensions. Second, Morocco has the objective of restoring the trust of Moroccans residing abroad towards the Moroccan government, and defending their interests by promoting their legal, social and humanitarian situation in the countries of residence. It then follows, from a political science point of view, the traditional rights/duties logic: 'I give you rights and you give me duties'. But this also seems to fail, especially concerning political rights.

Despite that there has been a diversification of economic activities, relatively few migrants seem inclined to have the financial capacity to start large-scale enterprises in Morocco (Haas 2007). Policies that try to enhance the development impacts of migration by specifically targeting migrants seem to have limited effects as long as they do not alter the general social, economic and political environment. Recent reforms have been primarily symbolical and, although they resulted in a better treatment of migrants-on-holiday and contributed to surging remittances, they still conceal a lack of structural change.

Symbolic politics, as it has been labelled by De Haas, will not convince migrants to invest as long as the general investment climate in Morocco continues to be unattractive due to failing legal systems, deficient credit markets, legal insecurity, corruption and excessive bureaucracy. This is exemplified by low levels of Foreign Direct Investment, sluggish and erratic economic growth and a deficient education system. These structural problems are unlikely to be solved by specific policies targeting skilled MLAs (Haas 2007). Our interviews also confirm the findings of one of the few surveys on Moroccan entrepreneurs (Bensouda et al. 2006). When reading the testimonies, the factors that block the return to Morocco of the skills installed abroad seem to be articulated around three points: the lack of information about job opportunities and the economic environment, the lack of transparency and seriousness in the workplace, and finally social problems. These last questions are of substantial importance since if we take the recent theories of policy paradigm change, if the new emerging policies are contradicted by evidence (this will be the role of interviews in this article), it is probably less likely that this new paradigm becomes consolidated through time, and can only survive if some changes are produced. This will be the underlying focus during the remaining part of the article.

Methodology and sources

In order to explore the relationship between policies and evidence by contrasting the Moroccan diaspora policy focus with actual practices, we performed a case study in Spain and Morocco. We conducted 31 interviews: 10 entrepreneurs, 4 Morocco experts, 4 policy-makers and 13 other stakeholders such as investment agencies, immigration officials, banks, chamber of commerce, entrepreneur associations, and business incubator directors. We visited businesses founded by Moroccan entrepreneurs in Spain and Morocco and participated in meetings with Moroccan politicians and policy-makers. Moreover we organized a roundtable inviting Moroccan actors (the Moroccan Ministry and Moroccan entrepreneurs, among others) in March 2017, titled *Moroccan Transnational Entrepreneurs: new social patterns, new narrative policies*. The interviewed Moroccan entrepreneurs were selected based on the criteria that they previously had migrated to Spain and either returned to Morocco to start a business, or chosen to develop their business project in the host country. They are all male (our repeated efforts to find female entrepreneurs matching our criteria failed, which may indicate that to the extent these exist, they are few in numbers, but also a certain inevitable selection bias as we depended on our contacts and no general information of our target group existed), and aged between 31-49.

Our stakeholder interviews confirmed that the entrepreneurs we interviewed appear representative for two main types of Moroccan migrant entrepreneurs, which we will describe in the following section. Nevertheless, it ought to be stated that the sampling was clearly the most challenging part of our empirical work. As we initiated our study we soon discovered that there were significant difficulties involved in finding any registers of entrepreneurs who matched this profile, as no such official records are kept, not even by Moroccan authorities. Despite the political interest in promoting business activities of Moroccan migrants, there are no existing data on the transnational economic activities of Moroccans abroad or the economic activities that returning Moroccans engage in (Aziz 2016; Mahdi 2016; Mesbah 2016; Mesbahi interviews 2016; Gabrielli and Franco-

Guillén 2018). It is therefore virtually impossible to estimate the frequency or character of these kinds of activities.

The municipal immigration department in Tangiers stated that they expect intensified return movements of Moroccans abroad due to the rapid economic growth that the region is undergoing, though the tendency is rather that many Spanish entrepreneurs invest in Morocco (Aziz, interview 2016). The large Catalan bank *La Caixa* has a department in Tangiers that offers assistance to Spanish companies who wish to establish themselves in Morocco; until October 2016 this had been the case of 850 companies. At *La Caixa* they find that many of these companies need to work with local Moroccans who have Spanish skills, which makes high skilled returning Moroccans ideal as consultants or employees, and consider this profile of return migrant more typical than that of the Moroccan entrepreneur (Mesbah, interview 2016).

Some Moroccan banks did have registers of entrepreneurs who are granted loans where the nationality of these entrepreneurs is stated, but would not share these with us due to their integrity policies. Instead, we had to rely on snowball sampling, limiting the recruitment of respondents to one person per initial contact in order to diversify the sample as much as possible. Some of our respondents were recruited through our contacts with Moroccan organisations and networks in Barcelona, some through the stakeholders we interviewed and some while visiting businesses and establishing contacts on the ground during the field work in Morocco. Needless to say we are unable to draw any general conclusions based on our limited sample; however it provides us with valuable information about the policies and the entrepreneurs' profiles, motivations and relationship both with the host country and the country of origin, as well as insights into some of the specific challenges that transnational migrant entrepreneurs face.

Case study of transnational migrant entrepreneurship in Spain and Morocco: identifying favourable factors and restrictions

In assessing whether Moroccan diaspora policies appear to succeed with their aim to attract Moroccans living abroad to develop their business projects in Morocco, we were mainly interested in the following questions: Who are these migrant entrepreneurs and what drives them? Does a sense of 'Moroccanness', identification with and loyalty towards the home country matter or are business choices made on merely rational-economic grounds? And, what obstacles or opportunities do these entrepreneurs encounter?

Transnational migrant entrepreneur profiles in the Spanish-Moroccan migration corridor

Moroccan migration to Spain is slightly different from that to other receiving countries as France or Belgium. It has been strongly dominated by the profile of a low-skilled male worker, who migrated for economic reasons and found work in sectors such as agriculture and construction during the years of economic growth, and then often lost his employment as a result of the financial crisis. Moroccans are the second largest immigrant nationality in Spain just marginally after the Romanians (15.4% and 15.7%, respectively) (ine.es 2018). Among our respondents, three of ten may be defined as belonging to this group, who migrated out of necessity and also returned and became entrepreneurs basically as a means to survive. The majority however, seven out of ten, has a different sociological profile: highly skilled and educated, with economic resources and a background from the higher social strata in Morocco. This profile would not be a typical Moroccan immigrant in Spain, but rather someone who may choose Spain just as he/she could choose France, Belgium or the US to study abroad or fulfil a professional project. This latter category of Moroccan residing abroad is probably the profile that Moroccan diaspora policies mainly aim to attract, though it is unclear whether they succeed in doing so, as most of the policy officers expressed.

In our analysis we draw on the well-known concepts of need-based vs. opportunity-based entrepreneurs (Newland and Tanaka 2010). Our initial fieldwork led us to partly question the usefulness of a clear-cut theoretical distinction between these categories. Applying these concepts, we would categorise four of the Moroccan entrepreneurs in our sample as driven by necessity, and six as mainly opportunity-driven entrepreneurs. The necessity entrepreneurs are defined as such because their need to have a basic income for subsistence drove them to become entrepreneurs, lacking other more attractive alternatives. All four had previously migrated to Spain, and returned to Morocco because they suffered from the effects of the financial crisis and could no longer find employment. Three of them have a basic educational level (primary school), while one is highly educated (Master degree from Spain); this entrepreneur aspires at returning to Spain once he has saved enough money to restart his life there, in his words out of both personal ('life quality is higher in Spain') and political reasons ('there is no democracy in Morocco'). What the six opportunity entrepreneurs have in common is that they are overall highly educated (five out of six have postgraduate university degrees) and comparably resourceful in terms of economic assets and useful social networks. Five of six acquired their education in Spain, and only one in Morocco. Studying a Master's degree (principally in law or business) was a central reason behind the decision to migrate for most of them. However in practice the categories of necessity or opportunity entrepreneur may intersect. For instance necessity entrepreneurship may indeed reflect more or less desperate life situations, but necessity could also drive the entrepreneur to focus on economic sustainability and identify opportunities to develop more pragmatic and realistic business projects:

> As I returned from Europe I looked for a job but there were none, and I had to make a living somehow. There [in Europe] I was able to save a little money, enough to pay the rent for the stand at the market place, buy some goods as fruit, vegetables, rice and couscous and get started. *Moroccan business owner, Ifrane (Fez region)*

We find no indications that opportunity entrepreneurship is inclined to be more successful than necessity driven initiatives, though the more precarious position among necessity entrepreneurs who lack economic resources or constructive social networks make them more vulnerable to failure. Moreover, all our respondents for whom the definition of opportunities is more central than plain necessity are also in need of their income from the business activities to make a living, to some degree making them necessity entrepreneurs as well. The distinction is thus not clear.

Beyond looking at the migrant entrepreneur profiles, we were interested in what motivated the choice of returning or not to Morocco, and to what degree the activities developed were really transnational.

Moroccan identity or pragmatism? The choice of where to develop TE projects

When enquiring into the potential that migrant TEs have for growth and development in both sending and receiving countries, the question of where the entrepreneur chooses to be based and whether the business activities actually involve transnational links between the countries becomes central. The Moroccan *Marhaba* policies assume that Moroccans abroad will be attracted by sentiments of belonging and solidarity with their country of origin as drivers behind entrepreneurship. However most of the respondents did not mention such sentiments as relevant for their business and migration decisions. Two of the respondents (both defined as opportunity-driven) claimed to feel strongly for Morocco and wanted to contribute to its development. The other opportunity entrepreneurs in our sample had instead chosen to be based in Spain. When asked why, personal preferences and motives (as having a Spanish spouse) dominate for three of them, while the fourth respondent had political motives and partly left Morocco for opposing the regime.

In looking at how the entrepreneurs made the choice of where to be based, we thus found variation, but motives were overall largely personal (family ties and lifestyle preferences dominate among the more resourceful respondents, while legal obstacles and unemployment are decisive for those in more precarious situations) and rational/pragmatic (one establishes a business where this is most economically favourable). Interesting is that the vast majority (eight out of ten) stated that they prefer to live in Spain (as *resident transnationals*), though four of them were unable to at present. Actually, the *possibility to choose* where to be based in itself appears to draw a dividing-line between different categories of TMEs. Three of the four necessity entrepreneurs in our sample had all returned from Spain against their personal desire, as remaining there was economically unsustainable. They were also entrepreneurs out of lack of other viable alternatives.

Looking closer at the level of transnationalism involved in the respondents' entrepreneurship initiatives, we see that just as the choice of where to be based, whether our respondents develop or not transnational businesses appears based on both personal motives and the identification of potential, as a respondent offering legal services to Spanish companies on the Moroccan market. Here, there is indeed a difference between the respondents we described as necessity entrepreneurs compared with those defined as opportunity entrepreneurs. None of the necessity entrepreneurs engage in transnational business activities; their small businesses are entirely focused on selling local products on the local market. Among the opportunity entrepreneurs instead, all six perform transnational business activities and maintain close links between Spain and Morocco. Reconnecting with Newland and Tanaka (2010), our findings appear consistent with their account that opportunity entrepreneurs more often have access to transnational networks and financial resources that facilitate their entrepreneurship. However, Newland and Tanaka (ibid) also suggest that transnationalism makes these businesses more likely to succeed, but there is a lack of empirical evidence to prove that this is so, and the fact that necessity entrepreneurs' businesses tend to be small, often one-person companies that focus on local markets does not necessarily make them less successful or economically sustainable. There is no given causal relationship between transnationalism and success, and there is a need to further explore what migrant businesses tend to be most beneficial and sustainable both in terms of personal success and economic development. Moreover, beyond mere economic success of individual business projects there may also be a need to analyze the potential multiple effects of returning and circulating migrants' transnationalism for national cultural and political life, for instance.

Focusing again on the economic dimension of these entrepreneurship projects, all our respondents agree that there are serious obstacles to doing business in Morocco. For several of them this is part of why they have chosen to be based in Spain. Our interviewed stakeholders confirm that few returning Moroccans set up their own businesses. They claim that the main reason for this is the lack of financial support for new companies in Morocco, whose only option are regular bank loans, which are difficult to access and have high interest rates. Therefore it is generally necessary to have substantial private savings to invest (Aziz 2016; Boukaich interviews 2016; Mahdi 2016; Mesbah 2016; Mesbahi 2016; Gabrielli and Franco-Guillén 2018). The lack of funding opportunities for start-ups or other forms of institutional support is the most important obstacle for setting up a business in Morocco according to the interviewed Moroccan entrepreneurs. Several of them also claim that Moroccan bureaucracy is difficult to manage, and that the informality of society makes useful social networks indispensable.

> There are no credits here for start-ups or anything like that, you must have capital of your own to set up a business. There are lots of people with a high education and ideas but with no money to invest. *Moroccan transnational entrepreneur, Tangiers*

> The main obstacle is without any doubts the bureaucracy, and the legal insecurity. The administration here works in a way that ... if you don't know the law very well they will destroy you. And you need friends who can help. And capital to invest. In Spain there are pretty favorable credit systems for companies, but in Morocco there are only regular bank loans with high interests. *Moroccan transnational entrepreneur, currently Madrid-based and circulates between Madrid and Tangiers*

The question of why some MTEs engage in a relation with their home countries, while others prefer to follow an international entrepreneurship venture, still remains under-researched (Solano 2016). Also, it was relevant to enquire if MTEs were aware or not of being considered as 'agents of change' of their home countries. We find that those who enter in contact with home policies are more aware of their potential influence beyond their own individual business benefits, but there is still not a general pattern on how MTEs build their projects beyond the individual business scope and take into consideration home policies, seeking to attract them. We also found that the MTEs indeed had ties with their home countries (mainly through family and friends networks), but these ties could not necessarily be interpreted under the national-identity premises, as seems to be the policy assumption of the Moroccan government. Our interviews cannot confirm that a given 'Moroccanness' influences on business decisions or entrepreneurial projects. On the contrary, our interviews show that ties to origin countries can be maintained for more pragmatic reasons. For the young transnational entrepreneur it is easier to do business in a context that you know and can 'control', than with unknown countries. To conclude, what our migrant entrepreneur respondents have in common is that they are mainly driven by pragmatism in their entrepreneurship activities. Even the very decision to become an entrepreneur, rather than an employee, is mainly pragmatic for most of them.

Discussion: the Moroccan diaspora as a tool for national economic development: limitations and further research

Encouraging the return of Moroccan expatriate skills abroad has marked government action since the 1990s. Institutions have been created specifically for this purpose. Moroccans residing abroad remain Moroccans regardless of the number of other nationalities acquired. This dual legal affiliation has several advantages for themselves and for the country of origin (cultural openness, currency transfers, etc.), even if it sometimes poses a problem: multiple obligations towards both the country of origin and the country of residence, the problem of integration in host countries, etc. Today the focus seems to be not only transnationalism but trans-generationalism, since Morocco wants to strengthen ties with young people in its diaspora. With the economic and political transitions, the potential of skilled Moroccans residing abroad constitutes an important force for revitalising and deepening the reform process.

Creating a favourable environment for professionals who are now abroad to further the development of innovation has been successful in some ways, but more needs to be done to direct the innovative potential of its highly educated workers towards entrepreneurial projects, which are still very few within this broad Marhaba policy. As for other developing countries, ensuring that the home country becomes more attractive to these migrants is an important early step. But to do that, more and better data are needed. There is a great need for further research in this area.

Other questions may arise for the migrant as transnational actor. Can the entrepreneur be transnational without being a political actor? The fact that Moroccan diaspora engagement policy is only economically justified is probably a limit in the current migration dynamic. The need of political action parallel to the economical one is probably one of the main recommendations we can infer both from interviews, but also from some critical, but constructive voices. Belguendouz (2010, 29) insists, for instance, that the full involvement of MLAs in the process of internal democratisation in Morocco remains on the agenda and will not succeed unless it is also supported by the Moroccan government.

This diaspora policy engagement also has some false premises that we have tried to uncover contrasting governance narratives with Moroccan entrepreneurs' motivations. Its insistence on linking their promotion of transnationalism as a means to make Moroccans keep a foot in Morocco seems to be unquestioned, and it is probably, as we have shown contrasting narrative policy with TMEs' motivations, another factor that distorts the Moroccan diaspora philosophy.

There may be a need to revise diaspora policies based on ideals (as a strong national identity and sense of solidarity with the 'motherland', or an overstatement of the potential for development in merely economic terms that returning migrant entrepreneurs bring with them) if they are not matched by reality, and aim at formulating more concrete actions that facilitate transnational migrant entrepreneurship in practice, and also recognises its potential for social, cultural and political transformation.

Notes

1. This may involve national, cultural, linguistic and/or religious identity (Planet Contreras and Hernando de Larramendi Martinez 2015).

2. Operation Marhaba is under the effective presidency of HM King Mohammed VI, highlighting the logistical, human, material and technical resources mobilized, in particular by the Mohammed V Foundation for solidarity, in order to ensure the operation. http://www.ccme.org.ma/en/what-s-new/53253.
3. At this stage we cannot enter deeply into the 'national identity' question in Morocco, but several dimensions could be a matter of dispute. There are Amazigh (officially described as a minority population, yet they are the majority), and the Arab populace (who generally do not intermarry with the Amazigh). In terms of language, there are huge battles over French or Arabic, or more recently English, as languages for teaching, official TV news, and other formal channels of communication. Whether people grew up in the North (with higher concentration of French influence) or in the South (that was never occupied by the French) is another central issue when speaking of 'national identity'. As for religion, there are different versions of Islam (e.g. Salafi, Sufi and more conventional and moderate).

Disclosure statement

No potential conflict of interest was reported by the authors.

Funding

This work as supported by Research Executive Agency, Project Number 645471.

ORCID

R. Zapata-Barrero http://orcid.org/0000-0002-3478-1330
Z. Hellgren http://orcid.org/0000-0003-1557-3779

References

Belguendouz, A. 2006. Le traitement institutionnel de la relation entre les Marocains résidant à l'étranger et le Maroc. http://hdl.handle.net/1814/6265.
Belguendouz, A. 2010. Compétences marocaines expatriées: Quelles politiques de mobilisation suivies pour le développement du Maroc? Du Tokten au Fincome WP Carim.
Bensouda, L., M. Bouzoubaa, H. Kadiri, and A. Khalil, coords. 2006. *Grande Enquête Maroc Entrepreneurs sur le thème du« Retour au Maroc »* Décembre.
Boukharouaa, N. E., coord. 2014. "The Moroccan Diaspora and its Contribution to the Development of Innovation in Morocco." In *The Global Innovation Index 2014: The Human Factor in Innovation*, edited by S. Dutta, B. Lanvin, and S. Wunsch-Vincent. Fontainebleau, Ithaca, and Geneva: Cornell University and WIPO.
Charef, M. 2008. Les migrations qualifiantes au Maghreb: Fuite de compétence ou mobilité de compétence? Diaspora Engagement in Morocco Understanding the Implications of a Changing Perspective on Capacity and Practices Migration policy brief No. 10 Maastricht Graduate School of Governance 2012.
El Asri, F., dir. 2012. Les compétences marocaines de l'étranger: 25 ans de politiques de mobilisation CCME.
Fondation européenne pour la formation. 2015. "Mesures de soutien aux migrants en matières d'emploi et de compétences (MISMES): Maroc." Fondation européenne pour la formation (FEF), mai 2015, Turin.
Gabrielli, L., and N. Franco-Guillén. 2018. Transnational Diaspora Entrepreneurship: The Case of Moroccans in Catalonia. GRITIM-UPF Policy Series 7.
Gamlen, A. 2006. *Diaspora Engagement Policies: Who Are They and What Kinds of States Use Them?* Oxford: Centre on Migration, Policy and Society. COMPAS working papers, no. 32.

Gubert, F., and C. J. Nordman. 2011. "Return Migration and Small Enterprise Development in the Maghreb." In *Diaspora for Development in Africa*, edited by S. Plaza and D. Ratha, Chapter 3, 103–126. Washington, DC: The World Bank.

Haas, H. De. 2007. "Between Courting and Controlling: The Moroccan State and 'Its' Emigrants." Centre on Migration, Policy and Society Working Paper No. 54, University of Oxford, 2007 WP-07-54.

Hamdouch, B., and J. Wahba. 2015. "Return Migration and Entrepreneurship in Morocco." *Middle East Development Journal* 7 (2): 129–148.

Hogan, J., and M. Howlett, eds. 2015. *Policy Paradigms in Theory and Practice*. Basingstoke, UK: Palgrave Macmillan.

McCormick, B., and J. Wahba. 2001. "Overseas Work Experience, Savings and Entrepreneurship Amongst Return Migrants to LDCS." *Scottish Journal of Political Economy* 48 (2): 164–178.

Newland, K., and H. Tanaka. 2010. *Mobilizing Diaspora Entrepreneurship for Development*. Washington, DC: Migration Policy Institute report.

OECD. 2016. *Talents à l'étranger : Une revue des émigrés marocains, Éditions OCDE*. Paris. http://doi.org/10.1787/9789264264304-fr

OECD. 2017. *Interactions entre politiques publiques, migrations et développement au Maroc, Les voies de développement, Éditions OCDE*. Paris. doi:10.1787/9789264279193-fr.

Østergaard-Nielsen, E. 2009. "Mobilising the Moroccans: Policies and Perceptions of Transnational Co-Development Engagement Among Moroccan Migrants in Catalonia." *Journal of Ethnic and Migration Studies* 35 (10): 1623–1641.

Planet Contreras, A. I., and M. Hernando de Larramendi Martinez. 2015. "Religion and Migration in Morocco: Governability and Diaspora." *New Diversities* 17 (1): 111–127.

Rezaei, S., I. Light, and E. Telles, eds. 2016. *Brain Circulation and Transnational Entrepreneurship: Guest Editorial – Special Issue* (International Journal of Business and Globalisation (IJBG)). Inderscience Publishers. https://rucforsk.ruc.dk/ws/portalfiles/portal/57114037/f109251131217468.pdf.

Royaume du Maroc (RdM). 2016a. *Politique Nationale d'Immigration et d'Asile 2013-2016*. Rabat: Ministère Chargé des Marocains Résidant à l'Étranger et des Affaires de la Migme voyration.

Royaume du Maroc (RdM). 2016b. "Stratégie Nationale pour les Marocains Résidant à l'Étranger: Bilan 2013–2016." Royaume du Maroc, septembre.

Saxenian, A. L. 1999. *Silicon Valley's New Immigrant Entrepreneurs San Francisco*. San Francisco, CA: Public Policy Institute of California.

Saxenian, A. L. 2006. *The New Argonauts: Regional Advantage in a Global Economy*. Cambridge, MA: Harvard University Press.

Solano, G. 2016. "Multifocal Entrepreneurial Practices: The Case of Moroccan Import/Export Businesses in Milan." *International Journal of Entrepreneurship and Small Business* 29 (2): 176–198.

VV.AA. 2009. Étude sur la contribution des Marocains Résidant à l'Étranger au développement économique et social du Maroc (Juin) Ministère Chargé de la Communauté Marocaine Résidant à l'Etranger.

Weimar, A., A. Unterreiner, and P. Fargues, eds. 2017. *Migrant Integration between Homeland and Host Society Volume 1*. Cham, Switzerland: Springer International Publishing.

Zapata-Barrero, R., and S. Rezaei. 2020. "Diaspora Governance and Transnational Entrepreneurship: The Rise of an Emerging Social Global Pattern in Migration Studies." *Journal of Ethnic and Migration Studies* 46 (10): 1959–1973. doi: 10.1080/1369183X.2018.1559990.

Stakeholder interviews

Aziz, Samir, immigration officer, City Council of Tangiers, 5/10/2016.
Basrire, K. General Secretary of Moroccan Entrepreneurs, 30 March 2017, Barcelona.
Benallal, Ahmed, representative of the Moroccan-Catalan cooperation association La Llum del Nord, 14/9/2016.
Boukaich, Khalid, professor of labor law, University of Tangiers, 3/10/2016.
Chaib, Mohammed, President of the Moroccan Ibn Battuta Foundation, 28/9/2016.
Claramunt, Maura, representative of international trade agreements at Acció (GenCat), 5/5/2016.
Khachani, Mohamed, Professor at l'Université Mohammed V-Agdal Rabat Coordinateur du Groupe de Recherches et d'Etudes sur les Migrations (GREM) Secrétaire Général de l'Association Marocaine d'Etudes et de Recherches sur les Migrations (AMERM), Rabat, 12/1/2017.
Lahlou, Mehdi, Professor of economy at the National Statistics and Applied Economics institutes (INSEA), Rabat. 9/1/2017.
Latifa, representative of the Catalan-Moroccan organization Nous Catalans, 5/10/2016.
Mahdi, Mohammed Bachir, president of the Chamber of commerce and industry in Tangiers, 4/10/2016.
Martin, I. European University Institute, working on a program cooperation with the EU Delegation in Rabat. 26/3/2016.
Mesbahi, Jamal, manager at the Regional investment center in Tangiers, 4/10/2016.
Mesbah, Mohammed, manager at La Caixa Tangiers, responsible for investment counseling targeting Spanish companies, 7/10/2016.
Rendón, G., SAIER, responsible for the Spanish government's voluntary return program in Barcelona, 26/2/2016.
Saliba, Ghassan, immigration responsible at Comisiones Obreras (Spanish trade union) in Barcelona, 8/2/2016.
Tem Samani, Youssef, representative of the Moroccan bank Banque Chaabi, Barcelona, 21/9/2016.

Policy Officers

Abdellah, B. General Secretary CCME (Conseil Communaute Marrocaine a l'Etranger) 24/3/2016, Rabat.
El Hasnaoui, A. Directeur Pôle Promotion Economique, Fondation Hassan II. 19/1/2017, Rabat.
Fonseca, A. Chef Mission, International Migration Organization, 7/3/2018, Rabat.
Ghislaine El Abid (Charge de Mission pour investisseurs Marrocains Resident à l'Etranger), CCME (Conseil Communaute Marrocaine a l'Etranger) 13/1/2017, Rabat.
Rami, A. policy officer (chargée de mission) CCME (Conseil Communaute Marrocaine a l'Etranger) 24/1/2017, Rabat.
Tigratine, F. Head of MRE Investor Support, Department Communication and Skills Mobilization, Ministry of Moroccans living abroad and migration affairs, 31/3/2017, Barcelona.

Prometheus, the double-troubled – migrant transnational entrepreneurs and the loyalty trap

Shahamak Rezaei and Marco Goli

ABSTRACT
Departing from the concept of Diaspora and practices of Ethnic Entrepreneurship (EE), much theoretical and empirical research on third-country Migrants' Transnational Entrepreneurship (MTE) emphasises, on a microlevel, the importance of individuals' social capital, dual habitus, ethno-cultural motivation, constrained self-efficacy and opportunity alertness. On a mesolevel much of the literature points out that both ethnic community (size and intensity) and group characteristics (survival strategies, networks, and social capital) are pivotal factors of the business development by third-country migrants in Europe. Circumstances around migrants' dual loyalty seem to overrule diasporic altruism and benefits of dual habitus. Above all, our empirical data show that the intersection between EE, MTE and integration policies are experienced by actors as interdependent fields of discursive practices, creating a fourth field of practice that is characterised by its own dynamic and opportunity structure. Attempting to understand the discourses dominating this fourth field of social practice we include other theories beyond those traditionally applied when studying migrants' transnational entreprenourship.

… TNE (Transnational Entrepreneurship) is not just a business. It is a lifestyle. As a business, TNE is an economic pursuit. As a lifestyle, it involves the whole person in drastic changes in the normal and preferred order of life … . (Light 2016)

Introduction

If globalisation was a tree, the international migration would be one of the oldest and largest branches on which integration of third-country migrants, Ethnic Entrepreneurship (EE) and Migrants' Transnational Entrepreneurship (MTE) would be younger and smaller branches. These fields of research have surprisingly and most typically been studied and addressed as separate fields and only occasionally as interdependent. One of the important causes of this conceptual disintegration and lack of focus on the interdependent nature of third-country MTE, international migration and integration policies is (Goli and Greve 2017), we believe, that Diaspora (Banton 1994; Brubaker

2005) most often, explicitly or implicitly, is considered the right premise and the point of departure (Ardichvili, Cardozo, and Ray 2003; Baron 2006; Bird and Jelinek 1988; Block, Thurik, and Zhou 2012; Bosma 2013; Drori, Honig, and Wright 2009; Rezaei and Goli 2009). Our results and analyses presented and discussed in the following will challenge these premises by focusing on the intersection of the three fields.

Most studies in social science have covered the intersections between migration and transnational entrepreneurship, between EE and transnational entrepreneurship, between international entrepreneurship and transnational entrepreneurship, etc. (see Zapata-Barrero and Rezaei 2020) Although the three fields as products of the root concept of globalisation and migration are related, they are not the same in character or dynamics. Studying the intersection between them therefore does not, and should not, only address the conceptual relationship. More importantly, it should include discursive (macrolevel), institutional (mesolevel), and practical/individual (microlevel) implications. The core aim here is the conceptual elaboration of each of the three fields' basic features, followed by elaboration on the intersection field and the consequences for MTE's practice. The primary data of our study is the analyses of DiasporaLink data (collected, coded, thematised and categorised) during 2016–2018, along with secondary data as background, including GEM (Global Entrepreneurship Monitor), Mipex (Migrant Integration Policy Index) and OECD.

The concept of brain gain and the new Argonauts that replaced the old and negative idea of brain drain (Saxenian 2005), brought the positive-sum game to the forefront and pushed back the idea of zero-sum game with regard to consequences of human mobility. It has, however, not been, we believe, a contribution to conceptualising the intersection fields at hand. It is acknowledged that the concept of brain gain has contributed to a recognition of MTE in both China and India, but a crucial question on why the phenomenon of brain circulation/gain does not occur in other countries in any scale close to the scale experienced in China and India remains unanswered. We see this contribution as a modest and first step towards finding an answer to the following question: operating in the field of intersection between EE, MTE and integration, who among migrants (i.e. except for 'the top-end of migrant entrepreneurs' that per definition is a non-generalizable substrata addressed by Saxenian's work (Saxenian 2005) can, under which conditions and how, evolve into transnational entrepreneurs?

Underlying this question, we are preoccupied with whether the driving forces and logic of the respective fields are complementary or counteracting. The 'Practice field' in Figure 1 illustrates these relationships.

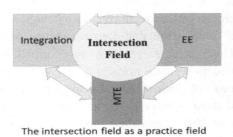

The intersection field as a practice field

Figure 1. The practice field. Source: Authors' own work.

Methodology and data

The study is based on DiasporaLink data including 126 interviews (15 explorative interviews followed by semi-structured, inductive, qualitative interviews in accordance with the phenomenological guidelines for conducting data collection). The goal is to describe the lived experience and the perspectives of migrant entrepreneurs. We therefore insistently excluded hypotheses or any other preconceived ideas (theoretical, empirical or practice-based) during the data collection and partial data analyses. The data collection is a result of collaboration with DiasporaLink colleagues working at the universities that are associated with DiasporaLink. Snowball technique was used, starting with explorative interviews with Immigrant cultural organisations and Immigrant business associations in the following countries:

U.S. (Princeton University, Yale University, University of California (UC) at Los Angeles and with UC Santa Barbara). The interviews were conducted in New York, Washington, D.C., Boston and Los Angeles;
U.K. (University of East London, University of Birmingham, Dublin Institute of Technology and University of Strathclyde). The interviews were conducted in London and Birmingham;
Sweden (Stockholm University, Uppsala University and the Swedish Ethiopian Chamber of Commerce). The interviews were conducted in Stockholm;
Germany (University of Hannover). The interviews were conducted in Hamburg;
Ethiopia (University of Addis Ababa). The interviews were conducted in Addis Ababa;
Morocco (Al Akhawayn University in Ifrane). The interviews were conducted in Ifrane and Casablanca;
Brazil (Campinas University). The interviews were conducted in São Paulo;
Chile (Universidad del Dessarrollo, UDD). The interviews were conducted in Santiago;
France (Montpellier Business School). The interviews were conducted in Paris;
Nigeria (Nigerian Entrepreneurship Center and University of East London). The interviews were conducted in London;
Denmark (Roskilde University). The interviews were conducted in Copenhagen.

Furthermore, DiasporaLink colleagues and partners from Chile (UDD, University of Desarrollo), Spain (Pompeu Fabra University), Netherlands (TNU University), Denmark (University of Southern Denmark) and Portugal (University of Lisbon, IGOT) have contributed with a variety of deliverables to the DiasporaLink Project and parts of the empirical data have been embedded as secondary data in this paper.

The interviewees included three groups: those who already are practicing transnational entrepreneurs, those who consider becoming transnational entrepreneurs, and those who tend to become or have an interest in becoming a future transnational entrepreneur. The majority of participants were males and in fields of production, manufacturing, tourism, supply and distribution, sales and imports/exports. There were two focal axes when conducting the semi-structured interviews: (1) conditions and circumstances in the home country that encourage/discourage transnational entrepreneurship; and (2) conditions and circumstances in the host country that motivate/demotivate transnational entrepreneurial activities. When appropriate, the interviewers followed the interviewees' lead. At the end of the interviews, the interviewees were encouraged to express any other thoughts or opinions that were not covered in the interview (i.e. other potential factors). The average duration of each interview was 90 minutes.

Linking insights from Transnational Research and Diaspora institutions and governance (see Zapata-Barrero and Rezaei 2020) the main objective of the content analyses was to identify common trends, rather than differences which describe the transnational business characteristics. It should be noted that at the very earliest stage of data collection, the issue of loyalty (Goli and Rezaei 2012) attracted attention. As a phenomenon the loyalty issue has been subject to many changes and challenges as a consequence of globalisation processes, while it simultaneously is an underlying requirement in the integration (and migration) discourse in Europe, and certainly is a core concern of home countries when confronted by migrants holding dual citizenship and wishing to do business in the home country. The empirical data collected in the project proved that the loyalty issue is one of the most important factors.

Results

Results from content analyses were summarised at the macrolevel and separated into: home country (Table 1), host country (Table 2) and a small group of 'Other factors' that were not suited to either of the two predominant categories (Table 3).

Content analyses – description of the data

According to the lived experiences of migrants in our study, a crucial factor in transnational entrepreneurship is to what degree the home country's economy is integrated

Table 1. Content analyses from 'Home country' question results.

Macrolevel	Characteristics reported in interviews
Home country Question: What are the conditions and circumstances that influence your transnational business? (If you already have one; or if you are considering starting one).	• Integration in the global economy • Access to other markets, namely to the host country market • Transparency, corruption, nepotism • Compatibility of products • Product quality (perceived and objective) • Compatibility of taste across borders • Formal institutions' perception of dual citizenship • Informal institutions' perception of dual loyalty status • Loyalty • Government planning • Government type (autocracy, democracy, dictatorship, etc.) • Government's attitude toward other nations (i.e. compromising, competing, conflicting) • Currency stability • Insurance and guarantees • Compatibility with dominant markets • Cultural compatibility • Bureaucracy • Bilateral relations (home-host country) • Competitive advantages

Source: Authors' own work.

Table 2. Content analyses from 'Host country' question results.

Macrolevel	Characteristics reported in interviews
Host country Question: What are the conditions and circumstances that influence your transnational business? (If you already have one; or if you are considering starting one)?	• The pattern of recognition and dual citizenship • Perception of the host countries • Perception of loyalty (dual, divided) • Government attitude towards migrants' transnational relations with home country (all kinds, including entrepreneurship) • Technological compatibility • Product compatibility • Competitive advantages • Discourse on integration • Bureaucracy and regulations • Market compatibility • Financial infrastructure and access to credits • Ethnic community (size and intensity) • Social capital of migrants • Migrants' attitudes towards home country • Human capital of migrants

Source: Authors' own work.

Table 3. 'Other factors' arising from the question results.

Macrolevel	Characteristics reported in interviews
Other factors Question: Are there other factors that influence your transnational business? (If you already have one; or if you are considering starting one)	• Importance of education acquired in the home country • Attitudes toward having an ethnic business in the host country • Access to entrepreneurial networks in home and host countries, and preferably transnational networks

Source: Authors' own work.

into the global market. Economic openness plays a key role and a critical question is whether there are any regional or global trade agreements with other countries. It is crucial for migrant entrepreneurs to have a good understanding of the terms and conditions, before starting a business.

The interviewees experienced, in varying degree depending on national context, the home country as less transparent, more corrupt, and with a higher degree of nepotism due to the importance of the traditional bonds that connect people. Whereas Western countries were experienced as societies ruled by meritocracy and adhering more to the rule of law, particularly in comparison with interviewees' home countries.

Another important issue that most interviewees emphasised is whether the markets at home and in the host country are compatible with each other concerning products, And whether there are products in the home country that could be substitute or complement goods that are consumed in the host country. Many interviewees felt that they lack the knowledge and competencies to accurately identify these instances and some declared that economic cultural knowledge is so important that they would prefer to wait, even sometimes too long, to avoid the risk of loss due to investing time and money in non-profitable products. Other interviewees confirmed this to be one of the reasons why transnational entrepreneurs normally invest in products they are familiar with, in markets they have a good understanding of in the host country among co-ethnics or third-country migrant populations in general.

Another major obstacle, when considering importing from the home country, is product quality. It is not uncommon that the home country lack safety regulations and/or measurable quality standards, or lack implementation of the regulations and/or quality standards by the relevant home country authorities.

Product quality is not limited to the product itself. Typically it goes beyond objective quality and involves other conditions, such as where and how the production took place, environmental concerns, the social image of the home country product in the host country, etc., as products in Western countries are embedded in cultural values and principles. Some interviewees expressed ideas of how they might meet Western standards, but at exorbitant costs making the adjustments too expensive to implement. It should be mentioned that a primary reason why transnational entrepreneurs import products from the home country to the host country is low cost: 'If we lose the cost advantage, then our products are no longer competitive'. one explained. The inability to identify quality characteristics valued by the host country market, rather than merely price, leads to opportunities likely to be overlooked.

The difficulty to interpret the host country's preferences appear again in other remarks from interviewees. Many indicated frustration at not being able to identify the market differences in terms of style, taste and design between the home country and the host country. Others expressed their concerns on how to address it effectively. Some felt they would have to considerably modify their products in order to compete in the mainstream for the largest number of customers. From the perspective of most interviewees, products available in Western countries normally have a nice product tag, a recognisable company logo and a standard package. Often in contrast to products in home countries, people have their own preferences and taste, and a notable number of customers care about the brand story.

Dual citizenship is a subject that many of the interviewees turn back to repeatedly. It is not only about whether they have the passports of two countries, but more about whether, specifically, the home country respects the citizenship of the host country. Sometimes when host countries learn of dual citizenship, especially in cases when negotiating financing, it becomes a disqualification. At other times, authorities treat the dual citizen as someone who has turned away from his/hers own people. In some countries, those who left are treated as guests or traitors. Suddenly credibility, accountability, loyalty and sense of belonging are questioned. Furthermore, interaction in the informally institutionalised arrangements can be affected by the dual citizenship, with an attitude that the individual, given the chance, can run away and hide in the host country if things go wrong; leaving former friends and neighbours in the home country to rely on themselves, as they are the ones who would have to stay and face the consequences.

Another challenge is underlined by a knowledge deficit in both host and home countries. The interviewees described difficulties in finding out what, if anything, local and national governments in the host country have planned for improving entrepreneurial skills. Even when plans exist, or after participating in training regarding innovation and entrepreneurship, the authorities in the home country often have completely different perceptions than the host country of what that means. Very few people are capable of carrying out business planning and as a result they often underestimate transnational competitiveness. Furthermore, for those trying to engage with potential partners in the home country, there is a high possibility of the authorities using political reasons as an excuse to turn plans down. One interviewee said:

> Having the passport of a Western country and a home abroad is a double blessing. It is good to feel at home in two different countries, but it is also a double-edged sword. In the West you are an African, in Africa you are a Westerner; in neither are you completely included. In the

West, they think you are loyal to your home country, while in your home country they think you prefer others and are, of course, more loyal to them.

Running a business in the home country is certainly an economic activity. However, it is more radically impacted by the political environment than in the more likely to be stable, host countries. A certain degree of instability is to be expected in the home country, as people tend not to emigrate when countries are stable and jobs are plentiful. But in some countries the degree of instability, particularly repetitive experiences of instability, becomes the 'way of life' and is very difficult for those who remain. One interviewee said that: 'Sometimes I got the impression that people back home were convinced that they were born to be underdogs', confirming that ongoing political and/or economic upheaval reinforces the notion that one should give up and be resigned to accept what fate has brought.

It is thus critical for the success of entrepreneurial activities in any part of the world what kind of government is in power, regardless of whether they are locals, migrants or foreign investors.

A majority of interviewees disassociated themselves from any strong desire to return to the home country and settle down permanently. Most were primarily concerned about currency stability. Though some banks are reticent to provide bank accounts for foreigners, most migrants prefer to deposit their savings in the banks of Western countries, and those who hold a Western country's passport are more likely to be aware of their rights and duties as citizens. They wish to do business in the home country primarily because they want to improve their own and their families' economic situation both in the home and the host country. They would like to start a business and after that travel between the two countries. This requires finding someone local they can trust as a collaborator. It is extremely difficult and family members are normally the first option in terms of the trust. But they are most often not the best candidate with the highest qualifications for running a business. For business people who haven't formally studied management, it is especially difficult to design a system that provides monitoring of remote functions at all times. Yet each business owner has to have insurance, legal contracts and adequate guaranties in place, in each business location.

Another obstacle noted by interviewees is bureaucratic regulations that either are not in place or operate in unproductive ways. If one abides by the bureaucratic regulations, the entrepreneur might just be the one who misses completion. One interviewee expressed it this way: 'If a majority of drivers do not care about traffic regulations and simply drive in the opposite direction (than the correct one) on an autobahn, but you abide by the regulations, who do you think would get hurt?'. There are also bureaucratic regulations with meanings and purposes that are simply not understood by the majority business owners.

An important issue for some interviewees is the specific relationship between their home and host countries: 'Thank God, it is not always troublesome, but the risk is there... suddenly all economic transactions get politicised... in that case, you'll be the loser'. The entrepreneurs and the 'could-be entrepreneurs' seem to be more aware of the potential competitive advantages their home country can offer in terms of the level of wages, production costs and transaction costs: 'If you can turn those general advantages into your own advantage, you'll be a winner; no matter if you are a smart migrant, Westerner or Easterner'. One interviewee said and asked: 'How come they can do it in China and India, but not in Morocco, Ethiopia and other places?'.

Macro circumstances in the host country

Even if the entrepreneur has formal citizenship, what counts as significant is whether the government and public institutions in the host country perceive transnational relations with the home country a positive or a negative characteristic. This perception is rarely about possible mutual economic benefits between home and host countries. It is more about the entrepreneur's loyalty to the home country becoming politicised for various reasons. When this happens on a general level, it has an impact on economic and transnational activities.

Consequences of the questioned loyalty could be difficulties applying for credit in the host country for doing business in the home country. The banks demonstrate an attitude 'of why are you coming to us if you want to do business in Africa or the Middle East?'.

Furthermore, on an individual level, a notable number of interviewees reported having experienced that co-ethnics automatically considered them as someone who will move back to the home country permanently when hearing that they are involved in businesses there. However, this is absolutely not the case. One interviewee explained that

> the majority of successful third-country migrant entrepreneurs who do business back home are well aware of the privilege of being a citizen in EU countries, such as France, Spain, Denmark and Sweden. If they were to give up one of their two citizenships, I am sure the majority – maybe even all – will give up the citizenship of the home country.

The attitudes of the formal and public institutions in the host country towards transnational entrepreneurs seem to be understandable for many migrant entrepreneurs. Unlike the Western countries, developing countries have their own less sophisticated standards and procedures of creditworthiness, business survivability and other issues related to doing business. One interviewee described home countries as 'Banana Republics' where one never knows the prospective outcome of investments due to currency instability, sudden governmental decisions, expropriations and other unexpected government interventions. While those incidents might rarely take place, some of the most important criteria are the perspectives of the three major credit ratings agencies (i.e. Standard and Poor's, Fitch and Moody's) as well as the International Monetary Fund (IMF) outlooks for financial performance of national governments. The ratings given by these four institutions impact currency stability, bond rates and bank lending. But, more importantly, as one interviewee explained, is the deeply rooted image of developing countries in the West: 'It takes centuries or at least decades to change that image, but one piece of bad news is usually enough to jeopardise the whole thing overnight'.

Loyalty as a theme related to the question of formal or substantial citizenship status was highlighted by many interviewees. It seems that doing business in the home country, or even expressing a desire to do so, is conceived as an indication of lacking loyalty toward the host country. One interviewee said that

> it seems to me that they (public institutions and specifically the governments) want you all the time to prove that you are one of them, that you belong to them ... there is a wide range of activities and attitudes that are considered as indications of the opposite. Unfortunately doing business in the home country is one of them.

Setting aside not being appreciated, it is not even desirable, accepted or tolerated that one can be loyal to two countries:

> They demand your very soul. Arriving at the airport, sometimes you are approached by some civil servants, usually backed up by a person in uniform, who ask '*Where you've been?*' If you name one of those 'bad image' troubled countries, they treat you like a suspect.... If you actually say that you've been doing business back home, you'll be in serious trouble,

a university-educated male interviewee explained, 'If you are a well-educated and highly-skilled person and wish to do business in your home country, they almost consider you as Prometheus, as if you were to steal the fire, the knowledge, the techniques, etc.', thus expressing a contradiction between the logic of Globalisation, on the one hand, and that of the Nation State and integration in Europe, on the other.

This scepticism is to be found on both sides of the border.

> Just like in your home country they treat you like: '*What are you doing here, really ...?*' Obviously, it does not make sense to many of them that you say 'goodbye', even for a short time, to a life in the West, which in their eyes represents paradise on earth, only to settle down there... Everybody knows about the money, the education and the social status in the West.

With a long residence in Western countries, it becomes second nature to depend on the very high level of nearly always functioning technology because the infrastructure is there. That is certainly not the case in many home countries.

> Doing business is a matter of waiting and waiting, waiting for permission, for stamps and documents and signatures – often in the specifically required colour of ink – that indicate approval of a license to operate. A lot of bureaucratic rules exist; some being followed or other times not. Technologies in the home and host countries do not talk together, they are often not compatible ... most probably because of the difference in cultures that fostered them.

The lack of compatibility is not only about technological culture and infrastructure but also the products themselves.

> I would really like to export things from here to my country ... there are so many good things here, that I know they want and they don't have ... but, first of all, they are very expensive; and second of all, the products are not compatible with what does exist in my home country, nor do they fit with the underlying culture ... they, so to speak, do not fit as a brick into an already existing wall. These kinds of problems could be solved by transnational entrepreneurs, and has been solved through communication with the producers here ... but first, you have to climb over the suspicion and the scepticism ... that also goes for private firms,

an interviewee reported.

Integration is a subject that heavily occupies transnational entrepreneurs. They are aware that the public and official attitudes in their host countries towards third-country migrant integration are changing, but not for the good, as many of them stress. The new attitudes create more suspicions towards people as well as other traditions and customs.

> If one does not behave exactly as 'they want one to', it does not take a long time to ask you why you do not just go back to your own home [country]. People become less tolerant, that is not good for business ... not for the business that we want to do ... loyalty towards two countries, and two peoples ... that is poison [for business in the host country].

It is a widespread experience among the interviewees that being part of an ethnic community and having a large number of relatives whom you trust based on familial ties, is a great deal of help if you are involved in a small business, like a cafeteria, in your own neighbourhood in Copenhagen, Amsterdam or Paris. However, if you want to go international, it is not of much help, neither in your host nor your home country. If you are dealing with a businessman, they will evaluate and assess your qualifications, competencies, resources, efforts and business ideas. Bear in mind, businessmen [i.e. experienced and already successful entrepreneurs] behave almost the same [worldwide], regardless of language, race, colour, religion and country …

> They don't open all the doors for you in Morocco and welcome you just because you happen to be a Moroccan … There are millions of Moroccans in Morocco. The only thing other parties care about is whether or not your business is going to make money.

Some of the interviewees say that the importance of ethnic community is probably overrated beyond what's reasonable. Some even report that a strong ethnic community and norm can be an obstacle when they want to think 'big'; both within the diaspora and in the home country.

They further report that the attitudes of migrants towards their own home country are changing rapidly as a result of a long residence in the West. Fewer migrants are dreaming of going back because they received education and built their own independent lifes and community in the host country. Unfortunately for the home country, these people are among the most successful in terms of education and participation in the labour market in the host country. A negative consequence is that more and more ethnic business owners who try to do business in the home country do not innovate. Without the interjection of new ideas from the diaspora – or elsewhere – the market for similar products/services in the home country becomes saturated. 'Additionally, you find that remittances sent back to the home country are used to finance your immediate family's consumption … not productive activities.'

Migrant Transnational Entrepreneurship (MTE)

There are many previous studies on MTE (Dana 1996; Davidsson and Honig 2003; Drori, Honig, and Wright 2009; Jensen, Rezaei, and Wherry 2014; Light, Rezaei, and Dana 2013; Mitchell et al. 2002; Portes and Celaya 2013; Portes and Fernandez-Kelly 2015; Rezaei and Goli 2016). Among all studies, the most established ones link MTE to ethnic business and diaspora. Portes, Haller, and Guarnizo (2002, 287) defines transnational entrepreneurs as ' … Self-employed immigrants whose business activities require frequent travel abroad … '. Light (2016) delivers a more concrete definition

> TNE involves entrepreneurs who slide back and forth across international borders to such an extent and with such frequency that they are said to be simultaneously resident in both places. TNEs are usually multi-lingual and they feel culturally at home in all the places where they operate. They frequently have more than one citizenship or, at least, a visa status that enables problem-free arrival and departures from airports.

Data for this paper indicates that the condition of 'feeling culturally at home in all the places where they operate' cannot be taken for granted as a premise, sometimes even quite to the contrary. Drori, Honig, and Wright (2009) formulate a theoretical framework towards transnational entrepreneurship, by introducing five factors/approaches that influence the transnational entrepreneur's individual capabilities and resources:

Agency. Highlights the transnational entrepreneurs' embeddedness, both in contexts of home and host country;

Cultural perspective. Views the cultural repertoires of transnational entrepreneurs' use of their entrepreneurial actions;

Institutional perspective. Focuses on the knowledge of the rules of the game that affect the performance of their venture. Studying TE from an institutional perspective will help one to understand the logic, actions, practices and rules that govern and coordinate organisational and human activities in certain national contexts;

Power relations perspective. Transnational entrepreneurs' business strategies inherently bear political meanings and consequences. This perspective underlines the strategic position transnational entrepreneurs can obtain by leveraging the political context in both worlds. Thus, the dimension of power relations and the political context shape both the choice and the meaning attached to a particular form of transnational entrepreneurs;

Social capital and network perspective. TE implies three domains for simultaneous network formation: a network of origin (ethnic, national), a network of destination, and a network of industry (Drori, Honig, and Wright 2009).

Inspired by Field and Capital Theory, Drori et al. (Drori, Honig, and Wright 2009; Terjesen and Elam 2009) establish the relationship between an agent and the context of the agent's surroundings, including the importance of success or failure of role models and peer groups on the formation of transnational entrepreneurship, which ' ... is grounded in the strength of relational economic geography' (Bathelt and Glückler 2003) and evolutionary economic geography (Boschma and Frenken 2006). Regional factors are conceived important because they shape: (1) beliefs about the desirability of founding a firm; (2) opportunities to learn about entrepreneurship; and (3) to build the abilities needed to succeed and the ease of acquiring critical resources (Wyrwich, Sternberg, and Stuetzer 2018). Like the field and capital theory, the important elements include primarily three core concepts: habitus, capital and field. It is argued that immigrants have been exposed to at least two cultural fields; that of the host and the country of origin. Hence, these individuals are able to combine their experiences and knowledge of both cultures (Hofstede 2001) together with their accumulated capital to form a dual habitus, i.e. an ability to navigate in the business world of both the country of origin and the host country. Authors' data deviates from this interpretation of the role of dual habitus.

Some of the aspects are already addressed explicitly in GEM surveys, namely the individual characteristics (i.e. perceived opportunities, perceived capabilities, fear of failure rate, entrepreneurial intentions, motivational index, high status to successful entrepreneurs, entrepreneurship as a good career choice) and several dimensions of the environmental aspects. The problem is that GEM data are not about MTEs and do not shed light on the intersection of the three fields; it is about entrepreneurship in general. Although the majority of the parameters under the heading 'Entrepreneurial Framework Conditions' in GEM data are of crucial importance for MTEs, important aspects of the national context at home, which according to our in-depth interviews are specifically relevant for migrant entrepreneurship, are not included.

Ethnic Entrepreneurship (EE)

EE has long been one of the most prominent expression of functionality of the ethnic community networks. As far as the celebrated cultural and demographic pluralism in, for instance, EU countries is concerned, a tangible presence of third-country immigrants in the public sphere is manifested through EE and the lives around them. Featuring EE's underlying compatibility with transnational entrepreneurship, Rezaei (2011) illustrate the interaction between Global, National and Minority businesses (Figure 2).

The authors' empirical data show clearly immigrants, in spite of their business priorities and activities on the surface appear to be ethnic-culturally embedded and generated, do have an instrumental attitude towards culture and tradition. Describing 'Ethnic strategies' including start-up as a business owner, Rezaei (2011) introduces, several factors of influence based on hundreds of qualitative interviews in European countries. The 'Ethnic strategy' is a result of reflection on the following aspects:

Sufficiency alternatives: What are earning possibilities under the given circumstances? There are three possibilities: (A) Being employed as a wage earner; (B) Living on welfare payments; (C) Being supported by spouse, parents, children et al.
Market conditions: Refers to the conditions in the market at hand. (A) Possibilities for ethnic products. (B) Starting business within the mainstream (mainstream products).
Ownership and property rights: Refers to the conditions for property rights and ownership. (A) Are there vacant locations available? (B) Is there competition for locations? (C) Which political/formal institutional conditions have to be met prior to action?
Other determinants: (A) The degree of your mobility? (B) Possibilities for inclusion in government priorities with regard to selective migrations and ownership? (C) Are you motivated enough?
Resource mobilisation: (A) Are there any ethnic community members around? (B) How is your accessibility to this ethnic network/community? (C) What are the relevant public priorities in the field?

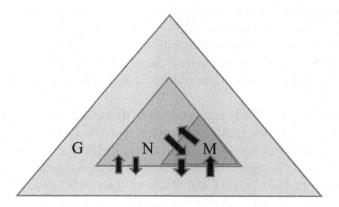

A model of business system. interaction between (G)lobal (N)ational (B) and (M)inority busines system

Figure 2. The interaction between the Global, the National and the Minority business system.

The compatibility between ethnic and transnational entrepreneurship

The strong co-ethnic networks (Granovetter 1973), which is the engine of the development of ethnic business, simultaneously becomes the equally embedded substantial inhibitor and weakness. Due to the very close (often family, relatives and co-ethnic) relations and the reproduction of exclusionary trust with few, if any, structural holes (Burt 2004; Rezaei and Goli 2009), ethnic businesses are believed to be at risk of becoming clustered spatially. With regard to breaches, they are usually enslaved and encapsulated in ethnically and divided identical sectors and businesses into relatively deprived residential urban areas. Short-run competitive advantages are obvious while opportunities for breaking out with regard to location, product, ownership and customer profiles are limited (Rath 2011).

In the social capital framework presented by Putnam (1993), EE is, as it has developed, partly based on vertically (as opposed to horizontally) structured and bonding (as opposed to bridging) of trust relationships. EE makes it possible for ethnic minorities to get by and simultaneously hold them back from getting ahead, prohibiting members from competing on larger scales, where there is much more potential, information, knowledge, skills and start-up finances available (Whitley 1992).

In many Western countries, over decades the phenomenon of EE has been rather dominantly perceived, framed and explained by host countries' public institutions and NGO's. EE is an expression of primarily unskilled, under-educated and less integrated third-country migrants' first choice. On the other hand, EE can also be an expression of the over-educated, under-skilled and better-integrated third-country migrants' second as well as third choice, or even last resort in case they do not apply or fail to be hired for jobs in the mainstream labour market. Comprehensive quantitative data indicates unambiguously that the overeducated, under-skilled migrants in ethnic businesses are not among the most successful (Rezaei and Goli 2006, 2007, 2009). Quite to the contrary, when speaking of the typical third-country migrant business operator, the individuals with least or no formal education are likely to perform better. The reason is that the qualifications required to run an ethnic business are of a completely different nature than those required to do a good job in mainstream business and certainly transnational entrepreneurship (Rezaei 2007; Nielsen 2007).

The tendency towards perceiving EE as the last resort for the less-integrated, poorly educated third-country immigrants can be expected to become even stronger in the future due to the rise of the so-called Competition state (Genschel and Seelkopf 2015; Pedersen 2011) and the so-called Performance society (Petersen 2016).

There is no doubt that strong ties dominate those processes and outcomes. The question is where these particular features and dynamics of EE, as it has developed in European countries, become the suitable engine for transnational entrepreneurial activities.

To answer this, it would be necessary to know which wage-earners could become transnational entrepreneurs (i.e. status change); and, who and how among ethnic entrepreneurs could go from 'Necessity entrepreneurs in the host country' to 'Opportunity entrepreneurs in the transitional arena' (i.e. quality change). The following groups have been identified with regard to status and quality changes:

- EEs with no or very low level of education and skills acquired in the mainstream labour market who are still operating ethnic businesses, where the employees (if there are any), customers, products and the business location are predominantly homogeneous;
- EEs with no or very low level of education and skills acquired in the mainstream labour market who have expanded their business footprint, but remained within the same line of business; e.g. from small café or restaurant to mainstream café or restaurant, with employees still predominantly co-ethnics;
- The overeducated and under-skilled EE who return to work as wage earners, due to increasing job openings in the wake of economic growth;
- The overeducated and under-skilled EE who continue to work in their own business in hopes of expanding within an equivalent line of products;
- Third-country migrants who have been working in the mainstream labour market as wage earners, divided into two sub-categories:
Employed as civil servants in the public sector (recognising that the public sector can be divided into many sub-categories dependent on the services delivered. For example, delivery of social services is completely different than providing healthcare or operating railways);
Employed in the private sector (with a regard for the characteristics of the particular business sector where the individuals were employed).

Prior research on transnational entrepreneurship indicated clearly (Stenholm, Acs, and Wuebker 2013; Tang, Kacmar, and Busenitz 2012; Waldinger and Fitzgerald 2004; Waldinger, Aldrich, and Ward 1990; Whitley 1992) that major differences at the individual level, where self-motivation, entrepreneurial commitment and alertness are decisive factors in relation to environmental dimensions (Jensen, Rezaei, and Wherry 2014; Kelly, Singer, and Herrington 2015; Kloosterman and Rath 2003; Mitchell et al. 2002).

The individual's motivation or lack of motivation can be divided into three main sub-categories related to the advantages and disadvantages of social capital (Coleman 1988), human capital and entrepreneurial mind-set. Furthermore, the motivations can be roughly typified as intrinsic or extrinsic. Some immigrants are extrinsically motivated to start a business because, for them, it was the only way to work legally in the host country, e.g. Czech Republic (OECD and EU 2014). Intrinsic motivations include the 'economy of self-fulfilment' (Bögenhold and Staber 1991). Not only conceptually but also with regard to formal institutional efforts to foster, improve and support the fields of EE (Rezaei and Goli 2009). A categorisation of individuals can be made alongside two aspects: those who 'can' as the consequence of the sum of human and social capital that they possess or can access; and those who 'choose to', i.e. those individuals who are motivated to become a transnational entrepreneur. These characteristics are illustrated as a matrix illustrating both outcomes: 'Those who can' (horizontal axis) and 'Those who choose to' (vertical axis), as seen in Figure 3.

Those who both can and choose to are either already running their businesses or won't have any extraordinary problems establishing themselves as such, as far as their skills and resources match the business they wish to establish. They have the competencies for the specific business they wish to develop, and they have access to finances either through their networks or through banks, according to their economic viability, and they are motivated. This group of individuals would be in need of assistance with regard to growth, or probably breaking-out. They need more structural holes as well as coordination between

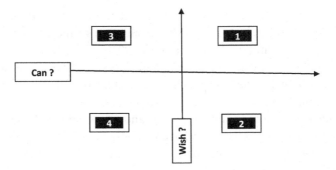

Figure 3. The 'Can' and 'Wish' model.

several influencing factors. Entrepreneurial skills training requires some two to four years of training to reach the level of having a product/service to present to potential investors. At the end of that term, it is still not certain that the team will be successful. Often, multiple products/services are developed before a 'winner' emerges. Success requires an effectively functioning entrepreneurship ecosystem involving several factors (Isenberg 2010).

Essentially, all categories of individuals interested in entrepreneurship require training:

> Those who *can* but do not *wish to*, have to first be motivated. After that, training can begin;
> Those who *cannot* but *wish to*, have to be helped acquire the necessary competencies. These individuals are most likely to succeed. Throughout the training, they accumulate skills and ideas, and potential investors would, based on assessments and evaluation of this development decide whether or not to make investments in further development.

And finally those who *cannot* or *do not wish to* should have access to training. Not everyone who is trained will be a successful entrepreneur. Some want less responsibility or more socialisation than working in a small unknown start-up and sometimes a student starts the learning process with a great idea, but by the time they've completed its development, the financial market has changed and no funds are available, or at least not at a borrowing rate that makes the product/service viable. Training and motivation are important, but success is also dependent on a number of external factors. Therefore, contingency plans need to be considered when indications of severe changes to the financial markets might be approaching.

Both the ability (self-efficacy) and the wish (entrepreneurial motivation) to become a transnational entrepreneur is according to our interviewees' experiences influenced by the particular perception of loyalty that is embedded in integration policy discourses in host countries.

Integration

The beginning of the new millennium was also the beginning of tremendous changes in the discourses on the integration of third-country immigrants in European countries. The changes can be characterised as a gradual paradigm shift (Goli 2002), or at least serious challenges to the migrant integration paradigm that previously dominated European migration and integration policy. The institutionalisation of the new discourses is taking place incrementally as institutional changes (Hall 1993) usually do.

There is no doubt that hijab, niqab, halal and haram, radicalisation, forced marriage, honour or shame killing, parallel society, ghetto, social control, challenges to gender equality and to interactions in labour market, hate crimes, circumcision of boys and girls, forced re-education journeys to home countries, gangs and crime, and challenges in schools and welfare system and other social spheres have not only been added to our vocabulary but also debated intensively as top issues of concern in societal and media discussions with top-level politicians' participation.

Parallel to this, European responses to these challenges, as well as challenges of international migration in many cases, have been the revival, reinvention and protection of the national identity and national borders. Cultural relativism and multiculturalism as perspectives, principals, and policy-making premises have been losing ground around Europe (Blaschke 2005). This development is likely to influence the (temporary or permanent) return migration and the motivation to go transnational, but there are plenty of intertwining factors. Research indicates that demographic characteristics of migrants, such as age, gender, marital status, and education are the major conventional control variables in quantitative analyses of return intentions. Conversely, Carling and Pettersen (2014) reported a nonlinear effect of educational attainment on return intentions (Bird and Jelinek 1988); more specifically, migrants with very low or very high levels of education have the lowest odds of intending to return. The much celebrated brain circulation does not seem to apply to migrants residing in Europe.

Strong integration in the host country and strong transnational (not necessarily entrepreneurial) activities could create the preconditions for becoming entrepreneurs, because moving back and forth between home and host country will develop dual habitus and knowledge, both being dynamic phenomena. Maintaining and developing the dual habitus depends, as Berry illustrated in his Acculturation model (Berry 1997) on whether the migrant community, as well as the majority society, consider the maintenance of one's identity and characteristics (dual habitus and dual loyalty) as valuable.

Sheffer (2003) put the question of loyalty orientation at the middle of individual immigrants and dependents' integration strategies, operating with three different kinds of (dynamic) loyalty strategies: at the beginning (arrival) the individual immigrant demonstrates a so-called ambivalent loyalty. The decision on whether the immigrant's loyalty would evolve into divided or dual loyalty (in our context loyalty toward home or host country) is dependent on five internal (to the ethnic community) circumstances that are interrelated and mutually reinforcing:

The minority group's identity and identification;
The intensity of the emotional belonging in the group;
The group's collective strategy towards assimilation or isolation;
The intensity, scope, and extent of the transnational networks;
The degree of group organisation.

Sheffer (2003) argued:

[...] Of these two sources of influence on loyalty patterns (the internal and external factors), the social and political situation in host countries is the more potent one... Thus, for example, greater openness and porosity of borders, substantial tolerance toward 'the other' and 'otherness', enhanced legitimacy for multiculturalism and pluralism and societal acquiescence in the establishment of diaspora communities and organizations, including diaspora transnational networks, are likely to promote diasporas' dual loyalties.

The following is only one example of a vast number of incidents that find their ways to media and public debate and questions third-country migrants and descendants' loyalty towards the host country:

'The German Football Federation (DFB) has criticised its internationals Mesut Özil and Ilkay Gündogan for posing in photos with Turkish President Recep Tayyip Erdogan. – Are we supposed to be impolite to the president of our families' homeland?' Özil asked, 'Whatever justified criticism there might be, we decided on a gesture of politeness, out of respect for the office of president and for our Turkish roots', he said, 'it was not our intention to make a political statement with this picture'.

Loyalty, surprisingly enough, is not, however, one of the parameters by which we in Europe usually measure integration. Mipex (Migrant Integration Policy Index) is the most comprehensive measurement of integration, covering 38 countries, alongside 8 indicators and 167 dimensions, providing a comprehensive assessment of the status quo in integration policies in different countries. The indicators include circumstances and conditions that influence migrants' participation in labour market mobility, education, and political participation, access to nationality, family reunion, health, permanent residence and anti-discrimination. Mipex' data primarily cover what government and public institutions do in order to improve the integration of migrants. The core of the Mipex study is the concept of citizenship, transnational citizenship, and its complications, but it almost exclusively addresses conditions for formal/nominal citizenship (Bauböck 1994), excluding aspects that have to do with substantial citizenship, such as sense of belonging, actual utilisation of participation rights, etc. Seen in Honneth's theoretical framework that with regard to the question of recognition goes way beyond the formal/nominal citizenship, legal right is only one: '... legal recognition split off from the hierarchical value order insofar as the individual was in principle to enjoy legal equality vis-à-vis all others'. The individual could then – certainly not in actual practice, but at least according to the normative idea – know that he or she was respected as a legal person with the same rights as all other members of society, while still owing his or her social esteem to a hierarchical scale of values – which had, however, also been set on a new foundation. Studying some of these substantial aspects is possible within the theoretical framework that was not originally designed and presented in relation to migrant integration, but will, we believe, make a great deal of sense, namely the three fields/spheres of recognition that are presented by Honneth.

The integration discourses' social practices (Fairclough 2013) at the institutional level of kindergarten and schools, where the secondary socialisation in the values of society and in interactions with peers and authorities take place has an impact on the development of self-confidence and self-efficacy (Bandura 1977). But an even more important sphere of recognition for developing self-efficacy and motivations for actions is what Honneth frames as 'self-respect' and 'self-esteem'. Self-respect has less to do with whether or not one has a good opinion of oneself than with one's sense of possessing the universal dignity of all persons. It is about recognition of an individual's status as an agent capable of acting based on reasons closely attached to what Habermas terms 'discursive will-formation'. Self-esteem as a product of recognition, on the other hand, is about developing a sense of what it is that makes one unique, and cannot inherently be based on a set of trivial or negative characteristics, but on something that is regarded valuable. 'It comes then as no surprise that members of denigrated groups have enormous difficulties being perceived in anything but stereotypical ways' (Anderson 1996). Even if this socialisation in values and proper modes of interaction is successful, there will still be challenges going transnational.

> Another important issue is whether immigrants who are established in advanced countries would be motivated to settle down permanently or for a longer period of time in less advanced homelands: … For someone already residing in an advanced country, deplorable social conditions in the developing world are unattractive. That case offers no lifestyle compensation for accepting the unpleasantness of the shuttlecock lifestyle. (Light 2016)

These differences are not the only ones. Applying Schein's model (Schein 2010) (originally exclusively applied to studies of organisational culture), one could say that MTEs, when in the homeland, are on a daily basis confronted with or challenged by a myriad of cultural phenomena that only they (due to the fact that they can compare to the equivalent practice in the host country) can elaborate explicitly on. Schein's model includes three interacting layers of cultural traits that characterise organisational (in our respect community) practices and relations including business relations: (1) Top level/layer is Behaviours and artefacts, which refer to the manifest level of culture, consisting of the constructed physical and social environment of an organisation. (2) Middle level/layer is Espoused values. The constituents of this level of culture provide the underlying meanings and interrelations by which the patterns of behaviours and artefacts may be deciphered. (3) Basic underlying assumptions that refer to the unconscious that is taken for granted as an acceptable way of perceiving the world. They are embedded in the social practices, leadership practices, and work traditions.

In order to grasp the fundamental cultural issues, it is inevitable to include Hofstede's operationalisation of fundamental cultural dimensions that transnational entrepreneurs meet when attempting to operate in the home country. Our data indicate that the scope and the intensity of these dimensions are far beyond the simple notion of dual habitus. Fundamental differences with regard to power distance, collectivism vs. individualism, masculinity vs. femininity, uncertainty vs. risk willingness and innovation (Brockhaus 1980), short-term normative orientation vs. long-term orientation, and restraint vs. indulgence, that they meet is not getting easier to accept and operate within solely because of awareness of their existence.

Conclusions and perspectives

Following the experiences of 'Actual Transnational Entrepreneurs' as well as the 'Could Become Transnational Entrepreneurs' expressed in the empirical data, we have scrutinised the core dynamics respectively, and the compatibility between the fields of EE, MTE and integration discourses. Being the first study of this intersection, it is too soon and too daring to conclude unambiguously based on our relatively limited empirical data. We see the modest contribution of this study being number one asking new questions/generating a new hypothesis, and number two opening up for the inclusion of theoretical concepts and frameworks that originally were not designed to study transnational entrepreneurship.

In spite of the limited scope, our study indicates rather clearly that a different kind of comprehensive research of circumstances around MTE is needed and has to include simultaneous studies of host countries' integration discourses, home countries' socio-cultural conditions, and their respective attitudes towards the question of loyalty. Furthermore our empirical analyses indicate that EE is, opposite to what is usually imagined, far from the suitable engine of the business and societal change that is inherit and appealing in MTE. Our empirical analyses also point out that currently developing integration discourses in Western countries do not bring about or support the kind of conditions and attitudes that foster and encourage transnational activities including transnational entrepreneurship among migrants and descendants. In order to study the intersections between these fields we will need a much more comprehensive comparative research design, which among other dimensions should map which host countries different migrant entrepreneurs (who operate or wish to operate in the specific home country) come from, what the net benefit is for specific home and host countries, and how fostering and supporting mutually beneficial developments are formally and informally institutionalised.

Disclosure statement

No potential conflict of interest was reported by the authors.

Funding

This work was supported by Research Executive Agency [grant number 645471].

References

Anderson, J. 1996. "Translator's Introduction." In *The Struggle for Recognition: The Moral Grammar of Social Conflicts*, edited by A. Honneth. Cambridge, MA: Polity Press.
Ardichvili, A., R. Cardozo, and S. Ray. 2003. "A Theory of Entrepreneurial Opportunity Identification and Development." *Journal of Business Venturing* 18 (1): 105–123.
Bandura, A. 1977. "Self-efficacy: Toward a Unifying Theory of Behavioural Change." *Psychological Review* 84 (2): 191–215.
Banton, M. 1994. "Modelling Ethnic and National Relations." In *Ethnicity*, edited by J. Hutchinson and A. Smith. Oxford: Oxford University Press.
Baron, R. A. 2006. "Opportunity Recognition as Pattern Recognition: How Entrepreneurs 'Connect the Dots' to Identify new Business Opportunities." *Academy of Management Perspectives* 20 (1): 104–119.
Bathelt, H., and J. Glückler. 2003. "Toward a Relational Economic Geography." *Journal of Economic Geography* 3 (2): 117–144.
Bauböck, R. 1994. *Transnational Citizenship. Membership and Rights in International Migration*. Aldershot: Edward Elgar.
Berry, J. W. 1997. "Immigration, Acculturation, and Adaptation." *Applied Psychology* 46 (1): 5–34.
Bird, B., and M. Jelinek. 1988. "The Operation of Entrepreneurial Intentions." *Entrepreneurship Theory and Practice* 3 (2): 21–29.
Blaschke, J. 2005. *Blasc Nation-State Building Processes and Cultural Diversity*. Berlin: Edition Parabolis.

Block, J. H., R. Thurik, and H. Zhou. 2012. "What Turns Knowledge Into Innovative Products? The Role of Entrepreneurship and Knowledge Spillovers." *Journal of Evolutionary Economics* 23 (4): 693–718.

Bögenhold, D., and U. Staber. 1991. "The Decline and Rise of Self-Employment." *Work, Employment and Society* 5: 223–239.

Boschma, R. A., and K. Frenken. 2006. "Why is Economic Geography Not an Evolutionary." *Journal of Economic Geography* 6: 273–302.

Bosma, N. S. 2013. "The Global Entrepreneurship Monitor (GEM) and Its Impact on Entrepreneurship Research." *Foundations and Trends in Entrepreneurship* 9 (2): 143–248.

Brockhaus, R. H. 1980. "Risk Taking Propensity of Entrepreneurs." *Academy of Management Journal* 23 (3): 509–520.

Brubaker, R. 2005. "The 'Diaspora' Diaspora." *Ethnic and Racial Studies* 28 (1): 1–19.

Burt, R. 2004. "Structural Holes and Good Ideas." *American Journal of Sociology* 110 (2): 349–399.

Carling, J., and S. V. Pettersen. 2014. "Return Migration Intentions in the Integration-Transnationalism Matrix." *International Migration* 52 (6): 13–30.

Coleman, J. S. 1988. "Social Capital in the Creation of Human Capital." *American Journal of Sociology* 94: S95–S120.

Dana, L. P. 1996. "Boomerang Entrepreneurs: Hong Kong to Canada and Back." *Journal of Small Business Management* 34 (2): 79–83.

Davidsson, P., and B. Honig. 2003. "The Role of Social and Human Capital among Nascent Entrepreneurs." *Journal of Business Venturing* 18 (3): 301–331.

Drori, I., B. Honig, and M. Wright. 2009. "Transnational Entrepreneurship: An Emergent Field of Study." *Entrepreneurship Theory and Practice* 33 (5): 1001–1022.

Fairclough, N. 2013. "Critical Discourse Analysis and Critical Policy Studies." *Critical Policy Studies* 7: 177–197.

Genschel, P., and L. Seelkopf. 2015. "The Competition State: The Modern State in a Global Economy." In *The Oxford Handbook of Transformations of the State*. Oxford: Oxford University Press.

Goli, M. 2002. *En Verden til Forskel. (Diskursive Inconsistancy and Institutional Inefficentcy)*. København: Københavns Universitet.

Goli, M., and B. Greve, eds. 2017. *Integration*. Copenhagen: Hans Reitzels Forlag.

Goli, M., and S. Rezaei. 2012. *Loyalitet – en Anthology om Værdighed*. Edited by M. Paustian. Aalborg: Aalborg Universitetsforlag.

Granovetter, M. 1973. "The Strength of Weak Ties." *American Journal of Sociology* 78 (6): 1360–1380.

Hall, P. A. 1993. "Policy Paradigms, Social Learning, and the State: The Case of Economic Policymaking in Britain." *Comparative Politics* 25 (3): 275–296.

Hofstede, G. 2001. *Culture's Consequences: Comparing Values, Behaviors, Institutions, and Organizations Across Nations*. 2nd ed. Thousand Oaks, CA: Sage. ISBN 978-0-8039-7323-7. OCLC 45093960.

Isenberg, D. 2010. "How to Start an Entrepreneurial Revolution." *Harvard Business Review*. https://institute.coop/sites/default/files/resources/Isenberg%20-%20How%20to%20Start%20an%20Entrepreneurial%20Revolution.pdf.

Jensen, K. W., S. Rezaei, and F. Wherry. 2014. "Cognitive Effects on Entrepreneurial Intentions: A Comparison of Chinese Émigrés and Their Descendants with Non-émigré Chinese." *International Journal of Entrepreneurship and Small Business* 23 (1–2): 252–277.

Kelly, D., S. Singer, and M. Herrington. 2015. "GEM Report." https://www.gemconsortium.org/report.

Kloosterman, R. C., and J. Rath. 2003. *Immigrant Entrepreneurs: Venturing Abroad in the Age of Globalization*. Oxford/New York, NY: Berg/University of New York Press.

Light, I. 2016. "Keynote Paper Prepared for the EU Horizon 2020 RISE Programme." DiasporaLink Project Mandatory Meeting Conference, at University of Birmingham, April 14–15.

Light, I., S. Rezaei, and L. P. Dana. 2013. "Ethnic Minority Entrepreneurs in the International Carpet Trade: An Empirical Study." *International Journal of Entrepreneurship and Small Business* 18 (2): 125–153.

Mitchell, R. K., J. B. Smith, E. A. Morse, K. W. Seawright, A. M. Peredo, and B. McKenzie. 2002. "Are Entrepreneurial Cognitions Universal? Assessing Entrepreneurial Cognitions Across Cultures." *Entrepreneurship: Theory and Practice* 26 (4): 9–32.

Nielsen, C. 2007. *Er indvandrere overkvalificeret til deres arbejde?* Copenhagen: SFI/VIVE.

OECD and EU. 2014. *The Missing Entrepreneurs 2014: Policies for Inclusive Entrepreneurship in Europe*. Paris: OECD. doi:10.1787/9789264213593-en.

Pedersen, O. K. 2011. *Konkurrencestaten*. Munksgaard.

Petersen, A. 2016. *Præstationssamfundet*. Hans Reitzels Forlag.

Portes, A., and A. Celaya. 2013. "Modernization for Emigration: Determinants and Consequences of the Brain Drain." *Journal of the American Academy of Arts and Sciences* 142 (3): 170–184.

Portes, A., and P. Fernandez-Kelly, eds. 2015. *The State and the Grassroots: Immigrant Transnational Organizations in Four Continents*, 212–235. New York: Berghahn Books.

Portes, A., W. J. Haller, and A. Guarnizo. 2002. "Transnational Entrepreneurs: An Alternative form of Immigrant Economic Adaptation." *American Sociological Review* 67 (2): 278–298.

Putnam, R. D. 1993. *Making Democracy Work. Civic Traditions in Modern Italy*. Princeton, NJ: Princeton University Press.

Rath, J. 2011. *Promoting EE in European Cities*. Luxembourg: Publications Office of the European Union.

Rezaei, S. 2007. "Breaking Out: The Dynamics of Immigrant-Owned Businesses." *Journal of Social Sciences* 3 (2): 94–105.

Rezaei, S. 2011. "Trust as a Competitive Strategy in a Global Co-Ethnic Market: Towards an Empirically Supported Theory." *International Journal of Business and Globalisation* 7 (3): 265–302.

Rezaei, S., and M. Goli. 2006. *Det Duale Arbejdsmarked i et Velfærdsstatsligtperspektiv – Et Studie af Dilemmaet Mellem Uformel økonomisk Praksis og Indvandreres Socio-økonomiske Integration. Hovedrapport. Delrapport 4*. Roskilde: Roskilde Universitetscenter.

Rezaei, S., and M. Goli. 2007. *Indvandreres Tætte Netværk: Katalysator Eller Hæmsko for Innovation og Vækst? Et Studie af Formelle og Uformelle Netværks Relationersbetydning for Dynamikken i Indvandrerejede Virksomheder*. Roskilde: Roskilde Universitetscenter.

Rezaei, S., and M. Goli. 2009. "Norm Divergence, Opportunity Structure and Utilization of Self-Employed Immigrant's Qualifications." *Journal of Social Sciences* 5 (3): 163–176.

Rezaei, S., and M. Goli. 2016. "Divided We Stand, Together We Fall: Iranians Immigrants in Scandinavian Countries: Sweden. Denmark and Norway." Unpublished Work.

Saxenian, A. 2005. "From Brain Drain to Brain Circulation: Transnational Communities and Regional Upgrading in India and China." *Studies in Comparative International Development* 40 (2): 35–61.

Schein, E. 2010. *Organizational Culture and Leadership*. 4th ed. John Wiley. ISBN 978-0-470-18586-5.

Sheffer, G. 2003. *Diaspora Politics. At Home Abroad*. Cambridge: Cambridge University Press.

Stenholm, P., Z. J. Acs, and R. Wuebker. 2013. "Exploring Country-Level Institutional Arrangements on the Rate and Type of Entrepreneurial Activity." *Journal of Business Venturing* 28 (1): 176–193.

Tang, J., K. M. Kacmar, and L. Busenitz. 2012. "Entrepreneurial Alertness in the Pursuit of new Opportunities." *Journal of Business Venturing* 27 (1): 77–94.

Terjesen, S., and A. Elam. 2009. "Transnational Entrepreneurs' Venture Internationalization Strategies: A Practice Theory Approach." *Entrepreneurship Theory and Practice* 33 (5): 1093–1120.

Waldinger, R., H. Aldrich, and R. Ward. 1990. "Opportunities, Group Characteristics and Strategies." In *Ethnic Entrepreneurs: Immigrant Business in Industrial Societies*, edited by R. Waldinger, H. Aldrich, and R. Ward, 13–48. London: Sage.

Waldinger, R., and D. Fitzgerald. 2004. "Transnationalism in Question." *American Journal of Sociology* 109: 1177–1195.

Whitley, R. 1992. *Business Systems in East Asia: Firms, Markets and Societies*. London: Sage.

Wyrwich, M., R. Sternberg, and M. Stuetzer. 2018. "Failing Role Models and the Formation of Fear of Entrepreneurial Failure: a Study of Regional Peer Effects in German Regions." *Journal of Economic Geography*. doi:10.1093/jeg/lby023.

Zapata-Barrero, R., and S. Rezaei. 2020. "Diaspora Governance and Transnational Entrepreneurship: The Rise of an Emerging Social Global Pattern in Migration Studies." *Journal of Ethnic and Migration Studies* 46 (10): 1959–1973. doi:10.1080/1369183X.2018.1559990.

The mixed embeddedness of transnational migrant entrepreneurs: Moroccans in Amsterdam and Milan

Giacomo Solano

ABSTRACT
This article addresses transnational migrant entrepreneurship – migrant entrepreneurs establishing businesses that span across borders. The article contributes to this field by applying the mixed embeddedness approach and revisiting it from a transnational perspective. The article uses an overall qualitative approach and analyses the case of Moroccan transnational entrepreneurs in Milan and Amsterdam (N = 35). This illustrates that, on the one hand, institutional embeddedness in different contexts (country of residence, country of origin, and other countries) influences respondents' business patterns through the opportunities and the constraints created by the political-institutional and economic features of these contexts. On the other hand, transnational entrepreneurs take advantage of their (often, previously-acquired) heterogeneous contacts (social embeddedness) and skills (e.g. linguistic knowledge, previous work experience) to conduct their business.

Introduction

Over the last thirty years, globalisation processes have changed contemporary society. New possibilities for communication and travel (Castells 1996; Elliott and Urry 2010) encourage people to build and maintain social relations with other people in different countries, and to access information from different places and contexts. Migrants develop new links and new contacts, but often keep their old ones as well. They are also exposed to new contexts, new habits and new opportunities. Migrants can use these connections and opportunities to carry out entrepreneurial activities with links outside their country of residence (Portes, Guarnizo, and Haller 2002; Levitt and Jaworsky 2007; Bagwell 2015).

In this changing global and migratory landscape (Castles, de Hass, and Miller 2014), it is thus relevant to focus on transnational business practices in order to understand how such new options have re-defined entrepreneurial practices. The field of transnational migrant entrepreneurship addresses this topic, namely migrant-owned entrepreneurial activities which do business in at least two countries – the country of residence and another country, often that of origin (Portes, Guarnizo, and Haller 2002; Drori, Honig, and Wright 2009; Honig, Drori, and Carmichael 2010). Therefore, transnational migrant entrepreneurs focus on other markets apart from that of their context of residence. Examples are import/export businesses or couriers (see, e.g. Ambrosini [2012]).

Focusing on transnational entrepreneurship seems particularly important because *the* literature shows that transnational migrant entrepreneurship seems to entail more profitable and more successful businesses than other experiences of migrant entrepreneurship (Portes, Guarnizo, and Haller 2002; Kariv et al. 2009; Wang and Liu 2015; Rath and Schutjens 2016).

The main questions are, what factors influence transnational migrant entrepreneurs, and what resources do they employ (Rath, Solano, and Schutjens 2019). As noted by Bagwell (2018), despite the fact that a good number of studies have addressed this topic (Portes, Guarnizo, and Haller 2002; Drori, Honig, and Wright 2009; Elo and Freiling 2015; Solano 2015; Rezaei, Light, and Telles 2016), an overall analysis of the driving factors and the resources employed for such businesses is still underexplored. Apart from a few exceptions (e.g. Portes, Guarnizo, and Haller 2002; Brzozowski, Cucculelli, and Surdej 2017; Bagwell 2018), the existing literature on transnational entrepreneurship has focused mainly either on individual characteristics and social networks (e.g. Portes, Guarnizo, and Haller 2002; Kariv et al. 2009; Patel and Conklin 2009; Terjesen and Elam 2009), or on contextual conditions and opportunities (e.g. Riddle, Hrivnak, and Nielsen 2010; Urbano, Toledano, and Ribeiro-Soriano 2011).

Therefore, this article aims to answer the following research question: *What are the factors influencing the transnational entrepreneurial patterns of migrants, and what resources do transnational migrant entrepreneurs employ to conduct their business?*

To answer these questions, the article applies a transnational mixed embeddedness approach (Bagwell 2018). The mixed embeddedness approach from Kloosterman and Rath (2001) provides a comprehensive theoretical framework by combining various levels of analysis (embeddedness in the context; embeddedness in social networks; individual characteristics). Indeed, the application of the mixed embeddedness approach allows us to fully grasp the phenomenon, and the factors influencing it.

Through 35 in-depth interviews, the article analyses the case of Moroccan transnational entrepreneurs in Amsterdam and Milan. I first introduce the mixed embeddedness approach. Then, I present the research on Moroccan transnational entrepreneurs in Amsterdam and Milan, and the findings from it. The article concludes with a discussion of these, together with some final remarks.

Conceptual approach: from mixed embeddedness to transnational mixed embeddedness

Embeddedness has been a powerful concept in explaining the economic activities of migrants (Portes and Sensenbrenner 1993), and, in particular, their entrepreneurial activities (Kloosterman 2010; Ram, Jones, and Villares-Varela 2017). The concept of embeddedness starts from the theoretical conviction that economic action is not driven only by individual and economic calculation; on the contrary, it is strongly structured by social contexts such as networks, institutions, norms and values (see Polanyi 1957; Granovetter 1985).

The concept has mainly been employed with regard to social networks (following Granovetter's definition, see Granovetter [1985], [2017]) – embeddedness in social relations, which influence the economic and entrepreneurial activities of migrants. However, a number of conceptual approaches and empirical studies in the field have addressed embeddedness in place-bounded institutions (following Polanyi's definition, see Polanyi [1957]).

Dutch scholars Kloosterman and Rath (Kloosterman, van der Leun, and Rath 1999; Kloosterman and Rath 2001) combined these two versions of embeddedness by introducing the so-called 'mixed embeddedness approach', which is now the leading approach in the field of migrant entrepreneurship (Ram, Jones, and Villares-Varela 2017). The approach rests on the assumption that migrants' entrepreneurial activities are influenced by:

(a) the structure (laws, rules, market characteristics, etc.) of the places where they live and conduct their business (*institutional embeddedness*);
(b) their social network – the contacts they have (*social embeddedness*);
(c) their human capital (skills and experiences).

The entrepreneurs' mixed embeddedness – namely, the combination of institutional and social embeddedness –, and the interplay between this and their human capital influence their entrepreneurial patterns (choice of sector, business performance, internationalisation, etc.). Therefore, by applying a mixed embeddedness approach, one can acquire an overall picture of the resources employed and the factors influencing transnational entrepreneurship.

Despite some exceptions (Miera 2008; Rusinovic 2008; Jones, Ram, and Theodorakopoulos 2010; Katila and Wahlbeck 2012; Bagwell 2015, 2018; Brzozowski, Cucculelli, and Surdej 2017) the focus of mixed embeddedness has so far been the country of residence. Given that migration trajectories have become more complex and varied (Castles, de Hass, and Miller 2014) and migrant communities have now spread all over the world (Levitt and Jaworsky 2007; Bauböck and Faist 2010), some authors suggested a shift in the mixed embeddedness approach (Schiller and Çağlar 2013; Solano 2016a; Bagwell 2018) in order to also incorporate the transnational level of the migrant entrepreneurial experience. In this vein, Bagwell (2018) called for a '*transnational mixed embeddedness*' approach. This aims at broadening the scope of the mixed embeddedness approach by expanding the focus from the country of residence to the country of origin and the countries where the diaspora is settled. This means that entrepreneurs might be *transnationally* embedded from both an institutional and a social standpoint. From the institutional standpoint (institutional embeddedness), transnational migrant entrepreneurs (henceforth, transnational entrepreneurs, for the sake of simplicity) have to deal with, and are influenced by, the institutional regimes and the market conditions of multiple places. Morawska (2004) and Miera (2008) highlighted the importance of the policies of the country of residence and the country of origin, and the relations between them, in shaping the degree of transnationalism of the business activity.

From the relational standpoint (social embeddedness), transnational entrepreneurs might have a transnational social capital, which can be used for the business. Insertion in social networks appears to be particularly important, especially in terms of taking advantage of contacts abroad (Portes, Guarnizo, and Haller 2002; Terjesen and Elam 2009; Jones, Ram, and Theodorakopoulos 2010; Valenzuela-García et al. 2014; Bagwell 2015).

Finally, the human capital of migrants is intrinsically transnational, since they have lived in different countries, they speak several languages, and they – formally or informally – have acquired skills in different countries. Differences in the skills possessed by an entrepreneur can influence the business outcomes connected to his/her institutional and social embeddedness (Portes, Guarnizo, and Haller 2002; Kariv et al. 2009; Patel and Conklin 2009).

Methodology

The research focuses on Moroccan entrepreneurs who own a transnational business, namely transnational entrepreneurs, who are:

> individuals who migrate from one country to another, concurrently maintaining business-related linkages with their former country of origin, and currently adopted countries and communities. By traveling both physically and virtually, ... (they) simultaneously engage in two or more socially embedded environments, allowing them to maintain critical global relations that enhance their ability to creatively, dynamically, and logistically maximize their resource base (Drori, Honig, and Wright 2009, 1001).

This study adopts a micro-level perspective in that it considers the individual experiences, strategies, networks, and narratives of fist-generation Moroccan transnational entrepreneurs who have migrated to Milan or Amsterdam. This research focuses on one national group across two cities in two national contexts, to understand how transnational practices may vary according to structural and institutional situations in different contexts.

The Moroccan group is one of the most significant migrant groups in both Amsterdam and Milan. Morocco is also a country with a stable political situation (see, e.g. Arieff [2015]). If this were not the case, political conditions might have discouraged links with the country of origin (Portes, Guarnizo, and Haller 2002; Baltar and Icart 2013).

Background to the study

Amsterdam and Milan present a combination of similarities and dissimilarities that are fruitful for the objective of this research.

The two cities play a key economic role in their country (Bontje and Sleutjes 2007; Mingione et al. 2007). Amsterdam (and Northern-Holland) is the Dutch central point for services and logistics (Bontje and Sleutjes 2007), and the service sector dominates the economy of Amsterdam (Kloosterman 2014). Milan (and, more generally, Lombardy) still has a strong industrial vocation (due to the presence of many SMEs), and it is a central node of import-export flows (Mingione et al. 2007). These create different opportunity structures for migrants. In Amsterdam, there are more opportunities in the service sectors (e.g. consultancy businesses), while the industrial/trade sector is still strong in Milan (Bontje and Sleutjes 2007; Mingione et al. 2007; Kloosterman 2014).

Furthermore, although the two cities have a considerable number of migrant residents, they differ in their migratory history, and in the size of their migrant populations. Amsterdam and the Netherlands have a longer tradition of being places of immigration (since 1960s) in comparison with Milan and Italy (since the late 1980s) (Colombo and Sciortino 2004; Rath 2009; Bijwaard 2010).

As a result of the different migration history, the migrant population in the two cities is partially different. Both cities have a considerable number of migrant residents, but the number of people of Moroccan background is higher in Amsterdam than in Milan.[1] The Moroccan group in the two cities is different in size and incidence: about 19,145 people in the Milan area (0.6% of the total population)[2] as opposed to 75,758 people in the Amsterdam area (9% of the total population).[3] The different migration history and number of Moroccan people might create different 'structures' and conditions in the country of residence, which in turn influences both transnational and entrepreneurial activities (Wang and Li 2007).

As for numbers of migrant entrepreneurs in the two cities, in Amsterdam foreign entrepreneurs are about 33% (Rath and Eurofound 2011), and in Milan this percentage is 27.9%.[4] There are about 3,109 Moroccan entrepreneurs in the Milan area, i.e. 2.5% of all entrepreneurs in the city.[5] Unfortunately, data sorted by nationality are not available for Amsterdam. However, just as an indication, there are 8,400 Moroccan entrepreneurs in the Netherlands (i.e. 0.6% of all entrepreneurs).[6]

Methods and sampling strategy

Overall, the approach is qualitative, employing in-depth face-to-face interviews. As noted by Bagwell (2018), this was considered the most appropriate to study this phenomenon, since an in-depth understanding of the patterns of transnational entrepreneurs and the factors influencing these was still needed. This allowed me to collect narratives regarding how migrants conduct their business. I also applied personal network analysis (Crossley et al. 2015) to collect information about entrepreneurs' networks.

A purposive sample was chosen based on qualitative typologies (Silverman 2000), which means that entrepreneurs were selected based on the different types of business within the category of Moroccan entrepreneurs with a transnational business.

In order to obtain a more comprehensive picture of Moroccan entrepreneurial activities in each city, different methods and sources were used to identify respondents: (1) a list provided by the Chamber of Commerce, with the indication of the business sector (e.g. import/export) and information on the business activities (in Milan only, as no list was available in Amsterdam); (2) contacts from Moroccan associations with a relevant role in the Moroccan group (e.g. Moroccan business networks and Islamic cultural associations); (3) entrepreneurs' business cards left in shops as advertisements; (4) the visibility of the business in the street.

By means of these strategies, 35 entrepreneurs running a transnational business[7] were interviewed (20 in Milan and 15 in Amsterdam). As emerged from the fieldwork conducted for the research, it is important to note that transnational businesses represent only a small part of total entrepreneurial activities carried out by Moroccans in Amsterdam and Milan. For example, based on the fieldwork, I estimated that there were only approximately 30 Moroccan entrepreneurs running a transnational business in Milan.

Table 1. Characteristics of the respondents and their businesses

	Amsterdam	Milan	Total
Gender			
Male	12	14	26
Female	3	6	9
Education[1]			
Low	1	6	7
Medium	4	8	12
High	10	6	16
Type of business			
Import/export	8	17	25
Consultancy	7	3	10
Number of employees			
0	6	3	9
1–3	6	14	20
>3	3	3	6
Total	15	20	35

[1]Low: none, primary school education, or junior secondary education; medium: professional or vocational diploma or High school degree; high: university degree or higher.

The interviews were conducted from September 2013 to November 2014 and these interviews lasted from one hour and a half to three hours. Besides socio-demographic information, questions regarding the entrepreneurial experience, daily working practices, business links, and resources used were investigated.

Entrepreneurs' profile

As illustrated in Table 1, the majority of the interviewees were male ($n = 26$), middle-aged (40 years old), with a medium-high level of education. The Amsterdam sample had a higher level of education than the Milan sample, which is consistent with the most recent figures from the OECD (2010, 2017). Respondent had decided to migrate for economic reasons or as a result of their parents' decision. Even though the Moroccan political situation was not very good in the past, during the interviews respondents mentioned that political persecution was not one of the reasons behind their emigration.

In keeping with the population trend, which emerged from the preparatory work before the fieldwork (Solano 2016a)– figures on transnational businesses were not available –, entrepreneurs owned businesses in both the goods-related sectors (specifically, import and/or export businesses – $N = 25$), and service sector (specifically, consultancy businesses – $N = 15$). The majority of businesses in Milan were in the import/export sector, while in Amsterdam there were also a relevant number of consultancy businesses. Respondents usually owned rather small companies: less than 20% had more than four employees.

Findings: the mixed embeddedness of transnational Moroccan entrepreneurs

Transnational entrepreneurial activities of Moroccan migrants in Amsterdam and Milan clearly emerge – even more so than for migrant entrepreneurship in general (Ram, Jones, and Villares-Varela 2017) – from their institutional embeddedness in the context(s), their social embeddedness, and the entrepreneurs' skills (human capital). It follows that, if I had not applied a mixed embeddedness approach and taken into account all aspects of this combination, I would not have been able to fully understand the processes involved in transnational entrepreneurship.

In general, Moroccan entrepreneurs in both Amsterdam and Milan are connected to different countries, and they have a multifocal perspective (Solano 2016b). They have links with multiple places, rather than bi-focal links, as suggested by most of the existing literature (Levitt and Jaworsky 2007).

Apart from the country of residence (Italy/the Netherlands), they have business links both with Morocco and with other countries (16/35), while a minority have contacts either with Morocco (10/35) or other countries (9/35) only. These links are mainly with Morocco, European countries where there is a high number of Moroccan migrants (e.g. Belgium and France), and Arab-speaking countries (North Africa, e.g. Egypt and Tunisia, and the Middle East, e.g. the United Arab Emirates and Saudi Arabia). The variety of countries that respondents are in contact with shows the multi-located (and not only bi-located) nature of their businesses.

Institutional embeddedness

The relevance of institutional embeddedness clearly emerges from the interviews; respondents stress the importance of the contextual features in which they are embedded, as mentioned by M. (M02), who produces fashion clothes which are then exported abroad: 'I could never have started my business in another city or country. Italy and Milan are the natural location for my business. Milan is very advanced in the fashion industry'.

The ME approach (Kloosterman and Rath 2001) identifies two spheres influencing migrants' entrepreneurial activities: political-institutional conditions (laws, rules, policies and politics); economic and market conditions (e.g. economic phases, industrial and productive structures, market concentration, and demand for particular products or services). The conditions in the country of residence, that of origin and other countries might play an important role (Solano 2016b; Zapata-Barrero and Rezaei 2020). This is the case of Moroccan entrepreneurs in Amsterdam and Milan.

Country of residence (Italy and the Netherlands)

The respondents described how the institutional and economic/market conditions of Amsterdam/the Netherlands and Milan/Italy played a role in shaping their business activities. The economic context seemed particularly powerful in influencing respondents' entrepreneurial patterns. Amsterdam's service-oriented economy (see Kloosterman, 2014) informed the decision to start a consultancy agency for Moroccan entrepreneurs there; in Milan, the strong industrial vocation led Moroccan entrepreneurs with a transnational business to focus more on the import/export sector.[8] In Amsterdam, respondents seemed keener to engage in the business-oriented service sector, while in Milan they tended to focus more on the goods-related sector (production or trade of goods).

Besides this, Moroccan entrepreneurs seized opportunities that emerged firstly in connection with their co-nationals' customs (e.g. consumer habits such as the demand for Moroccan tea or Moroccan food). The effect of these partially differs between the two cities. In Amsterdam, where there is a more numerous Moroccan group than in Milan, their co-nationals' customs lead entrepreneurs to import products from abroad and sell them at a national level. For example, J. (A20) provides fabrics and curtains for interior decorating, which he imports from Morocco because 'the fabrics are different from what I would be able to find in the Netherlands'. In Milan, their co-nationals' customs lead them to import products from abroad and export the products to other countries where there are greater numbers of Moroccan migrants (e.g. Belgium and France). This is also linked to the acknowledgement of the quality of Italian products, as explained by A. (M15), who sells Arab sofas wholesale:

> I knew that my co-nationals liked Arab furniture for their living rooms. They want to have high-quality products, manufactured here in Italy, but with a connection with Morocco. [...] I sell my products in Italy but I also export a lot of furniture abroad, especially in Europe, in countries where there are many of my co-nationals. (M15)

The production system of the country of residence, together with the demand for such products abroad, leads many entrepreneurs to export goods from Italy (e.g. industrial machinery; foods; clothing) and the Netherlands (e.g. trucks, flowers). For example, R. (M09) exports Italian machinery. Her business is particularly successful because many companies request Italian machinery for its high quality. Similarly, B. (A14) has a consultancy firm that helps companies from MENA (Middle Eastern and North African) countries, and in particular from the Arab Peninsula, to buy vehicles (trucks and vans) from the Netherlands and Germany, two countries where the production of these is particular advanced.

Consultancy businesses also take advantage of requests by many companies in the Netherlands and Italy wishing to expand their business to Morocco and other MENA countries. This is the case of many consultancy agencies, such as A.'s (M40), which helps Italian companies to establish contacts with people and other companies in those countries. Similarly, A. (A11) owns a consultancy business specialised in helping companies to start a business in Morocco.

The political and institutional contexts in the countries of residence seem to affect the business less than the economic conditions. Almost none of the interviewees mentioned any particular laws, regulations or institutional initiatives that helped or hindered their entrepreneurial activity. However, this underestimation of the effect of laws and regulations could be linked to the fact that respondents had overcome these particular barriers with ease (Kloosterman, van der Leun, and Rath 1999).

Institutional initiatives, such as policies to promote business start-ups or business internationalisation, do not appear to be incisive enough to create relevant opportunities. This is because policies are often inadequate and insufficient compared to the number of requests or the needs of entrepreneurs, especially when the target group is not limited to migrants:

> When I started, I tried to get some help but it was impossible. The Chamber of Commerce tries to do something but Milan is big and there are so many companies. The Region also offers some vouchers; there are vouchers for the internationalisation of the company, for example. The problem is that, on some very specific days, you have to go there early and wait. But all the available vouchers are used up immediately. So I didn't get any. (M02)

Respondents did not seem to be aware of policies targeting vulnerable people and areas. In the Netherlands, some years before the study, there was an initiative called IntEnt (Riddle,

Hrivnak, and Nielsen 2010), aimed at fostering business connections between the Netherlands and other countries (Morocco, Ghana and Suriname). However, none of the respondents were aware, or took advantage, of this. In Milan, there was a very interesting initiative called 'Tira su la Cler' [Open up your Shop] from the City of Milan (Barberis et al. 2017). This initiative consisted in offering help to start businesses in poor and disadvantaged areas of the city. However, only one respondent was aware of this, and almost all the respondents stated that there were no supporting policies from the government.

Country of origin (Morocco)

The role of the country of origin (especially in terms of the institutional setting) has rarely been analysed in-depth in the previous literature on transnational entrepreneurs (Zapata-Barrero and Rezaei 2020). In the case of Moroccan entrepreneurs, although mainly from an economic standpoint, respondents underlined how powerful the role of Morocco was in influencing their entrepreneurial patterns.

Many entrepreneurs in Amsterdam and Milan were influenced by, and took advantage of, the fact that Morocco specialises in making Arab products (e.g. particular types of food, furnishings, and furniture). For example, A. (A05) retails dresses and perfumes to a clientele of co-nationals in Amsterdam. He imports most of the goods from Morocco because these products are more common in that country: 'Most of the products I sell are only obtainable there, some in Morocco and some only in Saudi Arabia. It would be much more difficult to get these products here in the Netherlands.' (A05)

Furthermore, people in Morocco request particular products (e.g. clothes, shoes, furniture, foods). This works especially well for entrepreneurs in Milan since Italian products are generally well-known abroad. For example, B. (M01) exports Italian clothes, shoes and textiles to Morocco, where Italian products are highly in demand. He buys these goods in different regions, and he sends them to Morocco. Similarly, A. (M10) exports hydraulic and construction products to Morocco. He takes advantage of the demand for these and, more precisely, the lack of such high-quality products on the market in his city of origin.

From an institutional standpoint, as noted by Gabrielli and Franco-Guillén (2018), although the Moroccan government has implemented several initiatives targeting Moroccan emigrants – e.g. the FINCOME (the International Forum of Moroccan Skills Abroad) and the MDM (*Marocains du Monde*) Invest Fund –, those initiatives have not been very successful, especially with regard to Moroccan migrants in Italy and the Netherlands. Figures from the MDM fund showed that the majority of beneficiaries were from France, Belgium and Canada (Gabrielli and Franco-Guillén 2018). Entrepreneurs in both Amsterdam and Milan have underlined that they perceived such governmental initiatives and polices as very far from their interests. For example, H. (M06) states that 'in Morocco you always need to know someone, otherwise you do not go forward. The same is true with initiatives from the government'. Similarly, the role played by the Banque Populaire-Chaabi Bank in supporting transnational Moroccan businesses was not very relevant, as underlined by N. (M15): 'they [the bank] do not finance us; they look at the big companies, and they are not interested in our small businesses'. This confirms what Gabrielli and Franco-Guillén (2018) underlined regarding the Spanish situation.

Other countries

Apart from the country of residence (Italy/the Netherlands) and Morocco, respondents take advantage of, and are influenced by, the context of other countries. From an economic standpoint, they take advantage of the economic situation of certain countries to escape from the European economic crisis. For example, many entrepreneurs maintain business relations with Arab countries – especially with those in the Arab Peninsula –, where the economy is flourishing and demand for certain products is high (e.g. flowers from the Netherlands; industrial machineries from Italy). S. (A26), for example, sells decorative flowers to luxury hotels and restaurants in Dubai. In Europe, respondents take advantage of the request for Moroccan products by Moroccan migrants abroad. Indeed, the majority of business links are with countries with a big Moroccan group. For example, M. (M13) and M. (M16) export Arab living room furniture to other European countries such as Belgium and France, since Moroccans who live there create a demand for these products.

From an institutional standpoint, the free movement of goods and persons at the European level profoundly impacts the entrepreneurial patterns of the respondents. For their business, they are connected to many European countries and they often travel around Europe. M. (M07) is a case in point. He has a company that trades in various products. He imports tea and bazaar goods (such as fabrics, sheets, household products, etc.) from China to Italy (for Moroccans and other migrants), and he exports Italian products to various other countries (e.g. Belgium and France). He uses the possibilities offered by the free movement of persons and goods in Europe in different ways. When he started, he used to travel back and forth from France (by train or by car), exporting Italian products there and importing products for Moroccan migrants in Italy. Furthermore, he had had some problems with regulations linked to the international side of his business. He encountered difficulties when he wanted to import tea from China, because it did not meet Italian requirements. He finally resolved the situation by first importing the tea to France, where he has a branch of his business and where the rules are less strict, and then to Italy.

To sum up, embeddedness in different contexts (institutional embeddedness) influences transnational activities through the opportunities and constraints created by the political-institutional and economic features of these contexts.

Social embeddedness: transnational bridging social capital, with a strong role played by relatives

Beside institutional embeddedness, the mixed embeddedness approach stresses the importance of social embeddedness; the entrepreneurs' embeddedness in their social networks, which constitute their social capital. Transnational entrepreneurs need a set of social contacts in order to be active in multiple contexts and run a transnational business (Chen and Tan 2009). Embeddedness in different kinds of networks can have different effects on entrepreneurial activities (Portes and Sensenbrenner 1993; Anthias and Cederberg 2009; Patel and Conklin 2009).

Respondents have rather geographically-dispersed, non-homogeneous networks of people. They have business relations with them (e.g. exchanging products; providing, or receiving services) or they receive support from them (e.g. receiving information or help in conducting their business).

In the interviews, respondents made it clear that they had a transnational social capital; they used contacts located in different countries to conduct their business. They combined people from their country of residence (58.5% of total contacts mentioned, $N = 575$) and abroad (41.5%). Interestingly, the majority of their contacts abroad did not live in Morocco (27.2% out the total number of contacts lived in a third country, while only 14.3% were in Morocco).

Furthermore, they showed a capacity for bridging different kinds of people. Respondents made use of what the literature calls 'bridging social capital' (Putnam 2000; Baron 2015). Respondents had a mix of people of different national backgrounds among their contacts. The majority of these were of Moroccan background (43.7%), followed by people of other nationalities (29.3%). Natives of the country of residence represented 27.1% of the contacts.

The types of contacts also varied in terms of emotional closeness (Lubbers, Molina, and McCarty 2007; Vacca et al. 2018). Respondents combined weak ties (which were 65.2% of their total contacts), namely people with whom the entrepreneurs had no emotionally-close relations (Granovetter 1973), and strong ties (34.8%) – mainly relatives, but also friends.

Despite this, the role of family is still fundamental, even beyond what numbers show: relatives represent 12.8% of total contacts mentioned. Relatives are persons who can be trusted and on whom the migrants can rely for their business. In particular, they support transnational entrepreneurs in managing the foreign side of their business, and they also provide key pieces of information. M. (M06), for example, is a case in point. He owns a wholesale business of fruits and vegetables, which are mainly imported from Spain:

> My brother lives in Barcelona. Thanks to him I obtained all the information. He also has direct contacts with the suppliers there. He usually buys the fruit, he arranges everything and then he sends the fruit to Milan. (M06)

The importance of relatives – and of strong ties in general – is also due to the fact that they allow respondents to bridge different contacts and opportunities. This is well explained by A. (A18), who has a shop of traditional Moroccan women's clothing: 'That is a process of networking. I heard about certain individuals through family members or friends and I contacted them through relatives' (A18). Therefore, strong ties can represent links with weak ties operating in a wider social context (e.g. outside the residence country). The importance of relatives for building a bridging social capital was previously underlined by Katila and Wahlbeck (2012) in their study on Chinese and Turkish businesses in Finland. To start their businesses, Turkish entrepreneurs took advantage of the social capital made available by their Finnish spouses.

However, it is important to underline that entrepreneurs who conduct their businesses in connection with countries other than Morocco or those where there is a relevant group of Moroccan migrants, rely more on weak ties and less on relatives; they also have a higher number of co-nationals in their business networks.

Furthermore, a large group of these contacts was already present in the entrepreneur's network before the business start-up (40.3%), and so was not acquired in connection with the business. These contacts that pre-dated the business start-up were acquired mainly for work purposes (44%) or because they were relatives (28%). The findings suggest that entrepreneurs' contacts shaped their decision to either embark on a transnational business venture or to focus on a strictly domestic market:

> Many people I met before the business support me, both Italians and other migrants. Moreover, I rely on a number of Moroccan acquaintances for the part linked to Morocco. Most of these are friends from school or university. Now they have important jobs in the public or private sector. (M40)

> I chose Morocco and Jordan because I had reliable connections over there. I lived there for a long time, so I built up a huge network over there; it was easy, because I lived there. (A04)

This is a new finding, since previous studies have generally not considered temporality, and it underlines the fact that their networks led Moroccan entrepreneurs to internationalise their business, and not the other way around. This is in line with literature on mobility (Vandenbrande 2006; Recchi and Favell 2009), which underlines that the degree of rootedness in the local context affects the degree of transnationalism and mobility. That is, the more the migrant has contacts spread around the world, the more he or she engages in transnational (business) activities.

To sum up, their embeddedness in transnational heterogeneous networks allowed respondents to bridge different people from different places (transnational bridging social capital). In doing so, the role of family and strong ties remained central, as previously underlined by Bagwell (2008). The importance of this (transnational) social embeddedness is particularly evident as a relevant group of migrant entrepreneurs' contacts pre-dated the business start-up.

Transnational human capital

Transnational Moroccan entrepreneurs need to have certain individual characteristics that allow them to conduct their business. Both education and previous work experience – and the combination of these – are fundamental to have the right skills to conduct the business. Respondents generally had a level of education that equipped them with the skills necessary to manage an international business. They often had a degree in management, economics, or international business.

Furthermore, it appears that past work experience increases awareness of opportunities in a particular business sector. Moroccan entrepreneurs normally had previous work experience in a transnational environment. This provides the entrepreneur with the knowledge of a given sector and, often, with key contacts, as illustrated by the fact that 44% of entrepreneurs' contacts known before the business start-up were known for work purposes (see 'social embeddedness' section).

B. (A14) is a case in point. He 'worked for six years as an account manager in two trucking companies, both times in a department dealing with the Middle East and North Africa'. Thanks to his past work experience he developed the knowledge and the portfolio of clients to start his own consultancy agency in the same field. He is now a consultant for companies who wish to buy trucks and other vehicles from Germany and the Netherlands. However, his education also allowed him to take advantage of his past work experience. He studied Business and this helped him manage his company: 'I have a professional degree in Business; my degree has been very useful, since that's where I learned how to run a business'.

However, only a minority (9/35) combined education and work experience, or relied only on education (7/35), while a majority mainly took advantage of previous work experience (19/35). The trend seems to be that the most educated respondents tend to be in the consultancy business, while the ones that rely more on their previous work experience are more likely to be in the goods-related sector.

Linguistic skills are also fundamental. Respondents were generally able to speak at least one foreign language besides that of their country of residence (27/35), and a relevant number (14/35) had good knowledge of two or more languages (commonly English or French, but also Chinese, German or Spanish). Besides English, which has become the international language for the respondents as well as for all kinds of businesspeople, the most important language was Arabic. This allowed respondents to take advantage of the opportunities available in both Morocco and other countries, such as MENA countries. For example, A. (M40) had a consultancy business helping companies enter the market of MENA countries. During the interview, he underlined that 'to help companies that want to enter new markets I mainly exploit my knowledge of the Arabic language. It is fundamental'.

Respondents had a 'transnational linguistic capital' (Gerhards 2012), meaning that they knew other languages besides their mother tongue and the language of their country of residence. Having a transnational linguistic capital allowed them to be involved in transnational entrepreneurial activities. Indeed, fluency in several languages provided them with the skills they needed to maintain links with countries other than just Morocco.

It would be easy to hypothesise that these language skills are connected to the transnational business itself, namely that respondents had developed their language skills while running their business. However, the findings contradict this conclusion. Respondents usually knew several languages before starting a business: 'I can speak several languages. I always thought they were important, and I always invested in languages, even before opening my business' (A09). They usually learned these before the start-up of their business (at school, thanks to past work experience, or following personal interest). Another example is R. (M09), who exports Italian machinery to companies outside Italy. To handle the business, she needs to speak Arabic, English and Italian. Before starting the business, she had some experience with all three languages because she worked for an airline company:

> I was working at the airport ... so I spoke several languages, English mainly and also Italian, of course ... and I am a native speaker of Arabic. So I have the perfect profile for this kind of business. (M09)

Conclusions

The article applies the mixed embeddedness approach to the study of transnational migrant entrepreneurship. The study represents an endeavour in taking into account different elements that may influence transnational entrepreneurship: institutional embeddedness; social embeddedness; human capital (individual skills and experience).

Furthermore, as suggested by Bagwell (2018), the geographical scope of mixed embeddedness has been widened in order to take into account factors from the country of residence, the country of origin and other countries. By taking into consideration several contexts, the article sheds further light on the role of migrant embeddedness in contexts different from their country of residence (institutional embeddedness), and in networks of people living outside of it (social embeddedness). Overall, the article shows that, in order to truly understand the phenomenon, it is necessary to take into account several levels as well as the interplay between these levels. Focusing only on one aspect would have prevented us from fully understanding the resources employed by transnational entrepreneurs.

Their institutional embeddedness in several contexts, as well as the combination of social embeddedness and individual human capital, is the key to running a transnational business. Indeed, transnational entrepreneurship emerges as a combination of these three levels. The institutional embeddedness of Moroccan entrepreneurs influences them through the opportunities and the constraints created by the characteristics of these contexts. The characteristics of different contexts (the country of residence, the home country and other countries) and the combination of these shape transnational entrepreneurial patterns of migrants.

Opportunities are identified and seized thanks to their relational embeddedness, namely insertion in networks that are made up of different people (a mix of strong and weak ties; people with national background) and from different places (contacts that are geographically dispersed). The presence of geographically-dispersed and heterogeneous contacts does not make the relevance of family (and, more in general, of emotionally-close contacts) any lower. The importance of family completes the picture of Moroccan entrepreneurs who combine transnational networking strategies and have links with different kinds of contacts with deep embeddedness in (parts) of networks made up of more local and emotionally-close contacts. Interestingly, a relevant part of the respondents' contacts were acquired before the business start-up, and this clearly illustrates how much social embeddedness influences transnational businesses.

Similarly, opportunities would not have been seized without respondents employing their human capital. On the one hand, education is important to manage the business properly, and language skills are fundamental to expand the scope of the business. On the other hand, part of the transnational social capital of entrepreneurs is linked to their human capital, often in terms of previous work experience, since 44% of the entrepreneurs' contacts from before the business start-up were known for work purposes.

All in all, Moroccan transnational entrepreneurs in our sample represent an emerging group which are, as underlined by Saxenian (1999, ix), 'uniquely positioned because their language skills and technical and cultural know-how allow them to function effectively', in both the country of destination, the country of origin and globally.

The article also has some limitations, which pave the way for further research. The main limitation is that it addresses one specific group of migrants. As underlined by Portes, Guarnizo, and Haller (2002), different national groups can develop different transnational and entrepreneurial activities. Therefore, other studies should compare various national groups of migrants (as was done by Portes, Guarnizo, and Haller 2002, in the US context).

The article illustrates certain findings regarding temporality and causality. However, I traced these through a number of questions regarding the past. A longitudinal study could shed further light on the dynamics at play between entrepreneur profile and transnational migrant entrepreneurship, and could determine whether certain skills and contacts actually predate the decision to start a transnational business.

In addition, the article indirectly suggests that, by linking several European and non-European countries, migrant entrepreneurs might be able to partially avoid the effects of the European economic crisis (on this topic see, e.g. Fellini [2018]). Further studies might address this topic and investigate whether transnational entrepreneurship represents a strategy to escape from economic crises in the country of residence.

In conclusion, this article addresses the issue of transnational entrepreneurship, by comparing transnational Moroccan entrepreneurs in Amsterdam and Milan and applying a transnational mixed embeddedness approach. In particular, it provides new insights regarding the combination of factors influencing transnational migrant entrepreneurs.

Notes

1. All Dutch figures include both first- and second-generation migrants. Italian statistics consider only people born outside Italy.
2. Figures provided by the Italian National Statistics Institute (ISTAT); reference year: 2017.
3. Figures provided by the Dutch Centraal Bureau voor de Statistiek (CBS); reference year: 2017.
4. Figures provided by the Chamber of Commerce of Milan; reference year: 2017.
5. Figures provided by the Chamber of Commerce of Milan; reference year: 2017.
6. Figures provided by the Chamber of Commerce of Amsterdam; reference year: 2009. No more recently updated data is available.
7. I also interviewed 35 entrepreneurs running a domestic business, i.e. focusing on the domestic market of their country of residence. However, in line with the research question, I focus on the transnational part of the sample in this article.
8. This emerged particularly during the preparatory work done by the author before the fieldwork (see Solano 2016a).

Acknowledgements

I wish to thank Alberta Andreotti, Eduardo Barberis and José Luis Molina for their constructive comments on the first draft of this article. I am grateful to Shahamak Rezaei and Ricard Zapata-Barrero for their valuable remarks during the IEMed Interdisciplinary Research Seminar.

Disclosure statement

No potential conflict of interest was reported by the author.

Funding

This work was supported by a doctoral scholarship from the Italian Ministry of Education and a mobility scholarship from the European Commission (Erasmus Placement/Erasmus+ Traineeship). Furthermore, Fondazione Roberto Franceschi Onlus and Fondazione Isacchi Samaja (Young Professional Grant – 2013 edition) provided the financial support for the fieldwork on which this article is based.

ORCID

Giacomo Solano http://orcid.org/0000-0003-2339-8181

References

Ambrosini, Maurizio. 2012. "Migrants'Entrepreneurship in Transnational Social Fields: Research in the Italian Context." *International Review of Sociology* 22 (2): 273–292. doi:10.1080/03906701.2012.696970.

Anthias, Floya, and Maja Cederberg. 2009. "Using Ethnic Bonds in Self-Employment and the Issue of Social Capital." *Journal of Ethnic and Migration Studies* 35 (6): 901–917. doi:10.1080/13691830902957692.

Arieff, Alexis. 2015. "Morocco: Current Issues." Congressional Research Service Report. Washington D.C.: U.S. Congressional Research Service.

Bagwell, Susan. 2008. "Transnational Family Networks and Ethnic Minority Business Development: The Case of Vietnamese Nail-Shops in the UK." *International Journal of Entrepreneurial Behaviour & Research* 14 (6): 377–394. doi:10.1108/13552550810910960.

Bagwell, Susan. 2015. "Transnational Entrepreneurship Amongst Vietnamese Businesses in London." *Journal of Ethnic and Migration Studies* 41 (2): 329–349. doi:10.1080/1369183X.2014.907739.

Bagwell, Susan. 2018. "From Mixed Embeddedness to Transnational Mixed Embeddedness: An Exploration of Vietnamese Businesses in London." *International Journal of Entrepreneurial Behavior & Research* 24 (1): 104–120. doi:10.1108/IJEBR-01-2017-0035.

Baltar, Fabiola, and Ignasi Brunet Icart. 2013. "Entrepreneurial Gain, Cultural Similarity and Transnational Entrepreneurship." *Global Networks* 13 (2): 200–220. doi:10.1111/glob.12020.

Barberis, Eduardo, Alba Angelucci, Ryan Jepson, and Yuri Kazepov. 2017. *Divercities: Dealing with Urban Diversity – The Case of Milan*. Utrecht: Utrecht University. Faculty of Geosciences.

Baron, Robert A. 2015. "Social Capital." In *Wiley Encyclopedia of Management*, edited by Cary L Cooper, 1–3. Chichester, UK: John Wiley & Sons, Ltd. doi:10.1002/9781118785317.weom030086.

Bauböck, Rainer, and Thomas Faist, eds. 2010. *Diaspora and Transnationalism: Concepts, Theories and Methods*. Amsterdam: Amsterdam University Press.

Bijwaard, Govert E. 2010. "Immigrant Migration Dynamics Model for The Netherlands." *Journal of Population Economics* 23 (4): 1213–1247. doi:10.1007/s00148-008-0228-1.

Bontje, Marco, and Bart Sleutjes. 2007. *Accomodating Creative Knowledge: A Literature Review from a European Perspective*. Amsterdam: University of Amsterdam, Amsterdam institute for Metropolitan and International Development Studies (AMIDSt).

Brzozowski, Jan, Marco Cucculelli, and Aleksander Surdej. 2017. "The Determinants of Transnational Entrepreneurship and Transnational Ties' Dynamics among Immigrant Entrepreneurs in ICT Sector in Italy." *International Migration* 55 (3): 105–125. doi:10.1111/imig.12335.

Castells, Manuel. 1996. *The Rise of The Network Society: The Information Age: Economy, Society and Culture*. Hoboken: Wiley.

Castles, Stephen, Hein de Hass, and Mark Miller. 2014. *The Age of Migration, Fifth Edition: International Population Movements in the Modern World*. 5th ed. New York: The Guilford Press.

Chen, Wenhong, and Justin Tan. 2009. "Understanding Transnational Entrepreneurship Through a Network Lens: Theoretical and Methodological Considerations." *Entrepreneurship Theory and Practice* 33 (5): 1079–1091. doi:10.1111/etap.2009.33.issue-5.

Colombo, Asher, and Giuseppe Sciortino. 2004. "Italian Immigration: The Origins, Nature and Evolution of Italy's Migratory Systems." *Journal of Modern Italian Studies* 9 (1): 49–70. doi:10.1080/1354571042000179182.

Crossley, Nick, Elisa Bellotti, Gemma Edwards, Martin Everett, Johan Koskinen, and Mark Tranmer. 2015. *Social Network Analysis for Ego-Nets*. London: Sage Publications.

Drori, Israel, Benson Honig, and Mike Wright. 2009. "Transnational Entrepreneurship: An Emergent Field of Study." *Entrepreneurship Theory and Practice* 33 (5): 1001–1022. doi:10.1111/j.1540-6520.2009.00332.x.

Elliott, Anthony, and John Urry. 2010. *Mobile Lives. London* . New York, NY: Routledge.

Elo, Maria, and Jörg Freiling. 2015. "Transnational Entrepreneurship: An Introduction to the Volume." *American Journal of Entrepreneurship* 8 (2): 1–8.

Fellini, Ivana. 2018. "Immigrants' Labour Market Outcomes in Italy and Spain: Has the Southern European Model Disrupted During the Crisis?" *Migration Studies* 6 (1): 53–78. doi:10.1093/migration/mnx029.

Gabrielli, Lorenzo, and Núria Franco-Guillén. 2018. "Transnational Diaspora Entrepreneuship: The Case of Moroccans in Catalonia." 7. GRITIM-UPF Policy Series. Barcelona: Universitat Pompeu Fabra.

Gerhards, Jürgen. 2012. From Babel to Brussels. European Integration and the Importance of Transnational Linguistic Capital. Berlin Studies on the Sociology of Europe 28. Berlin.

Granovetter, Mark. 1973. "The Strength of Weak Ties." *American Journal of Sociology* 78 (6): 1360–1380.

Granovetter, Mark. 1985. "Economic Action and Social Structure: The Problem of Embeddedness." *American Journal of Sociology* 91 (3): 481–510. doi:10.1086/228311.

Granovetter, Mark. 2017. *Society and Economy: Framework and Principles*. Cambridge, MA: Harvard University Press.

Honig, Benson, Israel Drori, and Barbara Anne Carmichael. 2010. *Transnational and Immigrant Entrepreneurship in a Globalized World*. Toronto: University of Toronto Press.

Jones, Trevor, Monder Ram, and Nick Theodorakopoulos. 2010. "Transnationalism as a Force for Ethnic Minority Enterprise? The Case of Somalis in Leicester: Transnationalism and Ethnic Minority Enterprise in the UK." *International Journal of Urban and Regional Research* 34 (3): 565–585. doi:10.1111/j.1468-2427.2010.00913.x.

Kariv, Dafna, Teresa V. Menzies, Gabrielle A. Brenner, and Louis Jacques Filion. 2009. "Transnational Networking and Business Performance: Ethnic Entrepreneurs in Canada." *Entrepreneurship & Regional Development* 21 (3): 239–264. doi:10.1080/08985620802261641.

Katila, Saija, and Östen Wahlbeck. 2012. "The Role of (Transnational) Social Capital in the Start-up Processes of Immigrant Businesses: The Case of Chinese and Turkish Restaurant Businesses in Finland." *International Small Business Journal* 30 (3): 294–309. doi:10.1177/0266242610383789.

Kloosterman, Robert. 2010. "Matching Opportunities with Resources: A Framework for Analysing (Migrant) Entrepreneurship From a Mixed Embeddedness Perspective." *Entrepreneurship & Regional Development* 22 (1): 25–45. doi:10.1080/08985620903220488.

Kloosterman, Robert. 2014. "Faces of Migration: Migrants and the Transformation of Amsterdam." In *Migration and London's Growth*, edited by B. Kochan, 127–142. London: LSE London.

Kloosterman, Robert, and Jan Rath. 2001. "Immigrant Entrepreneurs in Advanced Economies: Mixed Embeddedness Further Explored." *Journal of Ethnic and Migration Studies* 27 (2): 189–201. doi:10.1080/13691830020041561.

Kloosterman, Robert, Joanne van der Leun, and Jan Rath. 1999. "Mixed Embeddedness: (In)Formal Economic Activities and Immigrant Businesses in the Netherlands." *International Journal of Urban and Regional Research* 23 (2): 252–266. doi:10.1111/1468-2427.00194.

Levitt, Peggy, and B. Nadya Jaworsky. 2007. "Transnational Migration Studies: Past Developments and Future Trends." *Annual Review of Sociology* 33 (1): 129–156. doi:10.1146/annurev.soc.33.040406.131816.

Lubbers, Miranda Jessica, José Luis Molina, and Christopher McCarty. 2007. "Personal Networks and Ethnic Identifications: The Case of Migrants in Spain." *International Sociology* 22 (6): 721–741. doi:10.1177/0268580907082255.

Miera, Frauke. 2008. "Transnational Strategies of Polish Migrant Entrepreneurs in Trade and Small Business in Berlin." *Journal of Ethnic and Migration Studies* 34 (5): 753–770. doi:10.1080/13691830802106010.

Mingione, Enzo, Elena Dell'Agnese, Silvia Mugnano, Marianna d'Ovidio, Bertram Niessen, and Carla Sedini. 2007. *Milan City-Region Is It Still Competitive and Charming?: Pathways to Creative and Knowledge-Based Regions*. Amsterdam: AMIDSt, University of Amsterdam.

Morawska, Ewa. 2004. "Immigrant Transnational Entrepreneurs in New York: Three Varieties and Their Correlates." *International Journal of Entrepreneurial Behavior & Research* 10 (5): 325–348. doi:10.1108/13552550410554311.

OECD. 2010. *Open for Business*. Paris: OECD Publishing.
OECD. 2017. *Missing Entrepreneurs 2017: Policies for Inclusive Entrepreneurship*. Paris: OECD Publishing.
Patel, Pankaj C., and Betty Conklin. 2009. "The Balancing Act: The Role of Transnational Habitus and Social Networks in Balancing Transnational Entrepreneurial Activities." *Entrepreneurship Theory and Practice* 33 (5): 1045–1078. doi:10.1111/j.1540-6520.2009.00334.x.
Polanyi, Karl. 1957. "The Economy as an Instituted Process." In *Trade and Market in the Early Empires: Economies in History and Theory*, edited by Karl Polanyi, Conrad M. Arensberg, and Harry W. Pearson, 243–269. London: McMillan.
Portes, Alejandro, Luis Eduardo Guarnizo, and William J. Haller. 2002. "Transnational Entrepreneurs: An Alternative Form of Immigrant Economic Adaptation." *American Sociological Review* 67 (2): 278–298. doi:10.2307/3088896.
Portes, Alejandro, and Julia Sensenbrenner. 1993. "Embeddedness and Immigration: Notes on the Social Determinants of Economic Action." *American Journal of Sociology* 98 (6): 1320–1350. doi:10.1086/230191.
Putnam, Robert D. 2000. *Bowling Alone: The Collapse and Revival of American Community*. 1. touchstone ed. New York, NY: Simon & Schuster.
Ram, Monder, Trevor Jones, and María Villares-Varela. 2017. "Migrant Entrepreneurship: Reflections on Research and Practice." *International Small Business Journal* 35 (1): 3–18. doi:10.1177/0266242616678051.
Rath, Jan. 2009. "The Netherlands. A Reluctant Country of Immigration." *Tijdschrift Voor Economische En Sociale Geografie* 100 (5): 674–681. doi:10.1111/j.1467-9663.2009.00579.x.
Rath, Jan, and Eurofound. 2011. *Promoting Ethnic Entrepreneurship in European Cities*. Luxembourg: European Union.
Rath, Jan, and Veronique Schutjens. 2016. "Migrant Entrepreneurship: Alternative Paradigms of Economic Integration." In *Routledge Handbook of Immigration and Refugee Studies*, edited by Anna Triandafyllidou, 96–103. New York, NY: Routledge.
Rath, Jan, Giacomo Solano, and Veronique Schutjens. 2019 (in press). "Migrant Entrepreneurship: Alternative Paradigms of Economic Integration." In *Migrant Entrepreneurship and Transnational Links*, edited by C. Inglis, B. Khadria, and W. Li. The Sage Handbook of International Migration. Sage.
Recchi, Ettore, and Adrian Favell. 2009. *Pioneers of European Integration: Citizenship and Mobility in the EU*. Northampton, MA: Edward Elgar.
Rezaei, Shahamak, Ivan Light, and Edward Telles. 2016. "Editorial of the Special Issue on Brain Circulation and Transnational Entrepreneurship." *International Journal of Business and Globalisation* 16 (3): 203–208.
Riddle, Liesl, George A. Hrivnak, and Tjai M. Nielsen. 2010. "Transnational Diaspora Entrepreneurship in Emerging Markets: Bridging Institutional Divides." *Journal of International Management* 16 (4): 398–411. doi:10.1016/j.intman.2010.09.009.
Rusinovic, Katja. 2008. "Transnational Embeddedness: Transnational Activities and Networks among First- and Second-Generation Immigrant Entrepreneurs in the Netherlands." *Journal of Ethnic and Migration Studies* 34 (3): 431–451. doi:10.1080/13691830701880285.
Saxenian, AnnaLee. 1999. *Silicon Valley's New Immigrant Entrepreneurs*. San Francisco, CA: Public Policy Institute of California.
Schiller, Nina Glick, and Ayse Çağlar. 2013. "Locating Migrant Pathways of Economic Emplacement: Thinking Beyond the Ethnic Lens." *Ethnicities* 13 (4): 494–514. doi:10.1177/1468796813483733.
Silverman, David. 2000. *Doing Qualitative Research*. London: SAGE Publications Ltd.
Solano, Giacomo. 2015. "Transnational vs. Domestic Immigrant Entrepreneurs: A Comparative Literature Analysis of the Use of Personal Skills and Social Networks." *American Journal of Entrepreneurship* 8 (2): 1–21.
Solano, Giacomo. 2016a. *Immigrant Self-Employment and Transnational Practices: The Case of Moroccan Entrepreneurs in Amsterdam and Milan*. Amsterdam-Milan: University of Amsterdam - University of Milan-Bicocca.

Solano, Giacomo. 2016b. "Multifocal Entrepreneurial Practices: The Case of Moroccan Import/Export Businesses in Milan." *International Journal Entrepreneurship and Small Business*. doi:10.1504/IJESB.2016.078698.

Terjesen, Siri, and Amanda Elam. 2009. "Transnational Entrepreneurs' Venture Internationalization Strategies: A Practice Theory Approach." *Entrepreneurship Theory and Practice* 33 (5): 1093–1120. doi:10.1111/j.1540-6520.2009.00336.x.

Urbano, David, Nuria Toledano, and Domingo Ribeiro-Soriano. 2011. "Socio-Cultural Factors and Transnational Entrepreneurship: A Multiple Case Study in Spain." *International Small Business Journal* 29 (2): 119–134. doi:10.1177/0266242610391934.

Vacca, Raffaele, Giacomo Solano, Miranda Jessica Lubbers, José Luis Molina, and Christopher McCarty. 2018. "A Personal Network Approach to the Study of Immigrant Structural Assimilation and Transnationalism." *Social Networks* 53 (May): 72–89. doi:10.1016/j.socnet.2016.08.007.

Valenzuela-García, Hugo, José Molina, Miranda Lubbers, Alejandro García-Macías, Judith Pampalona, and Juergen Lerner. 2014. "On Heterogeneous and Homogeneous Networks in a Multilayered Reality: Clashing Interests in the Ethnic Enclave of Lloret de Mar." *Societies* 4 (1): 85–104. doi:10.3390/soc4010085.

Vandenbrande, Tom, ed. 2006. "Mobility in Europe: Analysis of the 2005 Eurobarometer Survey on Geographical and Labour Market Mobility." European Union. EF, 06,59 EN. Luxembourg.

Wang, Qingfang, and Wei Li. 2007. "Entrepreneurship, Ethnicity and Local Contexts: Hispanic Entrepreneurs in Three U.S. Southern Metropolitan Areas." *GeoJournal* 68 (2–3): 167–182. doi:10.1007/s10708-007-9081-0.

Wang, Qingfang, and Cathy Yang Liu. 2015. "Transnational Activities of Immigrant-Owned Firms and Their Performances in the USA." *Small Business Economics* 44 (2): 345–359. doi:10.1007/s11187-014-9595-z.

Zapata-Barrero, Ricard, and Shahamak Rezaei. 2020. "Diaspora Governance and Transnational Entrepreneurship: the Rise of an Emerging Social Global Pattern in Migration Studies." *Journal of Ethnic and Migration Studies* 46 (10): 1959–1973. doi:10.1080/1369183X.2018.1559990.

Exploring the relationship between immigrant enclave theory and transnational diaspora entrepreneurial opportunity formation

Osa-Godwin Osaghae and Thomas M. Cooney

ABSTRACT
Immigrant Enclave Theory (IET) investigates the concentration and localisation of immigrants in a specific geographic area. Some IET studies have highlighted the resilience of these communities and described such enclaves as sources of mutual support, collective political power and beneficial social relationships. Other studies have examined the influence of IET on immigrant entrepreneurial activity within these geographic areas, although some of these studies have highlighted IET as a contributor to low profit margin businesses due to over-representation of immigrant enterprises within the same sector and geographic locality. This article considers the potential for Transnational Diaspora Entrepreneurship (TDE) as an alternative approach to business development within immigrant enclaves and proposes a new model for the relationship between IET and TDE opportunity formation. For the contextualisation of the relationship between IET and TDE, the article explores immigrant enclave related theories and transnational diaspora entrepreneurship frameworks to draw out the relationship between IET and TDE.

Introduction

People migrate from one country to another for various reasons ranging from war, unemployment, the chance of a better life, family reunification and the opportunity to pursue entrepreneurial opportunities (Hammar et al. 1997; Kingma 2007; Portes and Fernandez-Kelly 2015). In recent years, international immigration has been constantly rising and the number of migrants worldwide has continued to grow rapidly, reaching 244 million in 2015, up from 222 million in 2010 and 173 million in 2000. This substantial growth trend has caused immigration to become one of the most contentious political, economic and social issues of the twenty-first century (Honig 2020) and the focus of much attention amongst policymakers, governments and economic organisations around the world. Indeed, the 2016 Brexit referendum in the UK and the 2017 Presidential election in the USA were both events that generated substantial negative commentary surrounding the issue of immigration and caused significant reconsideration of the value of immigration to each country.

Schiller, Basch, and Blanc (1995) suggested that immigration was a process of cultural diffusion and that the concentration of foreign cultures within a geographical area in host countries will create market opportunities. Furthermore, Portes and Sensenbrenner (1993) argued that immigration into host countries can lead to the formation of an association of people of similar ethnic or immigration background in a specific locality, a concentration often referred to as an enclave. This geographical concentration of immigrants in a specific area provides much needed resources that aid immigrant and diaspora entrepreneurship start-ups. For example, in Canada, 17.5% of immigrants aged 18–69 were entrepreneurs compared with 14.4% of the Canadian-born population (Hou and Wang 2011). In the UK, immigrants are three times more likely to be entrepreneurial than people born in Britain, while in Ireland a higher percentage of migrants have recently started a business compared with the non-immigrant population (Jones et al. 2012). With this escalation in entrepreneurial activity by immigrants, the emergence of Transnational Diaspora Entrepreneurship (TDE) has also developed with expanded trade being initiated by immigrant entrepreneurs between their countries of origin and destination. Such a development is particularly noticeable in countries where immigration policies and economic development strategies are designed to maximise an immigrant's contribution to a national economy (OECD 2017). The growth in TDE has also become progressively simpler as travel and internet access make connecting between countries so much easier than in times past.

Diaspora describes immigrants who are 'forever' settled in a country other than their country of origin, plus they have a cultural understanding of both their host and home country (Aikins and White 2011). Transnational on the other hand highlights the circular flow of immigrants (Portes and Fernández-Kelly 2015), undertaken by people who create social, political and economic activities that span the national business environments of their country of origin and country of residence (Riddle, Hrivnak, and Nielsen 2010). Thus, Transnational Diaspora Entrepreneurs (TDEs) are specialised intermediaries whose actions typically serve to reduce transaction costs and encourage interaction between potential buyers and sellers within an immigrant enclave and across countries (Khanna and Palepu 2010). Scholars such as Dunning (2005), Kuznetsov (2006), and Sørensen (2007) have suggested that the ideas, resources and employment opportunities created by TDEs create a profound impact on the economic and social development of their home countries. From this perspective, TDEs fill a structural vacuum (human exchange and interaction) that may have arisen between many emerging and developed market economies (North 1991; Portes and Fernández-Kelly 2015). Furthermore, Khanna and Palepu (2010) argued that TDEs overcome significant challenges in emerging markets and enable firms to succeed in multiple environments.

TDE has long been associated with remittance and economic adaptation by immigrants in their country of residency. However, TDE is now viewed as a process of cultural diffusion that creates political, social and economic relationships between nations (Efendić, Babić, and Rebmann 2014), and the embeddedness of cultures in COR (Liu et al. 2020). This work examines transnational entrepreneurship through the cross-border movement of people and explores the relationship between Immigrant Enclave Theory (IET) and Transnational Diaspora Entrepreneurship (TDE) through theories and frameworks. As Aldrich and Waldinger (1990) and Neuman (2016) found, IET can create clustering, localisation and concentration of immigrants in a specific geographic area, while also expanding the availability of home countries' cultural resources in host countries. Therefore, IET and TDE offer an exciting entrepreneurial opportunity formation scenario for specific government policies to be developed that may proactively support the growth of international trade through this intersectionality, once a greater understanding of this relationship can be developed. A new model is proposed that seeks to offer greater insight into the relationship between IET and TDE. To achieve this, this article explores IET and TDE through the lens of immigration theories and frameworks to provide a possible relationship between the two theories.

Understanding Immigrant Enclave Theory (IET)

Immigrant Enclave Theory has its origins in the theory of labour market segmentation that implies a split between a primary and a secondary labour market (Wilson and Portes 1980). The primary labour market principally refers to large monopolistic corporations (Edwards 1975; Taubman and Wachter 1986), while the secondary market is the preserve of small competitive businesses that involve minority workers, employers and entrepreneurs (Pfeffer and Cohen 1984; Taubman and Wachter 1986). In the secondary markets, the sharing of same group identity, plus cultural and bounded solidarity, generate trust that reduces behavioural uncertainty that is essential for start-up and venture survival. Furthermore, this sharing of group identity may also prevent large firms from entering the markets of immigrants (Aldrich and Waldinger 1990), although research has shown that it is the low profit margins of the sector make it less interesting for large firms (Aldrich and Waldinger 1990). As Wilson and Portes (1980), Portes and Bach (1985), Aldrich and Waldinger (1990), and Gilbertson and Gurak (1993) found, immigrant businesses are frequently more harmonised with the needs of an immigrant enclave than with requirements outside the enclave, because of their understanding of the presence of distinctive conditions (immigrant cultural resources) that encourage immigrant enclave markets.

IET has been defined in a variety of ways, making comparisons across studies difficult. One of the most commonly used theories is by Portes (1981) who suggested that an immigrant enclave is a distinct spatial location and the organisation of a variety of enterprises serving an immigrant community. Portes and Jensen (1989) defined enclaves as the spatial gathering of businesses owned and run by immigrants serving immigrant groups. Waldinger (1986) and Neuman (2016) suggested that immigrant enclave theory described the location of an immigrant within a specific geographical area. Portes and Jensen (1989) highlighted enclaves such as Miami, West Little River, and Hialeah (all in the USA) as relevant examples due to the high concentration of Cubans and Cuban-owned firms in those areas. Zhou and Logan (1989) identified New York City as an ethnic enclave for Chinese immigrants, although any city that contains a Chinatown location could also have been suggested. These definitions and examples present enclaves as the geographical concentration of immigrants in a certain location and therefore IET is a condition whereby immigrants are situated in a specific geographic area and use their cultural resources and networking to form a closely knitted community of people from the same ethnic or immigrant background. This work adopts the definition of enclaves offered by Marcuse (1997, 242) which stated:

> An enclave is a spatially concentration area in which members of a particular population group, self-defined by ethnicity or religion or otherwise, congregate as a means of enhancing their economic, social and/or cultural development

This definition portrays enclaves as an environment that provides an immigrant with their home cultural resources, a social field for immigrant activity and encouragement for the geographical location of an immigrant in a specific neighbourhood within host countries. Drawing from Bourdieu and Nice's (1977) Theory of Practice, IET can be described as a social field (enclave) that generates immigrant infrastructures (habitus) and immigrant cultural capital (capital). According to Walther (2014), IET describes an environment that creates an infinite amount of interactions (discussions, negotiations or conflict) and rules, which determine and condition an individual's thoughts and behaviour amongst people of similar culture and immigration background.

A good example of a social field that generates immigrant infrastructures and capital for entrepreneurial start-ups is the concentration of Cuban Americans in Miami, which became noted for the occupation of localities that had been vacated by American-born people (Portes 1981). According to Waldinger (1986), such localities create environments whereby immigrants organise themselves into geographical, cultural, bounded communities where they trade exclusively or primarily with one another. Further, IET describes a scenario whereby through the utilisation of ethnic politics and ethnic mobilisation of resources, immigrants can combat cultural differences within their host countries (Portes and Manning 2012). Despres (1975) and Hechter (1977) described IET as a reactive formation on the part of the minority community to reaffirm its identity and interests in their own ethnic cultural element whilst located in their host countries.

IET portrays an environment where immigrants share an ethnic identity based on a common culture and cultural habits (Nagel and Olzak 1982; Berry et al. 2006; Chrysostome 2010). Furthermore, IET allows for an understanding of business development from which individual entrepreneurs can access typical immigrant resources such as (a) predisposing factors including cultural endowments and a sojourning orientation, and (b) modes of resource mobilisation such as ethnic social networks and access to co-ethnic labour (Light and Bonaich 1988; Boissevain et al. 1990, 132). It should be noted that Gold and Light (2000) and Riddle, Hrivnak, and Nielsen (2010) classified immigrant resources into two different groupings which were (a) tangible (e.g. financing), and (b) intangible (e.g. information, advice, guidance) resources. Although countries differ in numerous ways (such as in population densities, costs of living, educational opportunities, structural and institutional situations), immigrant resources are mostly similar in countries where there are immigrant enclaves (Birdseye and Hill 1995; Solano 2020). Thus, immigrant resources provide immigrant entrepreneurs with opportunities to convert their ideas and visions into rewarding ventures (Burt 1997). Hence, when an immigrant is starting an enterprise, resources are mostly about the benefits that allow an immigrant entrepreneur to use the resources that they do not own (e.g. immigrant network; human and social capital, and cultural resources). Frequently, this can be achieved through ethnic networks and building of trust within an enclave (Egbert 2009).

IET also explains the conditions through which immigrants gain market advantage and market protection (Waldinger 1986). For example, IET describes the importance of social and human capital in the immigrant entrepreneurial start-up process and with opportunity formation and recognition (Aldrich and Waldinger 1990). Further, as Granovetter (1992) suggested, networks are a way of understanding the embeddedness of entrepreneurial activity as networks provide a conceptualisation of the entrepreneurial process as a complex pluralistic pattern of interaction, exchange and the relationship between actors in a specified field. Social capital is a community characteristic that facilitates or inhibits the kind of innovation and risk-taking behaviour that is fundamental to entrepreneurship and it can be an endowment that can either be favourable or unfavourable to an immigrant entrepreneur (Westlund and Bolton 2003). Meanwhile, the human capital theory explains a situation whereby immigrants decide to go into entrepreneurial activity aided by skill gained through previous country knowledge (Sequeira and Rasheed 2006). Collectively these fundamentals of IET help to build understanding regarding how IET can create enclave resources in host countries, but unfortunately these resources and conditions can also frequently discourage transnational entrepreneurship and instead enhance opportunity formation solely within the confines of the enclave.

The findings by Portes and Manning (1986) on the Cuban Americans in Miami highlighted that immigrants are more likely to start a business when the culture of the home country is found within a specific geographical area in the host country. As found in the study of immigrant ventures in the UK, the presence of an ethnic minority community increases the number of ethnic businesses in a specific geographic area (Altinay and Altinay 2008). Furthermore, immigrant enclave ventures represented almost 6 per cent of the total SME population (approximately 218,000 businesses), employed almost a million people and generated revenues of over £58 billion for the UK economy. Table 1 below helps to describe the role of the enclave in promoting immigrant entrepreneurship.

Different empirical studies have confirmed these claims in Table 1 that an enclave provides immigrants with the environment, resources and infrastructures for venture development (Schiller, Basch, and Blanc 1995; Altinay and Altinay 2008; Neuman 2016). For example, the work by Altinay and Altinay (2008) suggests that the growth of both South Asian and Chinese entrepreneurship in the UK is a direct result of cultural factors (e.g. hard work, reliance on family labour and ethnic community networks) found within an immigrant enclave in the host country. Similarly, research on ventures by Indian immigrants by Metcalf, Modood, and Virdee (1996), Smallbone et al. (1999), Nwankwo (2005) and Altinay and Altinay (2008) suggest that cultural factors found within a specific geographical area are the principal reason behind successful Indian entrepreneurship in their host country. Finally, research by Portes and Sensenbrenner (1993) on immigrant enclaves of Cuban Americans in Miami highlighted that Cuban

Table 1. Showing the role of immigrant enclave within a national context.

Immigrant enclave	The Role of enclave
New start-ups	Account for 11 per cent of all new firms
Employment rate	It is estimated that there are 100,000 ethnic minority-owned businesses in London employing around 500,000 people
Culture	Diffusion of culture within a national context and creation of cultural resources, infrastructures and capital that impact on enclave entrepreneurial opportunity formation in host country
Economy	Creation of immigrant's economy and market niches. Engendering competition, creating employment and generating economic wealth and spending power
Environment	Demographic increase, settlement, human capital, co-ethnic labour and co-ethnic customers, interactions, attitude, networking
Infrastructures	Create start-ups resources, capital and infrastructures, that allow for future engagement with the enclave and native-born population Evidence from the Cuban construction firms, show that the Cuban firms started within their enclave and later operated beyond the enclave to serve the native-born population

Source: Compiled from articles by: Schiller, Basch, and Blanc 1995; Portes and Sensenbrenner 1993; Altinay and Altinay 2008; Neuman 2016

construction firms started within their enclave and later operated beyond the enclave to serve the native-born population. Collectively, these studies demonstrate that the presence of an enclave can create an opportunity that can transcend beyond the national and international context. Thus, it could be argued that the cultural resources, infrastructures, market, capital and environment that an enclave provides can create an entrepreneurial opportunity that drives diaspora transnationalism.

Understanding Transnational Diaspora Entrepreneurship (TDE)

Theoretically, diaspora and transnationalism often overlap and are sometimes used interchangeably, which makes defining diaspora and transnationalism a difficult task. Both concepts habitually involve using terminologies such as globalisation, cross-border, culture and integration/adaptation. Whilst each of these are important factors in defining diaspora and transnationalism, Bauböck and Faist (2010) argued that both diaspora and transnationalism occur within the limited social and geographic spaces of a specific environment. According to Levitt (2001), diaspora transnationalism is:

> A process of living within transnational social fields and the possibility of being exposed to a set of social expectations, cultural values and patterns of human interaction that are shaped by more than one social, economic and political system which enable one to engage in cross-border investment.

This definition embraces the current manner of understanding diaspora transnationalism as the interaction of diaspora between home and host countries, incorporating the bridging of social, economic and political relationships (Levitt 2001; Bauböck and Faist 2010; Portes and Fernández-Kelly 2015). Therefore, the human interaction in TDE occurs because of ethnic network and cultural resources across the host and home countries. Networks within TDE consists of ties or relationships built on trustworthiness between the investor and the community. What this symbolises is that networks improve ties between the transnational diaspora and the home country. Although a network may be regarded as informal relations that a person has with others (Reese and Aldrich 1995), in the TDE set-up it can serve as a contract-enforcement mechanism that promotes information flows across international borders (Javorcik et al. 2011).

TDE describes entrepreneurial models that involve the commuting of resources between host and home countries (Goldring 1996; Guarnizo 1997). By concurrently engaging in two or more socially embedded environments, diaspora transnationalism creates, develops and deploys its resource base to exploit economic comparative advantages in both host and home countries (Thieme 2008). Following the suggestions by Oviatt and McDougall (2005) and Riddle, Harivnak, and Nielsen (2010), TDE is considered as an entrepreneurial activity resulting from the sentiment that diaspora attach to their home country and the motivation to give back experiences acquired in their host country. Therefore, the motivation driving diaspora entrepreneurship is often complex and may involve pecuniary and non-pecuniary investment motivations, including feelings of duty and obligation to contribute to the development of their country of origin (Gillespie et al. 1999; Riddle, Harivnak, and Nielsen 2010).

Overall, TDE is understood to be a process of living within transnational social spheres and the possibility of being exposed to a set of social expectations, cultural values, and patterns of human interactions that are shaped by more than one social, economic and political system that allows a diaspora to engage in the cross-border activity (Gillespie et al. 1999; Bauböck and Faist 2010; Riddle, Harivnak, and Nielsen 2010; Portes and Fernández-Kelly 2015). The TDE concept conveys the idea of transnational populations living in a country of residence, while still maintaining economic, social and political relations with their country of origin (Debass and Ardovino 2009). Following the work of scholars such as Gillespie et al. (1999), Levitt (2001), Riddle, Harivnak, and Nielsen (2010), Bauböck and Faist (2010), Aikins and White (2011) and Portes and Fernández-Kelly (2015), this article defines TDE as those settled ethnic minority groups of migrant origins residing and acting in their country of residence, but maintaining strong sentimental, entrepreneurial and material links with their country of origin.

Understanding entrepreneurial opportunity formation for TDE

The desire to understand Entrepreneurial Opportunity Formation (EOF) has led to the question: where do opportunities come from (Shane 2003; Shane and Eckhardt 2003; Alvarez and Barney 2005; Alvarez and Barney 2007; Eckhardt and Ciuchta 2008; Alvarez and Parker 2009)? This discussion surrounding opportunity formation is embedded in a larger philosophy of scientific debate about realist and constructionist paradigms that have troubled organisational science scholars for many decades (Moldoveanu and Baum 2002). The core of the discussion lies between discovered realist opportunities and created evolutionary realist opportunities (Koppl and Minniti 2010). Recently, to avoid this discussion, scholars have begun to identify ways that apparent conflicts between realists and constructivists can be resolved. Two of the most commonly used concepts to describe entrepreneurial opportunity formation are the creation and discovery approaches.

The general perception regarding whether an opportunity is created or discovered is a manifestation of the individual/opportunity nexus approach. Kirzner (1997) argued that opportunities stem from imperfect knowledge, subject to the specific knowledge of time and place possessed by an entrepreneur. Shane and Eckhardt (2003) suggested that opportunities are there for the taking, but only for those who possess the qualities necessary to discover and exploit them. This suggestion has led to a debate asking if entrepreneurs have more cognitive skills than non-entrepreneurs. Furthermore, scholars such as Bandura (1991), Mills and Pawson (2006), and Pio and Dana (2014) have argued that entrepreneurs are individuals with the ability to take decisions and actions based on their beliefs about self, cultural disposition and how environmental factors affect their behaviour. As Ajzen identified, one's salient beliefs are determinants of a person's intentions and actions. What this suggests is that belief in one's actions drives one's own reality.

According to McMullen and Shepherd (2006), entrepreneurs are considered as possessing an accurate view of 'reality' as opposed to non-entrepreneurs. The realists assume that reality has an objective existence independent of individual perceptions (Popper and Popper 1979). According to Campbell (1974), the reality is independent of an individual's perception that plays a role in the selection and editing of an individual's beliefs and perceptions. Conversely, constructionists argue that reality is a social product based on the social interactions of individuals and does not have an existence independent of individual perception (Berger and Luckmann 1991). In the evolution of the field of entrepreneurship, the realist perspective has dominated the constructionist and evolutionary realist approaches (Venkataraman 2003). However, this does not suggest that constructionist or evolutionary realist views are not important in opportunity formation, but it does offer an indication that individual beliefs and perceptions of 'what is an opportunity' form the main foundations for the exploitation of an opportunity (Gartner 1985; Aldrich and Kenworthy 1999; Baker and Nelson 2005).

Kirzner (1997) claimed that opportunity is discovered (exogenously recognised) when individuals seise opportunities when they are alerted to them. Santos and Eisenhardt (2005) believe that opportunity formation occurs only when an entrepreneur perceives new opportunities for the creation of value and the construction of a market around these opportunities. However, according to enclave theorists, individual traits (cultural, personal knowledge, actions, attitude and behaviour) and immigrant networking capabilities combine to create opportunities for immigrant start-ups (Waldinger 1986; Portes and Sensenbrenner 1993). Waldinger, Aldrich and Waldinger (1990) suggested that such opportunity formation is a result of a complex interplay between political/economic and socio-cultural factors, and that a stable political situation (e.g. regulations, immigrant-friendly policies, healthy economy, entrepreneurial policies) helps to create increased entrepreneurial opportunities for immigrants. Similarly, Portes and Fernández-Kelly (2015) argued that a stable economic activity in a host country creates a structural opportunity for immigrants, while Aldrich and Waldinger (1990) and Neuman (2016) emphasised that government policies regarding the assimilation of immigrants and their diaspora create opportunities in the immigrant sector. Therefore, many authors would contend that context is a critical factor for entrepreneurial opportunities for immigrants.

It is arguable that achievement is also a defining trait of entrepreneurs and therefore entrepreneurial opportunity formation is driven by one of three kinds of needs: (1) need to affiliate; (2) need to achieve; and (3) need to be powerful (Murray 1938, later developed by McClelland 1965). According to Hornaday and Aboud (1971) and Wasdani and Mathew (2014), the need for power is an unconscious motive that pushes entrepreneurs to venture into creating organisations. From this perspective, it could be argued that the need for achievement drives an entrepreneur to a better cognitive way of thinking than non-entrepreneurs. Thus, opportunity formation is a result of an individual's ability to recognise an economic activity (old or new idea) and build a market around the found, discovered, or created product or service (Long and McMullan 1984; and Davidsson, Recker, and Von Briel 2017). This way of looking at opportunity formation suggests that opportunity can either be recognised, created or discovered, a discussion that has been challenged by many authors from a variety of theoretical perspectives (e.g. Sarasvathy and Dew 2005; Alvarez and Barney 2013; Guard and Giuliani, 2013).

Using the relational and temporal approach, Alvarez and Barney (2007) argued that opportunities are endogenously created, not discovered. Sarasvathy and Dew (2005), Guard and Giuliani (2013), and Alvarez and Barney (2013) were able to demonstrate that the process of opportunity recognition involves both creation and discovery, and that creation and discovery of opportunity occur simultaneously. According to the reality approach, unobservable opportunities exist independent of individual perception and therefore these opportunities can only be seen to be discovered (Kirzner 1973, 10). Thus, opportunities happen in an already existing reality and alert individuals are often familiar with the norms and laws or 'truth' of this reality (Koppl and Minniti 2010). From this perspective, it could be argued that entrepreneurial opportunity formation occurs when an individual is in a position to recognise and interpret the external elements that aid opportunity formation within a given location.

Given this understanding of existing literature relating to IET, TDE and opportunity formation, Figure 1 below suggests that immigrant entrepreneurial opportunity formation is the result of an individual enabler (previous country, knowledge, motivation, self-efficacy, need for achievement, power, and affiliation, persistence, direction, intensity) interacting with an external enabler (environment, infrastructures, and resources). On an individual level, elements such as entrepreneurial motivation, direction, intensity and persistence help opportunity formation. In clear terms, a motivated entrepreneur should be willing to exert a certain level of effort (intensity) for a certain time (persistence) towards a specific goal (direction). Furthermore, the environment (the presence of ethnic infrastructure, stable political and economic condition) in which a person lives (at that point in time) helps the development of the entrepreneurial opportunity formation. This indicates that human behaviour can react to events (because of several forces differing in both direction and intent) which may trigger certain behavioural objectives that help individual opportunity formation. Figure 1 inserted below

In line with the constructionist approach, individuals interpret a phenomenon, raw data or resources and give it a meaning that is different from another's interpretation

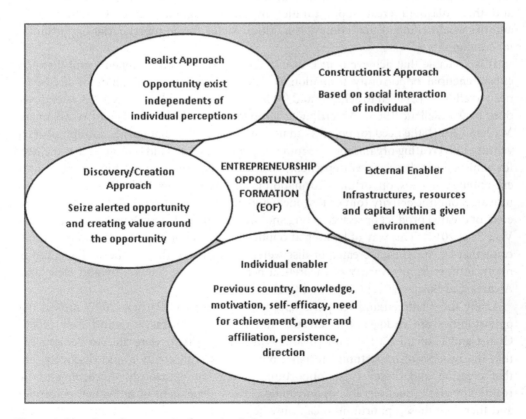

Figure 1. Mapping of opportunity formation in immigrant IET and TDE.

(Koppl and Minniti 2010). Hence, it is arguable that the way entrepreneurs interpret data and utilise resources gives them an advantage over non-entrepreneurs in terms of opportunity formation. According to Katz and Gartner (1988), individuals create realities and then mould their actions towards that reality. As such, opportunity formation lies in the ability of an individual to use the available resources (cultural, financial capital and previous country knowledge) to create opportunity (Davidsson 2016). Dimov (2010) argued that previous knowledge enhances one's confidence and ability to do something, and not because one individual has more cognitive ability than another person. In this way, an entrepreneur 'designs the future' based on the environment and the resources available to the entrepreneur (Baker and Nelson 2005).

In an immigrant enclave scenario, opportunity formation is a result of cultural resources found within the immigrant enclave (Santos and Eisenhardt 2005). As Waldinger (1986) determined, enclave resources create an opportunity for immigrant start-ups. Aldrich and Waldinger (1990) and Waldinger et al. (1990) argued that the reliance of co-ethnic habits by immigrants creates markets that encourage diaspora entrepreneurship within a national framework. In the enclave, immigrant opportunity formation involves the ability of an individual to use the enclave resources to identify niches and create enclave markets around those niches (Evans 1989). Hence, Figure 1 above suggests that opportunity formation is a result of the availability of several factors within the enclave that aid immigrant entrepreneurs in their start-ups.

The relationship between IET and TDE can be described as a 'Grand Theory', an abstract and normative theory of human nature and conduct (Skinner 1996). IET and TDE describe human nature and conduct within the enclaves and how an immigrant is bounded by home country, shared cultural meanings and norms in the host country (Bourdieu and Nice 1977). From this perspective, the environment is an essential factor to IET and TDE opportunity formation. The suggestion is that both IET and TDE explain how culture, environmental factors, infrastructures, capital and rules function to create an environment through which immigrants conduct their entrepreneurial activity. The evidence suggests that being part of a migrant enclave offers significant predictors of entrepreneurship, and together with being part of a diaspora community, this has become a significant factor to exploring TDE (Aldrich and Waldinger 1990; Portes and Fernández-Kelly 2015). By drawing from the work by Peroni, Riillo, and Sarracino (2016), this paper argues that the relationship between IET and TDE is based upon the reliance of specific cultural alignments between the infrastructures, environments and resources in the home and host countries. Clearly, what this suggests is that diaspora draws from the interaction that an immigrant enclave creates in host countries to engage in transnational entrepreneurship.

Discussion

As discussed earlier in the article, the literature has suggested that IET is a situation whereby people of similar immigration experiences concentrate in a specific geographical location and form a community bounded by immigrant resources. Meanwhile, TDE has been described as a:

social realm of immigrants operating in complex, cross-national domains, with dual cultural, institutional, and economic features that facilitate various entrepreneurial strategies (Drori, Honig, and Wright 2009, 1).

Understanding these two concepts and from mapping the elements of enclave entrepreneurship opportunity formation in Figure 1 above, it could be argued that IET provides a social field for immigrant entrepreneurship in host countries, while TDE is the engagement of an immigrant in cross-border entrepreneurship activity. Furthermore, it could also be reasoned that IET provides the cultural resources for TDE. As Aldrich and Waldinger (1990) and Portes and Fernández-Kelly (2015) found, home country culture in host countries frequently provide the market niches needed for immigrant entrepreneurship. As such, enclaves and TDE are culturally related and IET creates the resources for entrepreneurship in host countries, while the cultural understanding of a home country by TDE also allows for transnational activity by the diaspora.

Culture and the need to associate with one's ancestral home, as well as to be involved in entrepreneurial activity between home and host country, draw diaspora to their home countries in the same way that culture and national identity create immigrant entrepreneurial activity in host countries (Masurel et al. 2002). According to scholars such as Riddle and Marano (2008) and Riddle, Hrivnak, and Nielsen (2010), TDE occurs amongst those groups of entrepreneurs that avail of the cultural knowledge, social networking, electronic bulletin boards and other online venues of both host and home countries to engage in cross-border entrepreneurship. As such, diaspora transnationalism is a motivation of social recognition, friendliness, and receptiveness of the home country, as well as the integration of immigrants into their host countries (Nkongolo-Bakenda and Chrysostome 2013). According to Aldrich and Waldinger (1990), the enclave is a motivation of immigrant infrastructures and entrepreneurship environment in host countries. From this perspective, the relationship between IET and TDE arguably stems from the infrastructures and cultural resources that are available for start-ups and entrepreneurial activity in the host and home countries (Nkongolo-Bakenda and Chrysostome 2013).

The creation and discovery approaches suggest that an immigrant's enclave (the association of immigrants in a specific geographic area) and the individual (immigrant entrepreneur) are two important elements in the formation of opportunity. Immigrant enclaves create the cultural resources (immigrant market niches, human and social capital, networking and financial capital) that aid opportunity recognition. Discovery occurs at the point an individual (immigrant entrepreneur) recognises the available resources and creates a market around the discovered opportunity. Similarly, the cultural resources found within an enclave create an opportunity for TDE activity that encourages TDEs to take-up transnationalism leading to interaction with their ancestral home. Thus, immigrant enclave resources and an individual are the external and individual 'Enablers' of opportunity formation in immigrant/TDE activity, which suggests that enclave resources provide immigrant entrepreneurial activity in host countries and encourage transnationalism by the diaspora. This creates a relationship or link between IET and TDE.

As found in this work, the formation of immigrant enclave opportunity rests on the availability of three main factors: (a) environment, (b) infrastructures, and (c) resources. These factors also provide TDE with the opportunity to convert ideas and vision into rewarding ventures (Burt 1997; Portes and Sensenbrenner 1993). Further, the location and concentration of people of similar culture in a specific geographic area create enclave resources that encourage transitional entrepreneurship (Waldinger 1986). Thus, TDE describes diaspora entrepreneurial activity that spans between host and home country (Portes and Fernández-Kelly 2015). This cross-border entrepreneurial activity by diaspora is due to the increase in demand for immigrant markets caused by changes in the demographic conditions of immigrants and diaspora in host countries (Liebig and Sousa-Poza 2003). Thus, alterations in immigrants' demographic characteristics in host countries create infrastructures, resources and environments that provide market niches for start-ups and transnational entrepreneurship.

As Kloosterman, Van Der Leun, and Rath (1999) found in their study of Muslim Islamic butchers in the Netherlands, increases in the demographic condition of immigrants in host countries provide enclave opportunities and start-ups. What this suggests is that any increase in immigrant population creates market niches, capital (human and financial) resources and entrepreneurial opportunities. Following the suggestion by Drori, Meyer, and Hwang (2006) that the presence of immigrants creates institutional and economic features that facilitate various entrepreneurial strategies, this article argues that demographic conditions provided by the high rate of immigrants in a host country create an opportunity for TDE. According to Dimov (2010), entrepreneurial activity is a dependent of the external and individual enabler. TDE is a motivation of the resources, infrastructure and environment that an enclave provides and the individual ability to recognise the opportunity that these elements offer within a specific geographical area create transnationalism diaspora entrepreneurship opportunities. An entrepreneur aims to serve the cultural niches of immigrants in the host country, motivated by the diaspora need to give back to their country of origin the experience acquired in the country of residency (Gillespie et al. 1999; Riddle, Harivnak, and Nielsen 2010).

The work by scholars such as Newland and Tanaka (2010) and Nkongolo-Bakenda and Chrysostome (2013) have highlighted that entrepreneurial policies such as stable economy conditions, supportive government policies and immigrant networks are important factors that encourage immigrant start-ups and influence transnational entrepreneurship. According to Newland and Tanaka (2010) and Nkongolo-Bakenda and Chrysostome (2013), good entrepreneurship policies eradicate start-up administrative formalities, provide essential infrastructures and increase immigrant socio-demographic conditions in host countries. According to Dimov (2010) and Davidsson (2016), these factors enable opportunity formation and transnational entrepreneurship when found in an economy. Additionally, it could be argued that an individual entrepreneur's persistence, desire, need for achievement, power, affiliation and motivation, supported by an external enabler, form the main drivers to start-up opportunities and transnational entrepreneurship. As such, enclave demographic conditions, resources and entrepreneurial policies that encourage enclave opportunity formation, also influence transnational entrepreneurship opportunity formation.

Portes and Sensenbrenner (1993) argued that enclave resources and infrastructures can create start-up opportunity that aid venture development beyond an immigrant enclave. This article suggests that TDE opportunities are the consequence of an immigrant's capital (cultural, human, social capital) and networking that was created through immigrant enclave bounded solidarity and potential market opportunity formation. According to scholars such as Aldrich and Waldinger (1990) and Neuman (2016), IET helps to preserve an immigrant's home country cultural identity and provides immigrant resources that play an essential role in immigrant enclave opportunity formation. Egbert (2009) suggested that an immigrant's diaspora resources are mostly concerned with the benefits that entrepreneurs are offered by using resources that they do not own (i.e. immigrant network; human, social capital and cultural resources). Further, these resources allow for networking and building of trust within the enclave. Figure 2 below presents an amalgamation of these works into a new IET - TDE model that seeks to explain the relationship between the various elements.

According to the new model proposed in Figure 2, the pursuit of immigrant diaspora opportunity involves the ability of an individual entrepreneur to recognise and understand the capital, resources and infrastructures that are available from within their enclave and home country. Utilising these resources and building upon cultural interaction can lead to opportunity recognition for the entrepreneur. Dependent upon the nature of the opportunity, the support from enclave resources and the ability of the entrepreneur themselves, the opportunity can lead to (1) the birth of a new venture, (2) the opportunity is put on hold, or (3) it may be abandoned completely. Should it be pursued, then it can lead to TDE and business interaction between an immigrant's home and the host country. This proposed model contributes to existing literature by explaining the relationship between IET and TDE. The paper also suggests that factors such as (1) good entrepreneurial policies, (2) positive immigrant demographic conditions, (3) environmental factors, resources and infrastructures, and (4) immigrant culture, all encourage immigrant enclave entrepreneurial activity and have an influence on diaspora involvement in transnational entrepreneurship. In conclusion, cultural factors allow for immigrant entrepreneurship start-ups, survival and transcending of entrepreneurship beyond the enclave environment. Aldrich

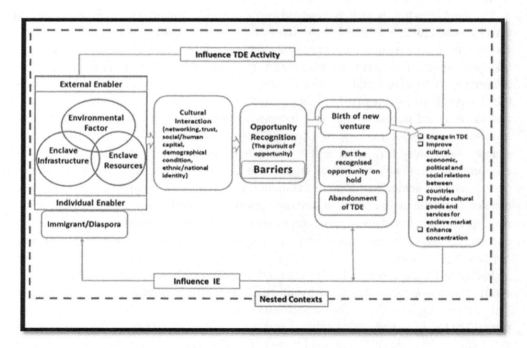

Figure 2. The relationship between IET and TDE.

and Waldinger (1990) and Riddle, Harivnak, and Nielsen (2010) both propounded that enclave and diaspora entrepreneurship are aimed at serving the ethnic niche of fellow immigrants or co-ethnic groups, and can lead to the development of economic, social and political opportunities for immigrants in their host countries.

Conclusion

The theories explored in this work suggest that immigrant enclaves in host countries offer immigrants valuable cultural resources and provide the external (environmental factors) and individual enablers that encourage enclave opportunity formation. Following these theories, this article suggests that IET influences on TDE opportunity formation are dependent on the external and the individual enabler factors within the enclave (see Figure 2). The individual enablers are those attributes (persistence, desire, and need for achievements, power, affiliation, and motivation) that aid opportunity formation (Dimov 2010; Davidsson 2016). The external enablers can include: (1) environmental factors such as socio-cultural factors, regulations, immigration-friendly policies, healthy economy, entrepreneurial policies, immigrant group, demographic characteristics; (2) infrastructures such as Government support networks; and (3) enclave resources such as financial capital, human capital, social capital, trustworthiness, community support, previous knowledge and networks that create start-up opportunities, as well as opportunity for transnational entrepreneurship (Nkongolo-Bakenda and Chrysostome 2013). Overall, immigrant entrepreneurship involves an understanding of home country cultural knowledge and enclave activity that provides the interaction for immigrant entrepreneurship (Aldrich and Waldinger 1990; Portes and Sensenbrenner 1993). Thus, cultural interaction when found in host countries can influence TDE in the following ways:

- Creates a home country culture in host countries
- Makes available market and immigrant resources necessary for immigrant activity
- Forms immigrant infrastructures, identity, social field, social and human capital
- Develops trustworthiness and bounded solidarity
- Provides community interaction and networking

These elements form the core of entrepreneurship opportunity formation for immigrants in their home and host countries (Aldrich and Waldinger 1990; Portes and Sensenbrenner 1993). As such, the presence of these home country cultural elements put the diaspora in the position to travel between their home and host country, and to avail of resources in both locations. Furthermore, immigrant enclaves provide an immigrant market, demographic characteristics, human and social capital, as well as trust and bounded solidarity, for the exploration of TDE within a host country (Waldinger 1986; Berry 2008). Thus, the presence of these elements in host countries act as stimulants to diaspora transnational entrepreneurship or can equally disincentives diaspora connectivity with one's ancestral home.

As evidenced in the literature, an understanding of their own home country cultural knowledge creates ease of adaptation for diaspora entrepreneurs engaging in transnational entrepreneurship and eliminates the adaptive processes that are undertaken by immigrants in an unfamiliar environment (Berry 2008; Bhatia and Ram

2009). As highlighted in Figure 2, enclave resources and demographic conditions in host countries provide diaspora with the opportunity to engage in transnational entrepreneurship. As suggested in various studies (e.g. Waldinger 1986; Aldrich and Waldinger 1990; Portes and Sensenbrenner 1993), immigrant markets mostly involve an understanding of ethnic preferences of the immigrant enclave customers. The understanding of immigrant preferences, the presence of immigrant demographic characteristics and the demand for the cultural goods that can only be supplied by people with similar cultural and immigration backgrounds, creates enclave markets and the need for the diaspora to engage in transnational entrepreneurship (Aldrich and Waldinger 1990; Neuman 2016). Thus, from the various theories explored in this work, it could be argued that the presence of IET resources in host countries encourages diaspora to undertake transnational entrepreneurship, plus IET protects enclave markets and makes immigrants and diaspora the main provider of transnational entrepreneurship.

An immigrant enclave provides the environment, resources and infrastructures that are pivotal to diaspora opportunity formation in the host country. Thus, TDE is dependent on the social-cultural resources and capital made available by the geographical concentration (enclave) of immigrants in a specific area in a host country. What this suggests is that the environment, resources and infrastructures that are found within the enclave create enclave market niches that can only be served by people with an immigrant's cultural knowledge and understanding of immigrant taste (Portes and Sensenbrenner 1993; Neuman 2016). Arguably, the immigration of people of diverse culture into host countries create enclave economics that support TDE, while the shuttling between host and host country by diaspora aid enclave entrepreneurship and increases the economic development of host and home countries. Overall, immigrant enclaves create opportunities not only for enclave entrepreneurship, but also for transcending entrepreneurship beyond the enclave (Portes and Sensenbrenner 1993).

Despite, the opportunities that immigrant enclaves provide and the ability of immigrants and diaspora to support the economics of both host and home country, enclave and transnational diaspora entrepreneurship remains an issue of national divide. But TDE is currently proposed as a builder of economic, social and political life within many nations (Portes and Fernández-Kelly 2015). Therefore, future research should seek to identify ways of highlighting the importance of enclave and transnational diaspora entrepreneurship, reducing the negativity surrounding immigration, immigrant enclaves and TDE activity within the national context, and help create a greater understanding of the economic and social benefits of immigration within a national context.

Disclosure statement

No potential conflict of interest was reported by the authors.

References

Aikins, K., and N. White. 2011. "Global Diaspora Strategies Toolkit." *Diaspora Matters, Impress Printing Works, Dublin* 1: 31–40.

Aldrich, H. E., and A. L. Kenworthy. 1999. "The Accidental Entrepreneur: Campbellian Antinomies and Organizational Foundings." In *Variations in Organization Science: in Honor of Donald T. Campbell*, edited by J. A. C. Baum and B. McKelvey, 19–33. Thousand Oaks, CA: Sage Publications. doi:10.4135/9781452204703.n2.

Aldrich, H., and R. Waldinger. 1990. "Trends in Ethnic Businesses in the United States." In *Ethnic Entrepreneurs: Immigrant Business in Industrial Societies*, edited by R. Waldinger, H. Aldrich, and R. Ward, 111–135. Newbury Park, CA: Sage.

Altinay, L., and E. Altinay. 2008. "Factors Influencing Business Growth: the Rise of Turkish Entrepreneurship in the UK." *International Journal of Entrepreneurial Behavior & Research* 14 (1): 24–46.

Alvarez, S. A., and J. B. Barney. 2005. "How do Entrepreneurs Organize Firms Under Conditions of Uncertainty?" *Journal of Management* 31 (5): 776–793.

Alvarez, S. A., and J. B. Barney. 2007. "The Entrepreneurial Theory of the Firm." *Journal of Management Studies* 44 (7): 1057–1063.

Alvarez, S. A., and J. B. Barney. 2013. "Epistemology, Opportunities, and Entrepreneurship: Comments on Venkataraman et al. (2012) and Shane (2012)." *Academy of Management Review* 38 (1): 154–157.

Alvarez, S. A., and S. C. Parker. 2009. "Emerging Firms and the Allocation of Control Rights: A Bayesian Approach." *Academy of Management Review* 34 (2): 209–227.

Baker, T., and R. E. Nelson. 2005. "Creating Something From Nothing: Resource Construction Through Entrepreneurial Bricolage." *Administrative Science Quarterly* 50 (3): 329–366.

Bandura, A. 1991. "Social Cognitive Theory of Moral Thought and Action." *Handbook of Moral Behavior and Development* 1: 45–103.

Bauböck, R., and T. Faist. 2010. "Diaspora and transnationalism: Concepts, theories and methods." In *Diaspora and Transnationalism: Concepts, Theories and Methods*, edited by R. Bauböck and T. Faist. Amsterdam: Amsterdam University Press.

Berger, P. L., and T. Luckmann. 1991. *The Social Construction of Reality: A Treatise in the Sociology of Knowledge (No. 10)*. London: Penguin.

Berry, J. W. 2008. "Globalisation and Acculturation." *International Journal of Intercultural Relations* 32 (4): 328–336.

Berry, J. W., J. S. Phinney, D. L. Sam, and P. Vedder. 2006. "Immigrant Youth: Acculturation, Identity, and Adaptation." *Applied Psychology* 55 (3): 303–332.

Bhatia, S., and A. Ram. 2009. "Theorizing Identity in Transnational and Diaspora Cultures: A Critical Approach to Acculturation." *International Journal of Intercultural Relations* 33 (2): 140–149.

Birdseye, M. G., and J. S. Hill. 1995. "Individual, Organizational/Work and Environmental Influences on Expatriate Turnover Tendencies: An Empirical Study." *Journal of International Business Studies* 26 (4): 787–813.

Boissevain, J., J. Blaschke, H. Grotenbreg, I. Joseph, I. Light, M. Sway, and P. Werbner. 1990. "Ethnic Entrepreneurs and Ethnic Strategies." *Ethnic Entrepreneurs: Immigrant Business in Industrial Societies*: 131–156.

Bourdieu, P., and R. Nice. 1977. *Outline of a Theory of Practice*. Vol. 16. Cambridge: Cambridge University Press.

Burt, R. S. 1997. "A Note on Social Capital and Network Content." *Social Networks* 19 (4): 355–373.

Campbell, R. B. 1974. Limited Liability for Corporate Shareholders: Myth or Matter-of-Fact. Ky. LJ, 63, 23.

Chrysostome, E. 2010. "The Success Factors of Necessity Immigrant Entrepreneurs: In Search of a Model." *Thunderbird International Business Review* 52 (2): 137–152.

Davidsson, P. 2016. *Researching Entrepreneurship: Conceptualization and Design (Vol. 33)*. Switzerland: Springer.

Davidsson, Recker, and Von Briel. 2017. "External Enablers in New Venture Creation Processes: A Framework." In *Academy of Management Proceedings Academy of Management*. Vol. 2017, 13126.

Debass, T., and M. Ardovino. 2009. Diaspora Direct Investment (DDI): The Untapped Resource for Development. United States Agency for International Development. USAID publication. http://pdf.usaid.gov/pdf_docs/PNADO983.pdf.

Despres, L.A. 1975. *Ethnicity and Resource Competition in Plural Societies*. Paris: Walter de Gruyter.

Dimov, D. 2010. "Nascent Entrepreneurs and Venture Emergence: Opportunity Confidence, Human Capital, and Early Planning." *Journal of Management Studies* 47 (6): 1123–1153.

Drori, I., B. Honig, and M. Wright. 2009. "Transnational Entrepreneurship: An Emergent Field of Study." *Entrepreneurship Theory and Practice* 33 (5): 1001–1022.

Drori, G. S., J. W. Meyer, and H. Hwang. 2006. *Globalization and Organization: World Society and Organizational Change*. Oxford: Oxford University Press.

Dunning, T. 2005. "Resource Dependence, Economic Performance, and Political Stability." *Journal of Conflict Resolution* 49 (4): 451–482.

Eckhardt, J. T., and M. P. Ciuchta. 2008. "Selected Variation: The Population-Level Implications of Multistage Selection in Entrepreneurship." *Strategic Entrepreneurship Journal* 2 (3): 209–224.

Edwards, R. C. 1975. "The Social Relations of Production in the Firm and Labour Market Structure." *Politics & Society* 5 (1): 83–108.

Efendić, A., B. Babić, and A. Rebmann. 2014. Diaspora and development. Embassy of Switzerland in Bosnia and Herzegovina.

Egbert, H. 2009. "Business Success Through Social Networks? A Comment on Social Networks and Business Success." *American Journal of Economics and Sociology* 68 (3): 665–677.

Evans, M. D. R. 1989. "Immigrant Entrepreneurship: Effects of Ethnic Market Size and Isolated Labor Pool." *American Sociological Review*: 950–962.

Gartner, W. B. 1985. "A Conceptual Framework for Describing the Phenomenon of New Venture Creation." *Academy of Management Review* 10 (4): 696–706.

Garud, R., and A. P. Giuliani. 2013. "A Narrative Perspective on Entrepreneurial Opportunities." *Academy of Management Review* 38: 157–160.

Gilbertson, G. A., and D. T. Gurak. 1993. "Broadening the Enclave Debate: The Labor Market Experiences of Dominican and Colombian men in New York City." In *Sociological Forum*, Vol. 8, 205–220. Switzerland: Kluwer Academic Publishers-Plenum Publishers.

Gillespie, K., L. Riddle, E. Sayre, and D. Sturges. 1999. "Diaspora Interest in Homeland Investment." *Journal of International Business Studies* 30 (3): 623–634.

Gold, S. J., and I. Light. 2000. "Ethnic Economies and Social Policy." In *Research in Social Movements, Conflicts and Change*, 165–191. Bingley: Emerald Group Publishing Limited.

Goldring, L. 1996. "Blurring Borders: Constructing Transnational Community in the Process of Mexico-US Migration." *Research in Community Sociology* 6 (2): 69–104.

Granovetter, M. 1992. "Economic Institutions as Social Constructions: A Framework for Analysis." *Acta Sociologica* 35 (1): 3–11.

Guarnizo, L. E. 1997. "The Emergence of a Transnational Social Formation and the Mirage of Return Migration among Dominican Transmigrants." *Identities Global Studies in Culture and Power* 4 (2): 281–322.

Hammar, T., G. Brochmann, K. Tamas, and T. Faist. 1997. International migration immobility and development: multidisciplinary perspectives.

Hechter, M. 1977. "Lineages of the Capitalist State." *The American Journal of Sociology* 82 (5) March: 1057–1074.

Honig, B. 2020. "Exploring the Intersection of Transnational, Ethnic, and Migration Entrepreneurship." *Journal of Ethnic and Migration Studies* 46 (10): 1974–1990. doi:10.1080/1369183X.2018.1559993.

Hornaday, J. A., and J. Aboud. 1971. "Characteristics of Successful Entrepreneurs." *Personnel Psychology* 24 (2): 141–153.

Hou, F., and S. Wang. 2011. "Immigrants in Self-employment." *Perspective on Labour and Income* 23 (3): 3.

Javorcik, B. S., Ç. Özden, M. Spatareanu, and C. Neagu. 2011. "Migrant Networks and Foreign Direct Investment." *Journal of Development Economics* 94 (2): 231–241.

Jones, T., M. Ram, P. Edwards, A. Kiselinchev, and L Muchenje. 2012. "New Migrant Enterprise: Novelty or Historical Continuity." *Urban Studies* 49 (14): 3159–3176.

Katz, J., and W. B. Gartner. 1988. "Properties of Emerging Organizations." *Academy of Management Review* 13 (3): 429–441.

Khanna, T., and K. G. Palepu. 2010. *Winning in Emerging Markets: A Road map for Strategy and Execution*. Virginia: Harvard Business Press.

Kingma, M. 2007. "Nurses on the Move: a Global Overview." *Health Services Research* 42 (3p2): 1281–1298.

Kirzner, I. M. 1973. *Competition and Entrepreneurship*. Chicago, IL: University of Chicago Press.

Kirzner, I. M. 1997. "Entrepreneurial Discovery and the Competitive Market Process: An Austrian Approach." *Journal of Economic Literature* 35 (1): 60–85.

Kloosterman, R., J. Van Der Leun, and J. Rath. 1999. "Mixed Embeddedness:(in) Formal Economic Activities and Immigrant Businesses in the Netherlands." *International Journal of Urban and Regional Research* 23 (2): 252–266.

Koppl, R., and M. Minniti. 2010. "Market Processes and Entrepreneurial Studies." In *Handbook of Entrepreneurship Research*, 217–248. New York: Springer.

Kuznetsov, Y. 2006. *Diaspora Networks and the International Migration of Skills: How Countries can Draw on Their Talent Abroad*. Washington, DC: World Bank Institute.

Levitt, P. 2001. "Transnational Migration: Taking Stock and Future Directions." *Global Networks* 1 (3): 195–216.

Liebig, T., and A. Sousa-Poza. 2003. How Does Income Inequality Influence International Migration?. European Regional Science Association Conference Papers, 472.

Light, I., and E. Bonacich. 1988. *Immigrant Entrepreneurs*. Berkeley, CA: University of California Press.

Liu, Y., R. Namatovu, E. Esra Karadeniz, T. Schøtt, and I. D. Minto-Coy. 2020. "'Entrepreneurs' Transnational Networks Channelling Exports: Diasporas From Central & South America, Sub-Sahara Africa, Middle East & North Africa, Asia, and the European Culture Region." *Journal of Ethnic and Migration Studies* 46 (10): 2106–2125. doi:10.1080/1369183X.2018.1560002.

Long, W. A., and W. E. McMullan. 1984. Mapping the New Venture Opportunity Identification Process. University of Calgary, Faculty of Management.

Marcuse, P. 1997. "The Enclave, The Citadel, and The Ghetto: What has Changed in the Post-Fordist US City." *Urban Affairs Review* 33 (2): 228–264.

Masurel, E., P. Nijkamp, M. Tastan, and G. Vindigni. 2002. "Motivations and Performance Conditions for Ethnic Entrepreneurship." *Growth and Change* 33(2): 238–260.

McClelland, D. C. 1965. "N Achievement and Entrepreneurship: A Longitudinal Study." *Journal of Personality and Social Psychology* 1 (4): 389.

McMullen, J. S., and D. A. Shepherd. 2006. "Entrepreneurial Action and the Role of Uncertainty in the Theory of the Entrepreneur." *Academy of Management Review* 31 (1): 132–152.

Metcalf, H., T. Modood, and S. Virdee. 1996. *Asian Self-Employment: The Interaction of Culture and Economics in England*. London: Policy Studies Institute.

Mills, C. E., and K. Pawson. 2006. "Enterprising Talk: a Case of Self-Construction." *International Journal of Entrepreneurial Behavior & Research* 12 (6): 328–344.

Moldoveanu, M. C., and J. A. Baum. 2002. "Contemporary Debates in Organizational Epistemology." *The Blackwell Companion to Organizations* Chapter 32: 733–751.

Murray, H. 1938. *Explorations in Personality*. New York: Oxford University Press.

Nagel, J., and S. Olzak. 1982. "Ethnic Mobilization in new and old States: An Extension of the Competition Model." *Social Problems* 30 (2): 127–143.

Neuman, E. 2016. "Ethnic Concentration and Economic Outcomes of Natives and Second-Generation Immigrants." *International Journal of Manpower* 37 (1): 157–187.

Newland, K., and H. Tanaka. 2010. *Mobilizing Diaspora Entrepreneurship for Development*. Washington, DC: Migration Policy Institute.

Nkongolo-Bakenda, Jean-Marie, and Elie Virgile Chrysostome. 2013. "Engaging Diasporas as International Entrepreneurs in Developing Countries: In Search of Determinants." *Journal of International Entrepreneurship* 11 (1): 30–64.

North, D. C. 1991. "Institutions." *Journal of Economic Perspectives* 5 (1): 97–112.

Nwankwo, S. 2005. "Characterisation of Black African Entrepreneurship in the UK: a Pilot Study." *Journal of Small Business and Enterprise Development* 12 (1): 120–136.

OECD Report. 2017. OECD Digital Economy Outlook. https://espas.secure.europarl.europa.eu/orbis/sites/default/files/generated/document/en/9317011e.pdf.

Oviatt, B. M., and P. P. McDougall. 2005. "Defining International Entrepreneurship and Modeling the Speed of Internationalization." *Entrepreneurship Theory and Practice* 29 (5): 537–553.

Peroni, C., C. A. Riillo, and F. Sarracino. 2016. "Entrepreneurship and Immigration: Evidence from GEM Luxembourg." *Small Business Economics* 46 (4): 639–656.

Pfeffer, J., and Y. Cohen. 1984. "Determinants of Internal Labour Markets in Organizations." *Administrative Science Quarterly* 29 (4): 550–572.

Pio, E., and L. P. Dana. 2014. "An Empirical Study of Indian Entrepreneurs in Christchurch, New Zealand." *International Journal of Entrepreneurship and Small Business* 22 (1): 17–35.

Popper, K. R., and K. R. Popper. 1979. *Truth, Rationality and the Growth of Scientific Knowledge*. Frankfurt: Vittorio Klosterman.

Portes, A. 1981. "13 Modes of Structural Incorporation and Present Theories of Labour Immigration." *International Migration Review* 15 (1_suppl): 279–297.

Portes, A., and R. L. Bach. 1985. *Latin Journey: Cuban and Mexican Immigrants in the United States*. Berkeley: Univ of California Press.

Portes, A., and P. Fernandez-Kelly. 2015. *The state and the grassroots: Immigrant transnational organizations in four continents*. New York: Berghahn Books.

Portes, A., and L. Jensen. 1989. "The Enclave and the Entrants: Patterns of Ethnic Enterprise in Miami Before and After Mariel." *American Sociological Review*: 929–949.

Portes, A., and R. D. Manning. 1986. "The Immigrant Enclave: Theory and Empirical Examples." In *Competitive Ethnic Relations*, edited by Susan Olzak and Joane Nagel. New York: Academic Press.

Portes, A., and R. D. Manning. 2012. The Immigrant Enclave: Theory and Empirical Examples. *The Urban Sociology Reader*, 38: 202.

Portes, A., and J. Sensenbrenner. 1993. "Embeddedness and Immigration: Notes on the Social Determinants of Economic Action." *American Journal of Sociology* 98 (6): 1320–1350.

Reese, P. R., and H. E. Aldrich. 1995. "Entrepreneurial Networks and Business Performance." *International Entrepreneurship*: 124–144.

Riddle, L., G. A. Hrivnak, and T. M. Nielsen. 2010. "Transnational Diaspora Entrepreneurship in Emerging Markets: Bridging Institutional Divides." *Journal of International Management* 16 (4): 398–411.

Riddle, L., and V. Marano. 2008. "Harnessing Investment Potential Through Homeland Export and Investment Promotion Agencies: The Case of Afghanistan." *Diasporas and Development: Exploring the Potential*: 91–112.

Santos, F. M., and K. M. Eisenhardt. 2005. "Organizational Boundaries and Theories of Organization." *Organization Science* 16 (5): 491–508.

Sarasvathy, S. D., and N. Dew. 2005. "New Market Creation Through Transformation." *Journal of Evolutionary Economics* 15 (5): 533–565.

Schiller, N. G., L. Basch, and C. S. Blanc. 1995. "From Immigrant to Transmigrant: Theorizing Transnational Migration." *Anthropological Quarterly* 68 (1): 48–63.

Sequeira, J. M., and A. A. Rasheed. 2006. "Start-up and Growth of Immigrant Small Businesses: The Impact of Social and Human Capital." *Journal of Developmental Entrepreneurship* 11 (04): 357–375.

Shane, S. A. 2003. *A General Theory of Entrepreneurship: The Individual-Opportunity Nexus*. Northampton, MA: Edward Elgar Publishing.

Shane, S., and J. Eckhardt. 2003. *The Individual-opportunity Nexus*, 161–191. Boston, MA: Springer.

Skinner, E. A. 1996. "A Guide to Constructs of Control." *Journal of Personality and Social Psychology* 71 (3): 549.

Smallbone, D., A. Fadahunsi, S. Supri, and A. Paddison. 1999. "The Diversity of Ethnic Minority Enterprises", Paper Presented at the RENT XIII, London, 25–26, November.

Solano, G. 2020. "The Mixed Embeddedness of Transnational Migrant Entrepreneurs: Moroccans in Amsterdam and Milan'." *Journal of Ethnic and Migration Studies* 46 (10): 2067–2085. doi:10.1080/1369183X.2018.1559999.

Sørensen, J. B. 2007. "Bureaucracy and Entrepreneurship: Workplace Effects on Entrepreneurial Entry." *Administrative Science Quarterly* 52 (3): 387–412.

Taubman, P., and M. L. Wachter. 1986. "Segmented Labor Markets." *Handbook of Labor Economics* 2: 1183–1217.

Thieme, S. 2008. "Sustaining Livelihoods in Multi-local Settings: Possible Theoretical Linkages Between Transnational Migration and Livelihood Studies." *Mobilities* 3 (1): 51–71.

Venkataraman, S. 2003. "Foreword." In *A General Theory of Entrepreneurship. The Individual-Opportunity Nexus*, edited by S. Shane , xi–xii. Northampton, MA: Edward Elgar Publishing.

Waldinger, R. D. 1986. *Through the eye of the Needle: Immigrants and Enterprise in New York's Garment Trades*. New York: New York University Press.

Waldinger, R., H. Aldrich, R. Ward, and J. Blaschke. 1990. *Ethnic Entrepreneurs: Immigrant Business in Industrial Societies*, 13–48. Newbury Park, CA: Sage.

Walther, M. 2014. "Bourdieu's Theory of Practice as Theoretical Framework." In *Repatriation to France and Germany*, 7–23. Switzerland: Springer Fachmedien Wiesbaden.

Wasdani, K. P., and M. Mathew. 2014. "Potential for Opportunity Recognition Along the Stages of Entrepreneurship." *Journal of Global Entrepreneurship Research* 4 (1): 7–22.

Westlund, H., and R. Bolton. 2003. "Local Social Capital and Entrepreneurship." *Small Business Economics* 21 (2): 77–113.

Wilson, K. L., and A. Portes. 1980. "Immigrant Enclaves: An Analysis of the Labour Market Experiences of Cubans in Miami." *American Journal of Sociology* 86 (2): 295–319.

Zhou, M., and J. R. Logan. 1989. "Returns on Human Capital in Ethnic Enclaves: New York City's Chinatown." *American Sociological Review* 54 (5): 809–820.

Entrepreneurs' transnational networks channelling exports: diasporas from Central & South America, Sub-Sahara Africa, Middle East & North Africa, Asia, and the European culture region

Ye Liu, Rebecca Namatovu, Emine Esra Karadeniz, Thomas Schøtt and Indianna D. Minto-Coy

ABSTRACT

Entrepreneurs located in the diaspora, compared to entrepreneurs located domestically, are well-known to export much, especially through transnational networking. This understanding has a gap: How is embeddedness of diasporic entrepreneurs in their origins shaping their transnational networking and trade? Globally representative samples of diasporic and domestic entrepreneurs have been surveyed, enabling comparisons of diasporas originating from the world's five regions: Central & South America, Sub-Sahara Africa, Middle East & North Africa, Asia, and the region of countries dominated by European culture. Entrepreneurs originating from European culture countries have larger transnational networks and more exports than entrepreneurs originating from any other region, particularly Sub-Sahara Africa. But diasporans from the other regions, especially Sub-Sahara Africa, have much larger transnational networks than their domestic peers. Transnational networking benefits exporting, in every location and every origin. Indeed, diasporans export more than domestics, by a direct effect and by additional indirect effects mediated through transnational networks, that differ across diasporas. By pioneering global comparisons of the diasporas from around the world, the study contributes to theorising by accounting for networking and trade, demonstrating that additional effects of being diasporan upon exporting are channelled through transnational networking, but differently across the heterogeneous diasporas.

1. Introduction

Entrepreneurs network transnationally and thereby export. Case studies also show that entrepreneurs in the diaspora network and export more than entrepreneurs staying at home (e.g. Baklanov et al. 2014; Portes, Guarnizo, and Haller 2002). The need remains for more encompassing studies, resulting in calls for comparative and global studies of heterogeneity of diasporas, voiced especially in this journal (e.g. Castles 2007; 2010).

Diasporas from different origins vary in their networking and trade. For example, entrepreneurs in the diaspora from Israel network densely with entrepreneurs in their home-country, with considerable brain circulation, and extensive transnational networks that channel knowledge and trade in global value chains. By contrast, the diaspora from Iran networks only sparsely with entrepreneurs in their home-country, essentially constituting a brain drain without reverse migration, and is hardly a conduit for business (Rezaei, Dana, and Ramadani 2017). This indicates a gap, how and why do various diasporas differ?

The well-supported propositions that diasporic entrepreneurs' transnational networks channel trade, but that diasporas differ, frame our research question: *How is embeddedness of diasporic entrepreneurs in their origins shaping their pursuits of transnational networks and trade?*

This question specifies an agenda for research on transnational entrepreneurship, TE,

> … how does the transnational entrepreneur actively develop and engage in business activities in an actual business environment? … How do national variations affect TE paths, modus operandi (including individual behavior and decision making, and the role of social networks), and outcomes? (Drori, Honig, and Wright 2009, 1016)

We analyse a globally representative sample, comprising domestic and diasporic entrepreneurs around the world. Our global perspective transcends the common national perspective by adopting a multi-level, multi-sited and comparative approach as called for (Portes 2010; Zapata-Barrero and Rezaei 2020). Our global approach brings several specific contributions. First, the design pioners global comparisons of entrepreneurial endeavours in the diasporas from around the World. Second, we ascertain endeavors that are common and efforts that differ across diasporas from various origins. Third, the findings contribute to theorising by demonstrating that the effect of being in a diaspora upon exporting is mediated by transnational networking, but differently across various diasporas.

2. Theoretical background and hypotheses

Theorising about migrants has focused on immigrants in a host-country, as they are embedded in the host-country, and as they have a mixed embeddedness, combining embeddedness in the host-country with embeddedness in the community of immigrants (Kloosterman and Rath 2001; Honig, Drori, and Carmichael 2010; Zapata-Barrero and Hellgren 2020). Recent theorising considers migrants as they have a dual embeddedness, simultaneously embedded in host- and home-society (Minto-Coy 2018a; Rezaei and Goli 2020; Solano 2019). Another line of theorising focuses on embeddedness of migrants in their home-society (Van Gelderen 2007; Wahba and Zenou 2012). People emigrating from their home-society carry with them their traditions and institutions, which continue to guide their lives in the diaspora, and thereby they remain embedded in their home-society (Froschauer 2001; Rusinovic 2008). For example, their pursuit of networks in the diaspora resembles networks they had in the home-society. Notably, if they were oriented toward family in home-society, they also pursue private networking in the diaspora. If they were globally oriented in home-society, then, in the diaspora, they also pursue transnational networks. This embeddedness in society of origin is pursued here.

A diaspora, specifically, denotes the people originating from a homeland from which they have dispersed (Bauböck and Faist 2010). The people in a diaspora are distinguished from others, notably from those in other diasporas and from domestics staying in their country of birth (van Tubergen 2015). Diasporans are often oriented toward their homeland and network with domestics back home, often with support of the homeland-government (Minto-Coy 2011). Their connections with the homeland are increasingly an object of policies by the home-country, aiming at development, financial support, and attraction of talent and entrepreneurs (Zhao and Zhu 2009). The diaspora is thus a dispersed but socially bounded population of migrants, which may be imagined as a community in minds of migrants (Harney 2007), with distinct organisations (Portes and Fernandez-Kelly 2015), and with ties within the diaspora in place of residence (Osaghae and Cooney 2020), and to the homeland and diasporans around the World (Faist 2010; Ojo and Nwankwo 2017; Solano 2015).

Diasporans share practices; notably, forms of assimilation and transnational practices such as networking emerging from embeddedness in the homeland (Drori, Honig, and Wright 2009). Indeed, diasporans often pursue business networks and trade with entrepreneurs in their homeland (Portes, Guarnizo, and Haller 2002; Chen and Tan 2009; Elo 2015; Rezaei 2009). At the same time, their transnational engagement with the homeland goes beyond business interests by utilising skills, knowledge and experience gained in the host context for the benefit of home (Elo and Riddle 2016). This includes novel ways of organising, innovative business models, networking and supporting domestic entrepreneurs as a way of giving back and transforming business culture back home (Minto-Coy and Séraphin 2017). Beyond this, the success in the host society has also led transnational diaspora entrepreneurs to fund philanthropic initiatives benefiting both their diasporic community and people at home (Minto-Coy 2018a, 2018b).

2.1. Diasporas from countries in the five regions of the World

Each country has its diaspora, so the World has several hundred diasporas (United Nations 2017). For our analysis, diasporas are aggregated according to their position in the global network of migration. Specifically, an aggregate has dense migration among countries within the aggregate, and less migration to and from countries outside the aggregate. We discern five aggregates,

- Countries dominated by European culture,
- Central & South America,
- Sub-Sahara Africa,
- Middle East & North Africa, and
- Asia.

Migration among these five regions is patterned. Migration has mostly been to the region dominated by European culture from the other regions. Thereby the European culture region is the centre and the other regions form the periphery. The periphery is linked to the centre by dense migration from the periphery to the centre. Migration is sparse from the centre to the periphery, and between regions in the periphery. Each region is cohesive, with dense migration within the region (United Nations 2017; Castles, de Haas, and Miller 2014). The five origins are described briefly.

2.1.1. The diasporas from countries dominated by European culture
European culture dominates in the countries in Europe, the United States, Canada, Australia, New Zealand, and Israel. This region has large diasporas originating from Russia, UK, USA and Israel (Collyer 2012; Lavenex 2016; Weinar 2017). Migrants from European culture countries mostly reside in other countries within the region (84% of this diaspora), and few reside in the other regions (16%) (United Nations 2017).

Migrants from European culture countries frequently consider themselves expatriates rather than migrants, consider their moves mobility rather than migration, and consider their residence abroad temporary. They usually maintain citizenship in their home country and intend to return home upon completing their mission (Andrejuk 2017; Boswell and Geddes 2011; Menz 2016).

They easily maintain ties to their homeland and to business partners in most other countries around the world, especially within the European Union (Brzozowski, Surdej, and Cucculelli 2017). This central region has more wealth, higher education, elaborate institutions, and larger business networks than peripheral regions.

2.1.2. The diasporas from countries in Central & South America
Central & South America has large diasporas originating from Argentina, Venezuela and Mexico. Many migrants from Central and South American countries reside in other countries within the region (16%), but by far most (83%) migrated to the European culture region, especially to USA, Canada, UK, Spain and Portugal, with a few to other regions (1%) (United Nations 2017).

Migration is driven mainly by economic motives, but students and some others emigrate with the intention to return but are tempted by opportunities in wealthier host-countries. Fewer migrants are refugees escaping persecution and violence. Brain drain is a feature of this migration. However, migrants have become transnational entrepreneurs remitting funds and creating opportunities which extend beyond their family to the place and community back home, e.g. Home Town Associations. Through transnational diaspora entrepreneurship, returnee entrepreneurship and reverse migration, opportunities emerge for brain circulation. Several governments in the region are pursuing policies to increase remittancing beyond family consumption to include knowledge transfer, trade and investments (Délano 2014); expanding diasporic entrepreneurs' business networks with domestic entrepreneurs.

2.1.3. The diasporas from countries in Sub-Sahara Africa
Sub-Sahara Africa has large diasporas originating from Angola, Zimbabwe, South Africa and Sudan (Akyeampong 2000; Bilger and Kraler 2005; Grillo and Mazzucato 2008). By far most diasporans from Sub-Sahara African countries reside in other countries within the region (69%), many migrants are in the former colonial powers and other countries in the European culture region (25%), and a few others in the other regions (6%) (United Nations 2017; Koser 2003).

Africans have mainly two motives for migrating: opportunities for work and escaping conflict (Ojo, Nwankwo, and Gbadamosi 2013). Many of those migrating outside Africa pursue citizenship in countries of residence, otherwise they will return home. African returnees often become entrepreneurs, and diasporic entrepreneurs contribute to the development of the region (Mayer, Harima, and Freiling 2015; Thomas and Inkpen 2013). The entrepreneurial endeavours of diasporans and returnees rely extensively on ethnic and familial social networks (Levin and Barnard 2013).

2.1.4. The diasporas from countries in the Middle East & North Africa
The Middle East & North Africa (here excluding Israel) has large diasporas originating from Morocco, Egypt, Turkey and Iran (Aboud 2000). Most migrants from countries in the Middle East and North Africa reside in other countries within the region (55%), and many reside in the European culture region, especially the former colonial rulers (44%). Only 1% reside in other regions (United Nations 2017).

A major motive for their emigration is war, and many flee to neighbouring countries. Another major motive is seeking work, attracted by opportunities in oil-rich countries and Europe. Many migrants become entrepreneurs in Europe, often also in second generation (Eroğlu 2017; Schøtt 2017a, 2017b). An illustration is the transnational network among entrepreneurs in Iran and in the Iranian diaspora which brings handwoven Iranian carpets to European markets (Rezaei 2009). Diasporans often feel connected to their homeland. Many want to open a business and trade with peers there. Some diasporan entrepreneurs residing in Europe eventually return home, also in second generation. They are not many, but are important for the practices they bring, and for serving as role models (Icduygu 2012).

2.1.5. The diasporas from countries in Asia
Asia (here excluding the Middle East) has large diasporas originating from China, India, Pakistan, Korea, Philippines and Vietnam (Bagwell 2015; Hugo 2005; Kim and Oh 2011). Many migrants from Asian countries reside in other countries within the region (32%), but more are in the European culture region, especially the former rulers of colonies in Asia (40%), and many also in oil-producing countries in the Middle East (28%), but hardly any in other regions (United Nations 2017; Watkins, Ho, and Butler 2017).

Diasporans from Asia cluster entrepreneurially in niches, with dense ethnic networks, as exemplified by Asian take-away restaurants and Asian high-tech entrepreneurs. Several emerging economies are turning the past brain drain into brain circulation, by adopting policies to attract diasporan entrepreneurs to return to their homelands where they become entrepreneurs and builders of eco-systems for entrepreneurship. Policies of supporting joint ventures between diasporan and domestic entrepreneurs are pursued in India and China (Saxenian 2005; Wang and Liu 2016).

The diasporas originating from these five regions of the world form the global network of migration, providing embedding for transnational business networks pursued by entrepreneurs.

2.2. Transnational networks around entrepreneurs
Entrepreneurs often network for resources such as advice (Jensen and Schøtt 2015). Entrepreneurs network in the private sphere with family and friends for advice. Entrepreneurs

also network in the sphere of business operations, with people in a work-place, professions, and the market. Entrepreneurs may also network for advice in the transnational sphere (Ashourizadeh et al. 2014).

A well-documented proposition is that location of entrepreneurs shapes networking, in that diasporans, compared to domestics, have more extensive transnational networks (Jensen et al. 2016); this proposition is briefly reconfirmed here (Table 2). Another well-researched proposition is that origin affects networking, in that culture moulds entrepreneurs' transnational networking (Cheraghi and Schøtt 2016; Schøtt 2018). This proposition of differences across origins is reconfirmed (Table 2). Specifically, entrepreneurs in countries dominated by secular-rational culture have extensive transnational networks, as also briefly reconfirmed (Table 2). These propositions motivate a new hypothesis:

> Hypothesis 1. Origin and location in combination are affecting transnational networking. Specifically, for the European culture origin, diasporans and domestics hardly differ in networking, whereas, for the other origins, diasporans are networking more than domestics.

2.3. Export, affected by origin and location

It is well-known that location affects exporting, in that diasporans, compared to domestics, export more (e.g. Ashourizadeh et al. 2015b); this is briefly reconfirmed here (Table 5). It is also well-documented that origin affects exporting, in that countries differ in their domestic entrepreneurs' exports (e.g. Baklanov et al. 2014); also this is reconfirmed (Table 5). Specifically, domestics in European culture countries have more exports than domestics within other regions, as reconfirmed (Table 5). Yet another well-researched proposition is that transnational networking promotes exporting (Ashourizadeh and Schøtt 2015; Li, Chen, and Schøtt 2016), as also reconfirmed (Table 6). These propositions motivate a new hypothesis,

> Hypothesis 2. Transnational networks are channeling effects of both origin and location upon exports, in that origin and location affect networking, and networking promotes exporting.

This channeling may be additional effects, indirect effects through networking in addition to the more direct effects; or may be mediating effects, so that much of the effect is not direct, but occurs through networks. Whether the channeling is mediating or is additional indirect effects will be analysed. The well-known propositions and the new hypotheses are illustrated in Figure 1.

The causal scheme summarises the three direct effects on exporting from origin, location and transnational networking, the two indirect effects of origin and location upon exporting, which are hypothesised to be channelled through transnational networking, and also the hypothesised joint effect of locational and origin upon transnational networking. These propositions and hypotheses are ascertained here.

3. Research design

The problematique calls for a design comparing across and comparing locations. Collecting data on a diaspora is difficult because of its dispersion around the World (Ghimire

Hypothesized effects of origin and location upon transnational networking and exporting.

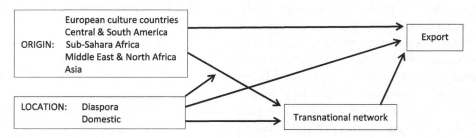

Figure 1. Hypothesised effects of origin and location upon transnational networking and exporting.

et al. 2017). Collecting data on all diasporas is only doable by global organisations (United Nations 2017). Fortunately, entrepreneurs around the World have been surveyed for the Global Entrepreneurship Monitor (Global Entrepreneurship Research Association 2018; Bosma et al. 2012). Questions asking about origin enable comparisons of the diasporas of the world.

3.1. Sampling

GEM samples in two stages (Bosma et al. 2012). First, countries are selected, by self-selection when a national team of researchers conducts the survey locally. Between 2012 and 2014 questions about origin were added to the survey of adults residing in 75 countries (von Bloh et al. 2019). This diverse sample seems representative of the societies around the World. Second, adults are sampled randomly in each participating country (Bosma et al. 2012). The survey identifies entrepreneurs as those who own and manage a starting or operating business, and asks about their business, e.g. exporting.

Our sample is the entrepreneurs, who reported their own and parents' country of birth, 55,068 entrepreneurs including 5,212 diasporans. This full sample is analysed for Tables 1 and 5. Networks were asked for entrepreneurs residing in 39 of the 75 countries. This subsample of 24,704 entrepreneurs is analysed for Table 2. For contrasting diasporans to domestics in multivariate analyses, domestics should not far outnumber diasporans. Therefore, in each country we randomly subsampled domestics, so the number of domestics is roughly four times the number of diasporans from the country. This subsample, 6,398 entrepreneurs, is analysed for Tables 3, 4 and 6.

3.2. Measurements

3.2.1. Location

An entrepreneur's location – domestic or diasporic – is indicated in the survey by asking (Global Entrepreneurship Research Association 2018):

Were you born in this country?

Was your mother born in this country?

Was your father born in this country?

If one or more of the three were born abroad, the respondent is considered diasporan. Conversely, if all three were born in the country, the respondent is considered domestic. This measurement of location is often used (e.g. Jensen, Rezaei, and Schøtt 2015; Jensen et al. 2016).

3.2.2. Origin

An entrepreneur's origin is the country that the person originates from. If the entrepreneur is domestic, the origin is the country the entrepreneur is living in. If the person is diasporan, the origin is identified by asking up to three questions. First, if the entrepreneur reported to not have been born in the country of residence, a follow-up question asked:

In what country were you born?

If the mother was reported to have been born abroad, a follow-up question asked,

In what country was she born?

If the father was reported to have been born abroad, a follow-up question asked,

In what country was he born?

The entrepreneur's origin is own country of birth, if born abroad; alternatively, country of birth of mother, if born abroad, and as another alternative, father's country of birth. This determines a diasporan's origin as a country other than country of residence. This determination of origin is used extensively (e.g. Ashourizadeh et al. 2015a).

3.2.3. Exporting

Exporting is measured by asking the entrepreneur:

What proportion of your customers will normally live outside your country?

The response is coded as a percentage. For multivariate analyses, the percentage is logged to reduce skew. This measure of exporting has been validated, and also used for researching diasporas (Ashourizadeh et al. 2015a; Liu and Schøtt 2019).

3.2.4. Networking

An entrepreneur's network is indicated by asking:

Various people may give you advice on your new business.

Have you received advice from any of the following:

Your spouse or life-companion? Your parents? Other family or relatives? Friends?

Somebody in another country? Somebody who has come from abroad?

A firm that you collaborate with? A firm that you compete with? A supplier? A customer? A lawyer? An accountant? A bank? A possible investor? A public advising services for business? A researcher or inventor? A current boss? Current work colleagues? Somebody who is starting a business? Somebody with much business experience?

These twenty potential advisors cluster in three spheres: the transnational, the private and the operations spheres, discerned in a cluster analysis (Jensen and Schøtt 2017).

Networking in the transnational sphere is measured as number of advisors reported of these two: somebody abroad and somebody from abroad (Cheraghi and Schøtt 2016). Networking in the private sphere is measured as the number of advisors of these four: spouse, parents, other family, and friends. Networking in the sphere of business operations is measured as the number of advisors among the other 14.

The measures of an entrepreneur's networks in various spheres have been used to research how networking is shaped by culture (Cheraghi and Schøtt 2016) and diasporic status (Jensen and Schøtt 2017), and how networks affect outcomes such as exporting (Li, Chen, and Schøtt 2016).

3.2.5. Control variables

Analyses should control for conditions affecting outcomes. The survey enables controlling for several characteristics (Bosma et al. 2012),

- Gender, coded 0 for women and 1 for men.
- Age, coded in years.
- Education, coded in years.
- Income of household, classified into lowest, middle, and highest third among the respondents in a country, coded 1, 2 and 3.
- Motive for starting the business, coded 0 if pushed by necessity, and 1 if pulled by opportunity.
- Age of business, as years since starting, logged to reduce skew.
- Owners of the business, a number of persons owning and managing the business, logged.
- Size of business, a number of persons working for it, logged.
- Innovativeness, as an index based on newness of product, uniqueness of product, and newness of technology, going from 1 to 3.
- Sector of business, with four categories: extractive sector, manufacturing sector, business services sector, and consumer services sector, which is the reference that each other sector is compared to.

We also control for a macro-level condition, economic wealth of country of residence, operationalised as Gross Domestic Product per capita, from the World Bank, logged to reduce skew.

3.3. Analytical strategy and modelling

An outcome such as networking and exporting is first indicated by the average for each origin and location (Tables 1, 2 and 5).

Causes of an outcome are better discerned by hierarchical linear modelling, which resembles regression, but also considers nesting of entrepreneurs within countries (Snijders and Bosker 2012). Effects on an outcome are modelled by using a dummy variable for location, coded 1 for diaspora and 0 for domestic, and a dummy variable for each origin, coded 1 if from that origin, and 0 if not. With five origins, we select one to be the reference to which each other origin is compared. The reference is the European culture region, as this seems most distinct from the other origins. This enables testing hypotheses about effects of origin and location upon networking and exporting.

4. Results

The following analyses background of diasporas, effects upon networking, and effects upon exports, partly channelled through the transnational network.

4.1. Background of the entrepreneurs

The background of entrepreneurs differs across origins and locations, Table 1.
Entrepreneurs differ in background across origins and across locations,

- Gender differs across place, in that women are less represented among diasporans than among domestics, except for the European culture origin.
- Age differs across place, in that diasporans are older than domestics, except for the European culture origin.
- Education of entrepreneurs is higher among diasporans than among domestics.
- Incomes among diasporan entrepreneurs and among domestic entrepreneurs are above average in the population of adults.
- Motives differ across location, in that diasporans, compared to the domestics, are more often pulled by opportunity than pushed by necessity.

Table 1. Background of the entrepreneurs, by origin and location.

	Location	European culture origin	Central & South American origin	Sub-Sahara African origin	Middle East & North African origin	Asian origin
Gender, per cent women	Diaspora	40%	44%	36%	20%	32%
	Domestic	36%	46%	48%	20%	44%
Age, years	Diaspora	42.5 y	39.3 y	35.5 y	36.7 y	42.0 y
	Domestic	43.4 y	38.8 y	34.8 y	36.4 y	40.5 y
Education, years	Diaspora	13.5 y	12.4 y	11.5 y	13.4 y	13.1 y
	Domestic	12.8 y	10.0 y	8.9 y	10.2 y	11.1 y
Income, 1–3 scale	Diaspora	2.3	2.2	2.1	2.2	2.3
	Domestic	2.3	2.2	2.1	2.1	2.0
Motive, per cent opportunity	Diaspora	59%	63%	60%	66%	66%
	Domestic	59%	63%	56%	49%	52%
Age of business, years	Diaspora	6.6 y	4.5 y	3.0	2.9	5.6
	Domestic	9.5 y	4.7 y	3.2	5.4	6.6
Owners of business, owners	Diaspora	1.8	1.7	2.0	2.4	1.9
	Domestic	1.7	1.6	1.5	1.7	1.5
Size of business, workers	Diaspora	6.7	1.9	2.7	11.9	9.4
	Domestic	5.8	1.8	1.9	5.3	5.7
Innovativeness of business	Diaspora	1.5	1.5	1.6	1.6	1.5
	Domestic	1.4	1.4	1.6	1.4	1.5
Sector: Extractive, per cent	Diaspora	4%	3%	4%	1%	2%
	Domestic	9%	5%	7%	9%	10%
Sector: Manufacturing, per cent	Diaspora	23%	21%	24%	32%	24%
	Domestic	24%	25%	16%	33%	17%
Sector: Business services, pct	Diaspora	30%	21%	12%	21%	26%
	Domestic	25%	12%	5%	11%	8%
Sector: Consumer services, pct	Diaspora	43%	56%	60%	46%	48%
	Domestic	42%	58%	72%	48%	65%
GDP per capita in host-country, logged	Diaspora	10.3	10.0	9.5	11.1	10.4
	Domestic	10.3	9.3	8.2	9.3	9.3
Export volume from host-country, per cent of GDP, logged	Diaspora	3.9	3.4	3.7	3.9	4.1
	Domestic	3.5	3.2	3.4	3.2	3.7

Note: Table 1 is based on the full sample of 55,068 entrepreneurs including 5,212 diasporans.

- Businesses differ, in that diasporans, compared to domestics, have businesses that are younger, with more owners, staff, and innovativion.
- Sectors differ, in that diasporans, compared to domestics, have businesses less often in the sector of extraction, but more often in the sector of business services.

Table 1 also reconfirms that diasporans have migrated to regions, that are wealthier in terms of Gross Domestic Product per capita, and more export-oriented.

4.2. Networks affected by origin and location

Networking differs across origins and locations, Table 2.

Transnational networks around domestics are largest in the European culture countries, Table 2. As expected, for every origin, diasporans have larger transnational networks than domestics. As hypothesised, the European culture origin has the smallest difference between diasporans and domestics in their transnational networks. This is explained partly by the already extensive transnational networks among domestics, and by the circumstance that the diasporans from European culture countries are not in any region with larger transnational networks.

Causal effects are better ascertained by modelling networking as a function of location and origin, using a dummy variable for diasporic contrasted domestic location and a dummy for having a certain origin contrasted having a European culture origin, Table 3.

Transnational networking is positively affected by being diasporan rather than domestic, Model 1 in Table 3. Transnational networking is negatively affected by being domestic within any region other than within the European culture region, Model 1. The combined effects of location and origin are the interaction effects in Model 2. The interaction effects are positive, showing that the difference in networking between domestics and diasporans from every origin is bigger than the difference for the European culture origin. The effects of location and origin are estimated by the coefficients in Table 3, and the summed coefficients are listed in Table 4.

Table 4 shows the combined effects of location and origin upon transnational networking. The domestics in the European culture countries form the reference to which each other kind of entrepreneur is compared. Compared to the European domestics, the domestics in every other region have smaller transnational networks, especially domestics in Asia. The diaspora from European culture countries has transnational networks that are hardly larger than the transnational networks around the domestics in the European

Table 2. Networks around entrepreneurs, by origin and location.

	Range	Location	European culture origin	Central & South American origin	Sub-Sahara African origin	Middle East & North African origin	Asian origin
Transnational network	0–2	Diaspora	.48	.34	.57	.57	.21
		Domestic	.43	.19	.18	.19	.08
Operational sphere network	0–14	Diaspora	3.65	2.25	3.63	4.47	2.36
		Domestic	3.63	1.94	2.17	2.09	1.49
Private sphere network	0–4	Diaspora	1.71	1.78	2.62	1.99	1.66
		Domestic	1.70	1.93	2.50	1.94	2.14
Whole network	0–20	Diaspora	5.85	4.38	6.80	7.03	4.23
		Domestic	5.75	4.05	4.83	4.17	3.71

Note: Table 2 is based on the 24,704 entrepreneurs with measured networks.

Table 3. Transnational networks around entrepreneurs, affected by location and origin.

	Model 1 Main effects	Model 2 Interaction effects
Location: Diaspora versus domestic	.24 ***	.02[a]
Origin: Central & South America	−.31 ***	−.37[a]
Origin: Sub-Sahara Africa	−.21 ***	−.37[a]
Origin: Middle East & North Africa	−.23 ***	−.28[a]
Origin: Asia	−.56 ***	−.62[a]
Diaspora * Central & South America		.16 *
Diaspora * Sub-Sahara Africa		.62 ***
Diaspora * Middle East & North Africa		.20 *
Diaspora * Asia		.19 *
Gender (males 1, females 0)	.07 **	.06 *
Age	−.01	−.01
Education	.05 ***	.05 ***
Income	.05 ***	.05 ***
Motive: opportunity	.11 ***	.11 ***
Age of business	−.06 ***	−.06 ***
Owners of business	.05 ***	.04 ***
Size of business	.07 ***	.07 ***
Innovativeness of business	.06 ***	.06 ***
Sector: extractive	−.03	−.05
Sector: manufacture	−.01	−.02
Sector: business services	.08 *	.09 *
GDP per capita in country of residence	.06	.05
Intercept	.10 **	.17 ***

Notes: Hierarchical linear modelling (using a subsample of 6,100 entrepreneurs; cf. Section 3.1). Origin has European culture countries as reference, to which each other origin is compared. Sector has business services as reference, to which each other sector is compared. The dependent variable and the macro-level independent variable are standardised. Each micro-level numerical independent variable is standardised and centred in country of residence. Each dichotomous variable is a 0–1 dummy.
*$p < .05$.
**$p < .01$.
***$p < .001$.
[a]Significance is not tested (significance is tested in the model of main effects).

culture region. The diasporas from other regions differ in transnational networks, small in the Asian diasporas and large in the Sub-Sahara African diasporas.

4.3. Export affected by origin, location, and networks

Exporting differs across origins and locations, Table 5. Among domestics, exporting is highest in the European culture countries. For every origin, diasporans are exporting more than domestics, especially for those originating from Central & South America, from Middle East & North Africa, and from Asia.

Causal effects are ascertained by modelling exporting as a function of origin and location, Table 6. Exporting is positively affected by being diasporan rather than domestic.

Table 4. Effects of combinations of location and origin upon transnational networks.

		Location	
		Domestic	Diaspora
Origin	European culture countries	0 (reference)	.02
	Central and South America	−.37	−.21
	Sub-Sahara Africa	−.37	.25
	Middle East & North Africa	−.28	−.08
	Asia	−.62	−.43

Note: Table 4 is derived from Table 3; cf. section 4.2.

Table 5. Exports, by origin and location.

	European culture origin	Central & South American origin	Sub-Sahara African origin	Middle East & North African origin	Asian Origin
Diaspora	19.9%	12.6%	17.0%	18.0%	18.6%
Domestic	10.5%	5.2%	10.4%	6.9%	4.6%

Note: Table 5 is based on the 50,794 entrepreneurs with measured exports.

Table 6. Export, affected by origin, location, and networking.

Origin: Central & South America	−.67 ***
Origin: Sub-Sahara Africa	−.09 ***
Origin: Middle East & North Africa	−.58 ***
Origin: Asia	−.82 ***
Location: diaspora versus domestic	.13 ***
Transnational network	.33 ***
Operations sphere network	.03 ***
Private sphere network	.002
Gender (males 1, females 0)	.01
Age	−.03 *
Education	.05
Income	.00
Motive, opportunity	.08 ***
Age of business	−.01
Owners of business	.05 ***
Size of business	.10 ***
Innovativeness of business	.09 ***
Sector: Extractive	−.14 **
Sector: Manufacturing	−.02
Sector: Business services	.06
GDP per capita in host-country	.09
Intercept	.30 ***

Notes: Hierarchical linear modelling (using a subsample of 5,710 entrepreneurs; cf. Section 3.1). Origin has European culture as reference, to which each other origin is compared. Sector has business services as reference, to which each other sector is compared. The dependent variable and the macro-level independent variable are standardised. Each micro-level numerical independent variable is standardised and centred in country of residence. Each dichotomous variable is a 0–1 dummy.

*$p < .05$.
**$p < .01$.
***$p < .001$.

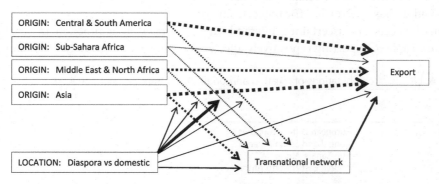

Figure 2. Estimated effects of origin and location upon transnational networking and exporting.

Exporting is negatively affected by being domestic within any region other than within the European culture countries.

Hypothesis 2 posited that effects of origin and location upon exporting are channelled through transnational networking. This is indicated by a positive effect of transnational networking upon exporting, Table 6. The networks in the operations sphere and the private sphere are included in Table 6. These two networks hardly affect exporting, so they hardly channel effects of location and origin upon exporting or otherwise expand the account. This reemphasises benefits of transnational networking.

In short, location and origin affect exporting, with direct effects and indirect effects channelled through transnational networking, but effects differ across diasporas.

5. Conclusions

The research question has been: *How is embeddedness of diasporic entrepreneurs in their origins shaping their pursuits of transnational networks and trade?* Analyses revealed direct effects of origin and location and indirect effects, through transnational networking, upon exporting. The estimated effects are summarised in Figure 2.

The direct effect of location on export is drawn as a solid arrow indicating that the effect of being diasporan, compared to domestic, is positive. The indirect effect of location on export, through transnational networking, is drawn as an arrow from location to networking, which is solid, signifying that diasporans are networking more extensively, followed by an arrow from networking to exporting that is also solid, signifying that this effect is positive. Thickness of arrows symbolises strength of effects, as indicated by standardised coefficients. So, in short, diasporas differ considerably in their networking, and partly through this channel they differ considerably in their exporting. Origin directly affects exporting as indicated by four arrows. Originating from Central & South America, rather than the European culture region, entails less exports, indicated by a dashed arrow. Likewise, originating from Sub-Sahara Africa, from Middle East & North Africa and from Asia, rather than from the European culture region, entail less exports, indicated by dashed arrows.

Furthermore, origin indirectly affects exporting through networking. Originating from Central & South America, from Sub-Sahara Africa, from Middle East & North Africa, and from Asia, rather than from the European culture countries, reduces networking as indicated by the four dashed arrows, and thereby entails less exporting. However, these four reductions are alleviated by being diasporan rather than domestic, as indicated by the four positive interaction effects represented as the four solid arrows from location to the four dashed arrows.

We briefly conclude for each region of origin. The European culture countries evidence only small gains for their diasporans, compared to their domestics, in transnational networking and exporting. That the gains are small is due partly to the already extensive networks and exports in the European culture countries, and partly to the circumstance that the diasporans are not residing in any region with more networking and exporting. These gains of diasporans relative to domestics in the European culture countries are smaller than the gains of diasporans relative to domestics in any of the four other regions.

Diasporans from Asian countries differ from their domestic peers, in that they are networking much more in the transnational sphere, and also more in the operational sphere, but less in the private sphere. Although these diasporans originate from countries with little exporting, they are intensive exporters in the diaspora. This shift is partly because of the diasporans' extensive transnational networks, that are a conduit for exporting. Such transnational networking is exemplified in ventures undertaken by diasporic entrepreneurs from India, jointly with entrepreneurs back home (Pruthi, Basu, and Wright 2018).

Diasporans from Africa are also more likely to export through networks than their domestic peers. These gains in exporting by diasporans may be attributed to the dense network of social relations and their embeddedness in the cultural and institutional environment of their home countries. Moreover, the nature of ventures they found may increase their export, for example circuit, cultural and ethnic enterprises relying on tangible and intangible resources that flow from home- and host-countries and promote exporting.

Diasporans from Central and South America are also shown to export more than domestics, demonstrating their potential in helping to secure more equitable engagement for peripheral contexts via diaspora trade. When we see that networking promotes exporting, then domestic entrepeneurs from the region can increase their exports via networking with their diasporan peers. This is consistent with case-studies (Kumar and Steenkamp 2013; Minto-Coy 2016), suggesting diasporic networks help firms from emerging markets to internationalise and overcome challenges such as liability of foreignness.

Diasporans from Middle East and North Africa originate from societies with much networking in the private sphere, but little operational sphere networking and little transnational networking. Despite this background, the diasporans pursue transnational networking and thereby enhance trade. Thereby they can serve as business partners for peers in their home countries. A classical example is Iranian carpets that are marketed in Europe through a transnational network of entrepreneurs in Iran and in the Iranian diaspora (Rezaei 2009). With anti-Islamic sentiment rising in societies of residence, more diasporans are likely to return home. The diasporan entrepreneurs have a hitherto unrealised potential for carrying institutional arrangements and becoming role-models.

The European culture region is thus a centre of diasporan networking and trade with the other regions forming a periphery.

5.1. Contributions

The study addresses calls for research on how transnational entrepreneurs are networking for business outcomes, as embedded in societies of residence and societies of origin (Drori, Honig, and Wright 2009; Honig, Drori, and Carmichael 2010). The study also addresses the need for research more encompassing than the common case-studies, a need voiced in calls for comparative and global studies of heterogenous diasporas (e.g. Castles 2007; 2010).

The study makes several contributions. Firstly, it addresses the dearth of global comparisons of diasporas originating from around the World. Second, the account contributes to theorising by demonstrating how transnational networking benefits exporting, in every location and every origin. Indeed, diasporans export more than domestics, by direct effect and by additional indirect effects mediated through transnational networks. Third, the findings demonstrate considerable differences among the diasporas from various origins. The findings are also relevant from a managerial and policy perspective, suggesting strategies for export-led growth via transnational diaspora entrepreneurship.

5.2. Limitations

The strength of our study is its coverage of the diasporas from the various regions around the World. This implies omission of detail. A major limitation is that heterogeneity within each diaspora is ignored. For example, the differences between the second-generation and first-generation migrants, notably in the balance of dual embeddedness in home-society and in host-society, has been ignored. As another example, the diaspora from countries in Central and South America comprises the segment that has migrated within the region and the segment that has migrated to the European culture region, and these two segments differ, in both networking and exporting (Schøtt 2018).

5.3. Future research

Our account intimate possibilities for future research. Firstly, it would be fruitful to distinguish between different segments of a diaspora (Portes and Martinez 2020), especially between the segment that resides in proximate and similar host-societies, and the segment in distant societies (Baltar and Icart 2013). Secondly, it would be fruitful to compare entrepreneurs originating from the centre with entrepreneurs originating from the peripheral regions (Honig 2020; Schøtt 2016). A third line of investigation may aim at understanding the experiences of returnee diaspora entrepreneurs as they bring institutional arrangements, knowledge and transnational networks for conducting international trade (Filatotchev et al. 2009). Finally, future research could also assess the role of transnational diaspora entrepreneurs in helping domestic firms to internationalise and overcome liabilities of foreignness (Minto-Coy 2016).

Acknowledgements

The study benefited from comments by reviewers and editors, and from discussion with Alejandro Portes and hospitality at the Center for Migration and Development, Princeton University.

Disclosure statement

No potential conflict of interest was reported by the authors.

Funding

Schøtt visited as a Marie Curie Fellow in the DiasporaLink project, funded by EU Horizon 2020 grant 645471. Liu was supported by an award for her research project 'On the collaborative ability and improvement of hybrid organization in entrepreneurial universities' from the National Natural Science Foundation of China, grant number 71603241.

References

Aboud, B. 2000. "Re-reading Arab World-New World Immigration History: Beyond the Prewar/Postwar Divide." *Journal of Ethnic and Migration Studies* 26 (4): 653–673.

Akyeampong, E. 2000. "Africans in the Diaspora: The Diaspora and Africa." *African Affairs* 99 (395): 183–215.

Andrejuk, K. 2017. "Self-employed Migrants From EU Member States in Poland: Differentiated Professional Trajectories and Explanations of Entrepreneurial Success." *Journal of Ethnic and Migration Studies* 43 (4): 560–577.

Ashourizadeh, S., S. Rezaei, T. Schøtt, and K. W. Jensen. 2015a. "People's Human and Social Capital Benefiting Careers in Entrepreneurship: Adults in China and in the Chinese Diaspora." *International Journal of Business and Globalisation* 16 (3): 378–400.

Ashourizadeh, S., S. Rezaei, T. Schøtt, and J. Vang. 2014. "Entrepreneurs' Human and Social Capital: Direct and Reinforcing Benefits for Export." *International Journal of Entrepreneurship and Small Business* 21 (2): 246–267.

Ashourizadeh, S., and T. Schøtt. 2015. "Exporting Embedded in Culture and Transnational Networks Around Entrepreneurs: a Global Study." *International Journal of Business and Globalisation* 16 (3): 314–334.

Ashourizadeh, S., T. Schøtt, E. P. Şengüler, and Y. Wang. 2015b. "Exporting by Migrants and Indigenous Entrepreneurs: Contingent on Gender and Education." *International Journal of Business and Globalisation* 16 (3): 264–283.

Bagwell, S. 2015. "Transnational Entrepreneurship Amongst Vietnamese Businesses in London." *Journal of Ethnic and Migration Studies* 41 (2): 329–349.

Baklanov, N., S. Rezaei, J. Vang, and L.-P. Dana. 2014. "Migrant Entrepreneurship, Economic Activity and Export Performance: Mapping the Danish Trends." *International Journal of Entrepreneurship and Small Business* 23 (1/2): 63–93.

Baltar, F., and I. B. Icart. 2013. "Entrepreneurial Gain, Cultural Similarity and Transnational Entrepreneurship." *Global Networks* 13 (2): 200–220.

Bauböck, R., and T. Faist. 2010. *Diaspora and Transnationalism: Concepts, Theories and Methods*. Amsterdam: Amsterdam University Press.

Bilger, V., and A. Kraler. (eds.) 2005. "African Migrations: Historical Perspectives and Contemporary Dynamics." *Stichproben* 5 (8): 1–328.

Bosma, N., A. Coduras, Y. Litovsky, and J. Seaman. 2012. *GEM Manual. A Report of the Design, Data and Quality Control of the Global Entrepreneurship Monitor*. Accessed April 2018. www.gemconsortium.org.

Boswell, C., and A. Geddes. 2011. *Migration and Mobility in the European Union*. Basingstoke: Palgrave.

Brzozowski, J., A. Surdej, and M. Cucculelli. 2017. "The Determinants of Transnational Entrepreneurship and Transnational Ties' Dynamics among Immigrant Entrepreneurs in ICT Sector in Italy." *International Migration* 55 (3): 105–125.

Castles, S. 2007. "Twenty-first-century Migration as a Challenge to Sociology." *Journal of Ethnic and Migration Studies* 33 (3): 351–371.

Castles, S. 2010. "Understanding Global Migration: A Social Transformation Perspective." *Journal of Ethnic and Migration Studies* 36 (10): 1565–1586.

Castles, S., H. de Haas, and M. J. Miller. 2014. *The Age of Migration, 5th ed.: International Population Movements*. New York: Guilford.

Chen, W., and J. Tan. 2009. "Understanding Transnational Entrepreneurship Through a Network Lens: Theoretical and Methodological Considerations." *Entrepreneurship Theory and Practice* 33 (5): 1079–1091.

Cheraghi, M., and T. Schøtt. 2016. "Conceived Globals: Entrepreneurs' Transnational Networking, Across Phases, and Embedded in Culture." *International Journal of Business and Globalisation* 16 (3): 209–227.

Collyer, M. 2012. "Migrants as Strategic Actors in the European Union's Global Approach to Migration and Mobility." *Global Networks* 12 (4): 505–524.

Délano, A. 2014. "The Diffusion of Diaspora Engagement Policies: A Latin American Agenda." *Political Geography* 41: 90–100.

Drori, I., B. Honig, and M. Wright. 2009. "Transnational Entrepreneurship: An Emergent Field of Study." *Entrepreneurship Theory and Practice* 33 (5): 1001–1022.

Elo, M. 2015. "Diaspora Networks in International Business: A Review on an Emerging Stream of Research." In *Handbook on International Alliance and Network Research*, edited by J. Larimo, N. Nummela, and T. Mainela, 13–41. Cheltenham: Elgar.

Elo, M., and L. Riddle. 2016. *Diaspora Business*. Oxford: Interdisciplinary Press.
Eroğlu, S. 2017. "Trapped in Small Business? An Investigation of Three Generations of Migrants From Turkey to Western Europe." *Journal of Ethnic and Migration Studies, Online*, doi:10.1080/1369183X.2017.1323629.
Faist, T. 2010. "Towards Transnational Studies: World Theories, Transnationalisation and Changing Institutions." *Journal of Ethnic and Migration Studies* 36 (10): 1665–1687.
Filatotchev, I., X. Liu, T. Buck, and M. Wright. 2009. "The Export Orientation and Export Performance of High-Technology SMEs in Emerging Markets: The Effects of Knowledge Transfer by Returnee Entrepreneurs." *Journal of International Business Studies* 40: 1005–1021.
Froschauer, K. 2001. "East Asian and European Entrepreneur Immigrants in British Columbia, Canada: Post-Migration Conduct and Pre-migration Context." *Journal of Ethnic and Migration Studies* 27 (2): 225–240.
Ghimire, D. J., N. E. Williams, A. Thornton, Linda Young-DeMarco, and P. Bhandari. 2017. "Strategies for Origin-Based Surveying of International Migrants." *Journal of Ethnic and Migration Studies*, Online. doi:10.1080/1369183X.2017.1394178.
Global Entrepreneurship Research Association. 2018. www.gemconsortium.org Accessed April 2018.
Grillo, R., and V. Mazzucato. 2008. "Africa < > Europe: A Double Engagement." *Journal of Ethnic and Migration Studies* 34 (2): 175–198.
Harney, N. D. 2007. "Transnationalism and Entrepreneurial Migrancy in Naples, Italy." *Journal of Ethnic and Migration Studies* 33 (2): 219–232.
Honig, B., I. Drori, and B. Carmichael. 2010. *Transnational and Immigrant Entrepreneurship in a Globalized World*. Toronto: University of Toronto Press.
Honig, B. 2020. "Exploring the Intersection of Transnational, Ethnic, and Migration Entrepreneurship." *Journal of Ethnic and Migration Studies* 46 (10): 1974–1990. doi:10.1080/1369183X.2018.1559993.
Hugo, G. 2005. "The New International Migration in Asia." *Asian Population Studies* 1 (1): 93–120.
Icduygu, A. 2012. "50 Years After the Labour Recruitment Agreement with Germany: The Consequences of Emigration for Turkey." *Perceptions Journal of International Affairs* 17 (2): 11–36.
Jensen, K. W., S. Rezaei, and T. Schøtt. 2015. "Talent among Chinese Entrepreneurs at Home and Abroad." In *Entrepreneurship and Talent Management From a Global Perspective: Global Returnees*, edited by H. Wang, and Y. Liu, 62–91. Cheltenham: Elgar.
Jensen, K. W., S. Rezaei, T. Schøtt, S. Ashourizadeh, and J. Li. 2016. "Chinese Entrepreneurs' Human and Social Capital Benefiting Innovation: in China and in the Chinese Diaspora." *International Journal of Business and Globalisation* 16 (3): 350–377.
Jensen, K. W., and T. Schøtt. 2015. "Verification of Lack of Emergent Behavior in Extending a Social Network of Agents." *Social Network Analysis and Mining* 5 (1): 1–17. Article 48, doi:10.1007/s13278-015-0287-8.
Jensen, K. W., and T. Schøtt. 2017. "Components of the Network Around an Actor." In *Encyclopedia of Social Network Analysis and Mining*, Vol 1, 2nd edition., edited by R. Alhajj and J. Rokne. New York: Springer.
Kim, H.-R., and I. Oh. 2011. "Migration and Multicultural Contention in East Asia." *Journal of Ethnic and Migration Studies* 37 (10): 1563–1581.
Kloosterman, R., and J. Rath. 2001. "Immigrant Entrepreneurs in Advanced Economies: Mixed Embeddedness Further Explored." *Journal of Ethnic and Migration Studies* 27 (2): 189–201.
Koser, K. 2003. *New African Diasporas*. London: Routledge.
Kumar, N., and J.-B. Steenkamp. 2013. *'The Diaspora Route'. Brand Breakout How Emerging Market Brands Will Go Global*. Houndmills. Basingstoke: Hampshire: Palgrave.
Lavenex, S. 2016. "Multilevelling EU External Governance: The Role of International Organizations in the Diffusion of EU Migration Policies." *Journal of Ethnic and Migration Studies* 42 (4): 554–570.
Levin, D., and H. Barnard. 2013. "Connections to Distant Knowledge: Interpersonal Ties Between More- and Less-Developed Countries." *Journal of International Business Studies* 44 (7): 676–698.
Li, J., Z. Chen, and T. Schøtt. 2016. "Innovation Benefitting Exporting: Benefit Enhanced by Transnational Networking." *International Journal of Business and Globalisation* 16 (3): 245–263.

Liu, Y., and T. Schøtt. 2019. "Life-satisfaction of Entrepreneurs in the Diaspora: Embedded in Transnational Networks and in International Business." In *Diaspora Networks in International Business: Perspectives for Understanding and Managing Diaspora Resources and Business*, edited by M. Elo and I. Minto-Coy, 257–275. Heidelberg: Springer.

Mayer, S. D., A. Harima, and J. Freiling. 2015. "Network Benefits for Ghanaian Diaspora and Returnee Entrepreneurs." *Entrepreneurial Business and Economics Review* 3 (3): 95–121.

Menz, G. 2016. "Framing Competitiveness: The Advocacy of Migration as an Essential Human Resources Strategy in Europe." *Journal of Ethnic and Migration Studies* 42 (4): 625–642.

Minto-Coy, I. D. 2011. "'Beyond Remittancing': An Investigation of the Role of ICTs in Facilitating and Extending the Diaspora's Contribution to the Caribbean." *Canadian Foreign Policy Journal* 17 (2): 129–141.

Minto-Coy, I. D. 2016. "The Role of Diasporas in the Growth and Internationalization of Businesses in Countries of Origin." In *Diaspora Business*, edited by M. Elo and L. Riddle. Oxford: Inter-Disciplinary Press.

Minto-Coy, I. D. 2018a. "From the Periphery to the Centre: Start-up and Growth Strategies for Minority Diaspora Entrepreneurs." *International Journal of Entrepreneurship and Small Business* (in press).

Minto-Coy, I. D. 2018b. "Marshalling Transnational Partners for Caribbean Development: The Role of the Diaspora." In *Caribbean Realities and Endogenous Sustainability, Barbados*, edited by N. Karagiannis, and D. A. Mohammed. Jamaica & T&T: University of West Indies Press. (in press).

Minto-Coy, I. D., and H. Séraphin. 2017. "The Role of the Diaspora in the Emergence and Territorial Intelligence in Haiti." *International Journal of Business and Emerging Markets* 9 (1): 48–67.

Ojo, S., and S. Nwankwo. 2017. "Diaspora and Transnational Entrepreneurship: A Conceptual Exploration." In *Diaspora and Transnational Entrepreneurship in Global Contexts*, edited by S. Ojo and S. Nwankwo, 1–22. Hershey: IGI Global.

Ojo, S., S. Nwankwo, and A. Gbadamosi. 2013. "Ethnic Entrepreneurship: The Myths of Informal and Illegal Enterprises in the UK." *Entrepreneurship & Regional Development* 25 (7-8): 587–611.

Osaghae, O., and T. Cooney. 2020. "Exploring the Relationship Between Immigrant Enclave Theory and Transnational Diaspora Entrepreneurial Opportunity Formation." *Journal of Ethnic and Migration Studies* 46 (10): 2086–2105. doi:10.1080/1369183X.2018.1560001.

Portes, A. 2010. "Migration and Social Change: Some Conceptual Reflections." *Journal of Ethnic and Migration Studies* 36 (10): 1537–1563.

Portes, A., and P. Fernandez-Kelly. 2015. *The State and the Grassroots: Immigrant Transnational Organizations in Four Continents*. New York: Berghahn Press.

Portes, A., L. Guarnizo, and W. Haller. 2002. "Transnational Entrepreneurs: An Alternative Form of Immigrant Economic Adaptation." *American Sociological Review* 67 (2): 278–298.

Portes, A., and B. P. Martinez. 2020. "They are not all the Same: Immigrant Enterprises, Transnationalism, and Development." *Journal of Ethnic and Migration Studies* 46 (10): 1991–2007. doi:10.1080/1369183X.2018.1559995.

Pruthi, S., A. Basu, and M. Wright. 2018. "Ethnic Ties, Motivations, and Home Country Entry Strategy of Transnational Entrepreneurs." *Journal of International Entrepreneurship (Online)*, doi:10.1007/s10843-017-0223-2.

Rezaei, S. 2009. "The Marginalization of Globally-Born Businesses: Ethnically Divided Trade in Hamburg and the World Economy-The Case of Global Persian Carpet Trade Through Ethnic Networks." *American Journal of Economics and Business Administration* 1 (2): 79–96.

Rezaei, S., L.-P. Dana, and V. Ramadani. (eds.). 2017. *Iranian Entrepreneurship: Deciphering the Entrepreneurial Eco-System in Iran and in the Iranian Diaspora*. Cham: Springer.

Rezaei, S., and M. Goli. 2020. "Prometheus, the Double-troubled – Migrant Transnational Entrepreneurs and the Loyalty Trap." *Journal of Ethnic and Migration Studies* 46 (10): 2045–2066. doi:10.1080/1369183X.2018.1559998.

Rusinovic, K. 2008. "Transnational Embeddedness: Transnational Activities and Networks among First- and Second-Generation Immigrant Entrepreneurs in the Netherlands." *Journal of Ethnic and Migration Studies* 34 (3): 431–451.

Saxenian, A. 2005. "From Brain Drain to Brain Circulation: Transnational Communities and Regional Upgrading in India and China." *Studies in Comparative International Development* 40: 35–61.

Schøtt, T. 2016. "Entrepreneurs' Satisfaction with job and Life in the Sub-Sahara African Diaspora: Dual Embeddedness in Home-Society and Host-Society." *FUTA Journal of Management and Technology* 1 (1): 75–83.

Schøtt, T. 2017a. "Immigrant and Indigenous Youth in Europe: Entrepreneurial Intention Building on Human, Financial and Social Capital." *International Journal of Entrepreneurship and Small Business* 30 (3): 374–394.

Schøtt, T. 2017b. "Networks Around Women and men Entrepreneurs in the Iranian Diaspora: Dual Embeddedness in Iran and in Host-Society." In *Iranian Entrepreneurship: Deciphering the Entrepreneurial Eco-System in Iran and in the Iranian Diaspora*, edited by S. Rezaei, L.-P. Dana, and V. Ramadani, 231–247. Berlin: Springer.

Schøtt, T. 2018. "Entrepreneurial Pursuits in the Caribbean Diaspora: Networks and Their Mixed Effects." *Entrepreneurship & Regional Development* 30 (9–10): 1069–1090. doi:10.1080/08985626.2018.1515825.

Snijders, T. A. B., and R. J. Bosker. 2012. *Multilevel Analysis: An Introduction to Basic and Advanced Multilevel Modeling*. Los Angeles: Sage.

Solano, G. 2015. "Transnational vs. Domestic Immigrant Entrepreneurs: A Comparative Literature Analysis of the use of Personal Skills and Social Networks." *American Journal of Entrepreneurship* 8 (2): 1–21.

Solano, G. 2020. "The Mixed Embeddedness of Transnational Migrant Entrepreneurs: Moroccans in Amsterdam and Milan." *Journal of Ethnic and Migration Studies* 46 (10): 2067–2085. doi:10.1080/1369183X.2018.1559999.

Thomas, K. J. A., and C. Inkpen. 2013. "Migration Dynamics, Entrepreneurship, and African Development: Lessons From Malawi." *International Migration Review* 47: 844–873.

United Nations. 2017. "International Migration Stock: The 2017 Revision." (UN_MigrantStockByOriginAndDestination_2017.xlsx). http://www.un.org/en/development/desa/population/migration/data/estimates2/estimates17.shtml. Accessed April 2018.

Van Gelderen, M. 2007. "Country of Origin as a Source of Business Opportunities." *International Journal of Entrepreneurship and Small Business* 4 (4): 419–430.

van Tubergen, F. 2015. "Ethnic Boundaries in Core Discussion Networks: A Multilevel Social Network Study of Turks and Moroccans in the Netherlands." *Journal of Ethnic and Migration Studies* 41 (1): 101–116.

von Bloh, J., V. Mandakovic, M. Apablaza, J. E. Amorós, and R. Sternberg. 2020. "Transnational Entrepreneurs: Opportunity or Necessity Driven? Empirical Evidence From two Dynamic Economies From Latin America and Europe." *Journal of Ethnic and Migration Studies* 46 (10): 2008–2026. doi:10.1080/1369183X.2018.1559996.

Wahba, J., and Y. Zenou. 2012. "Out of Sight, out of Mind: Migration, Entrepreneurship and Social Capital." *Regional Science and Urban Economics* 42: 890–903.

Wang, H., and Y. Liu. 2016. *Entrepreneurship and Talent Management From a Global Perspective: Global Returnees*. Cheltenham: Elgar.

Watkins, M., C. Ho, and R. Butler. 2017. "Asian Migration and Education Cultures in the Anglo-Sphere." *Journal of Ethnic and Migration Studies* 43 (14): 2283–2299.

Weinar, A. 2017. "From Emigrants to Free Movers: Whither European Emigration and Diaspora Policy?" *Journal of Ethnic and Migration Studies* 43 (13): 2228–2246.

Zapata-Barrero, R., and Z. Hellgren. 2020. "Harnessing the Potential of Moroccans Living Abroad Through Diaspora Policies? Assessing the Factors of Success and Failure of a new Structure of Opportunities for Transnational Entrepreneurs." *Journal of Ethnic and Migration Studies* 46 (10): 2027–2044. doi:10.1080/1369183X.2018.1559997.

Zapata-Barrero, R., and S. Rezaei. 2020. "Diaspora Governance and Transnational Entrepreneurship: The Rise of an Emerging Social Global Pattern in Migration Studies." *Journal of Ethnic and Migration Studies* 46 (10): 1959–1973. doi:10.1080/1369183X.2018.1559990.

Zhao, L., and J. Zhu. 2009. "China Attracting Global Talent: Central and Local Initiatives." *China: An International Journal* 07: 323–335.

Index

Aboud, J. 135
Adult Population Survey (APS) 56
Agarwala, Rina 43
Aldrich, H. 129–131, 135, 137–138, 140–141
Altinay, E. 132
Altinay, L. 132
Alvarez, S. A. 135
ambivalent loyalty 102
Amsterdam 7–8, 96, 109–110, 112–115, 117, 123
Arab sofas 116

Bach, R. L. 130
Bagwell, S. 110–111, 113, 120–121
Barney, J. B. 135
Basch, L. 129
Bauböck, R. 133
Belgium 79–80, 115–118
Belguendouz, A. 83
Blanc, C. S. 129
Bourdieu, P. 131
brain gain 12, 46, 73, 88
Brzozowski, J. 54
business 3–6, 8, 10, 54–56, 58–59, 64–65, 76–82, 87, 90–91, 93–96, 99–100, 109–111, 113–116, 118–122, 129–130, 132, 154–156, 158; activities 23, 34, 43, 80–81, 96, 111, 113, 115, 149; cultures 10, 12; development 8, 131; networks 119, 150–151; outcomes 112, 162; sector 113, 156; services 158

Campbell, R. B. 134
capital 22–23, 39–40, 42, 55, 59, 63, 82, 97, 131, 133, 137, 139–140, 142
Carling, J. 102
Central America 9, 148, 150–151, 159, 161
Chile 6, 52–53, 56–59, 61, 63–65, 89
Chilean economic development agency (CORFO) 59
Chilean entrepreneurs 63
Chilean Government 6, 53, 58, 64
China 19, 22–23, 43, 46, 88, 93, 118, 152
Chinese Immigrants 130
Chrysostome, Elie Virgile 139

circular transnationalism 74, 77
co-ethnics 91, 94, 100
consultancy businesses 112, 114, 116, 121
control variables 102, 156
Cooney, Thomas 8
Cucculelli, M. 54
cultural knowledge 138, 141–142
cultural resources 129–131, 133, 137–138, 140–141

data collection 89–90
Davidsson, P. 139
demographic conditions 139, 142
dense migration 150–151
Despres, L.A. 131
developing countries 11, 54, 83, 94
Dew, N. 135
diaspora engagement policy 6, 72, 74
diaspora entrepreneurs 2, 11, 141, 152, 157, 162
diaspora entrepreneurship 2, 4, 133, 137, 141
diasporans 9, 150–155, 157–159, 161–162
diaspora policies 3, 12, 69–70, 74, 77, 83
diaspora policy paradigm 73; change 71
diaspora politics 3–4, 11–12
diaspora transnationalism 133, 138
diasporic entrepreneurs 9, 149, 152, 161–162; embeddedness of 9, 149, 161
Dimov, D. 137, 139
direct effects 153, 161–162
domestic entrepreneurs 44, 46, 151–153, 157
double taxation avoidance agreements 58
Drori, G. S. 139
Drori, I. 96–97
dual citizenship 7, 70, 90, 92
dual habitus 97, 102, 104
dynamic economies 50

Eckhardt, J. 134
EES 51–52, 56–57, 64–66, 100
Egbert, H. 140
Eisenhardt, K. M. 135
embeddedness 54, 97, 110–111, 118, 120, 122, 129, 131, 149–150, 162

enclave resources 132, 137–142
entrepreneurial culture 61, 64
entrepreneurial environments 21, 52
entrepreneurial motivations 54, 101, 136
entrepreneurial opportunity formation (EOF) 128, 134–136
entrepreneurial projects 2, 12, 82–83
entrepreneurs 4–6, 9–10, 18, 52–53, 55–56, 58–59, 61, 63–66, 73–74, 77–83, 93–94, 111–114, 116–120, 122, 134–135, 137–138, 140, 148–150, 152–158, 162–163
entrepreneurship 4–6, 11, 17–19, 23, 25, 34, 38–39, 41–42, 44–45, 51–58, 61, 63–64, 81, 97, 137–138
entrepreneurship motivations 54
entrepreneurs network 119, 148, 152, 155–156
ethnic businesses 33, 96, 99, 132
ethnic enclaves 19, 24, 26, 33, 39, 43, 46, 130
ethnic enterprises 38–39, 162
ethnic entrepreneurship (EE) 2, 4, 7, 16–29, 34, 46, 87–88, 98–100, 104–105
ethnic firms 36, 38, 40
ethnic mobilisation 131
ethnic politics 131
European culture countries 151, 153, 158–159, 161
European culture origin 153, 157–158
European culture region 148, 150–152, 156, 158, 161–163
exporting 9, 23, 54, 149, 153–156, 159, 161–163

Faist, T. 133
Fernández-Kelly, P. 138
foreign investors 58, 93
Franco-Guillén, N. 117

Gabrielli, L. 117
Gamlen, A. 71
Gartner, W. B. 137
Germany 6, 20, 22, 25, 51–53, 56–57, 59, 61, 63–66, 73, 76, 116, 120
Gilbertson, G. A. 130
Giuliani 135
Global Entrepreneurship Monitor (GEM) 56
Gold, S. J. 131
Goli, M. 7
Granovetter, M. 131
Grasmuck, Sherri 40
Guard 135
Guarnizo, A. 9, 53, 96, 122
Guarnizo, L. E. 9, 40, 51, 53, 122
Gurak, D. T. 130

Haas, H. De 71, 74
Haller, W. J. 9, 53, 96, 122
Hartley, Scott 9

Hechter, M. 131
Hellgren, Zenia 6
high-tech transnational firms 40
home countries 2–4, 7–13, 38–40, 42, 70, 72–73, 82–83, 89–96, 102, 104–105, 129, 132–133, 137–142, 162
Honig, B. 5, 96
Hornaday, J. A. 135
Hrivnak, George A. 54, 131, 133, 141
human capital 5–6, 18–19, 25–26, 28, 34, 36, 40, 42, 44, 53–55, 111–112, 114, 120–122, 141
Hwang, H. 139

immigrant enclave theory (IET) 4, 8, 128–132, 136–139, 141–142
immigrants 5–7, 9–10, 16–18, 20–21, 23–26, 28–29, 38–40, 46, 55–57, 59, 97–98, 129–132, 135–139, 141–142, 149; businesses 45, 130; community 19, 40, 130, 149; enterprises 33, 38–40, 44, 46; entrepreneurs 13, 33, 129, 131–132, 138; entrepreneurship 26, 33–34, 44, 138, 141; groups 5, 28, 33, 36, 40–41, 46, 130, 141; infrastructures 131, 138; markets 130, 139, 141–142; resources 131, 137, 140–141; transnational entrepreneurs 59, 61, 64
informal enterprise 38
informal immigrant enterprise 38
infrastructures 8, 95, 132–133, 136–142
institutional embeddedness 8, 111, 114–115, 118, 121–122
international business 120
Iranian Diaspora 152, 162
Itizigsohn 40

Jensen, L. 130

Katila, Saija 119
Katz, J. 137
Khanna, T. 129
Kirzner, I. M. 135
Kloosterman, R. 110, 139

Lamont, M. 22
Landolt, P. 9, 40, 51, 53, 122
larger transnational networks 158
Lee, Renne 43
Levitt, Peggy 133
Light, I. 11, 77, 96, 131
linguistic skills 121
Liu, Y. 9
Logan, J. R. 43, 130
loyalty trap 87

Maâzouz, Abdallatif 76
Manning, R. D. 132
Marcuse, P. 130

INDEX

Marhaba Operation 76
Martinez, B. P. 5–7
Mathew, M. 135
McDougall, P. P. 133
McMullen, J. S. 134
MENA countries 116, 121
Metcalf, H. 132
Meyer, J. W. 139
Middle East 9, 148, 150, 152, 159, 161
Miera, Frauke 111
migrant entrepreneurs 2, 51, 54, 79, 88–89, 91, 94, 105, 113, 120, 123
migrant entrepreneurship 64, 97, 110–111, 114, 123
migrant transnational entrepreneurs 87
migrant transnational entrepreneurship 4, 7, 96
migration entrepreneurship 16
migration studies 2–5, 9, 12, 17, 70
Milan 7–8, 109–110, 112–117, 119, 123
mixed embeddedness approach 7, 26, 28, 109–111, 114–115, 121, 123, 149
Modood, T. 132
Molnar, V. 22
Morawska, Ewa 111
Moroccan diaspora 71, 74, 83; engagement policy paradigm 69; engagement policy philosophy 72; policies 74, 77, 79–80
Moroccan entrepreneurs 72, 75, 78–80, 82–83, 112–113, 115, 117, 120, 122
Moroccan identity 6, 73–74, 77, 81
Moroccan migrants 7, 77–78, 114–119
Moroccans 7–8, 69–70, 72–73, 75, 77–81, 83, 96, 113–114, 118
Moroccans Living Abroad (MLAs) 69–70, 72, 74–76, 83
Moroccan transnational entrepreneurs 7, 70, 75, 82, 122
Moroccan Transnational Entrepreneurs (MTEs) 4, 7, 70, 77, 82, 87–88, 96–97, 104–105
Morocco 7, 61, 64, 70–83, 89, 93, 96, 112, 115–121, 152
motivations 4, 10–12, 46, 55–56, 75, 79, 83, 100–103, 133, 136, 138–139, 141

necessity-based entrepreneurial activity (NEC) 55
necessity entrepreneurs 4, 80–81, 99
networking 64, 119, 130, 138–141, 149–150, 153, 155–158, 161–163
Neuman, E. 129–130
Newland, K. 81, 139
Ng, M. 53
Nice, R. 131
Nielsen, Tjai M. 54, 131, 133, 141
Nkongolo-Bakenda, Jean-Marie 139
non-entrepreneurs 134–135, 137

North Africa 9, 18, 115, 120, 148, 150, 152, 159, 161–162
Nwankwo, S. 132

opportunity-based entrepreneurship (OPP) 54–55
opportunity entrepreneurs 4, 80–81, 99
opportunity entrepreneurship 51, 80
opportunity formation 8, 131–132, 135–139
Osaghae, Osa-Godwin 8
Oviatt, B. M. 133

Palepu, K. G. 129
Peroni, C. 137
Pessar, Patricia 40
Pettersen, S. V. 102
petty entrepreneurship 39
petty immigrant enterprise 39
Portes, A. 5–7, 9, 51, 53, 96, 122, 129–130, 132, 138–139
Prometheus 87, 95
Putnam, R. D. 99

Rath, J. 110, 139
Rezaei, S. 6–7, 11, 70, 77, 98
Riddle, Liesl 54, 131, 133, 141
Riillo, C. A. 137

Santos, F. M. 135
Sarasvathy, S. D. 135
Sarracino, F. 137
Saxenian, A. 10–11, 50, 77, 122
Schiller, N. G. 129
Schumpeter, J. A. 4
self-employment 5, 18, 26, 34, 36, 40–41, 46, 66
Sensenbrenner, J. 129, 132, 139
Shane, S. 134
Sheffer, G. 102
Shepherd, D. A. 134
Smallbone, D. 132
social capital 10, 13, 17, 25–26, 39–40, 44, 52, 55, 100, 118–119, 122, 131–132, 138–141; bridging 118–120
social embeddedness 8, 111–112, 114, 118, 120–122
social global pattern 9
social networks 40, 46, 80, 82, 110–112, 118, 149, 152
Solano, G. 7–8
South America 9, 148, 150–151, 159, 161–163
Spain 70, 78–82, 89, 94, 119, 151
Spanish-Moroccan migration corridor 79
Sub-Sahara Africa 9, 148, 150–151, 161
super-diversity 17, 28
Surdej, A. 54

Tanaka, H. 81, 139
Telles, Edward 11, 77
transnational businesses 8, 28, 73, 81, 112–115, 118, 121–123
transnational diaspora 128, 133
transnational diaspora entrepreneurs 129, 150, 163
transnational diaspora entrepreneurship (TDE) 8–9, 56, 129–130, 133–134, 137–142, 151, 162
transnational enterprise 12, 44, 46
transnational entrepreneurs 50–57, 59, 61, 63, 65–66, 69, 88–89, 91, 94–97, 100–101, 104, 111–113, 117–118
transnational human capital 120
transnationalism 2–3, 33–34, 40, 42, 53, 55, 71, 76, 81–83, 133, 138
transnational migrant entrepreneurs 64, 79, 109–111, 123
transnational migrant entrepreneurship 6, 70, 79, 83, 109–110, 121
transnational Moroccan entrepreneurs 73, 114, 120, 123
transnational networking 9, 149, 153, 158, 161–162
transnational networks 9, 39, 81, 102, 149–150, 152–153, 157–159, 161–163
transnational policy 69–71, 74, 77
Turkish Immigrants 20

Van Der Leun, J. 139
Vertovec, S. 17
Virdee, S. 132
Von Bloh, J. 6

Wahlbeck, Östen 119
Waldinger, R. 130, 137–138, 141
Walther, M. 131
Wasdani, K. P. 135
Wilson, K. L. 130
Wong, L. L. 53
World Economic Forum (WEF) 53
Wright, M. 96

Zapata-Barrero, R. 6, 11, 70, 77
Zhou, M. 40, 43, 130